COUNTRY
Satan's Sinners M.C.
BOOK 2

COLBIE KAY

Cathy
Thank you for the support.
Hope you love it.
♡ Colbie Kay

QUIET COUNTRY

Quiet Country

Satan's Sinners M.C. Book 2

Copyright© 2015 Colbie Kay

Cover Design & Formatting: Jersey Girl & Co. Design

Editors: Jana Whaley and Tonya Bright

Final Editor: Casey Heiter with Cat's Eye Editing and Design

ALL RIGHTS RESERVED.

No part of this book may be reproduced or transmitted in any form or by any means, electronic or mechanical, without permission from the publisher, except in the case of brief quotations embodied in critical articles or reviews.

This is a work of fiction. Names, characters, businesses, places, events, and incidents are products of the author's imagination and are used fictitiously. Any resemblance to actual persons, living or dead, events or locales is purely coincidental.

The use of artists, song titles, and brand names throughout this book are done so for storytelling purposes and should in no way be seen as advertisement. Trademark names are used in an editorial fashion with no intention of infringement of the respective owner's trademark.

This book is licensed for your personal enjoyment. This book may not be re-sold or given away to other people. If you would like to share this book with another person, please purchase an additional copy for each recipient. If you are reading this book and did not purchase it, or if it was not purchased for your use only, then you should return it to the seller and please purchase your own copy.

ISBN-13: 978-1515370727

ISBN-10: 1515370720

COLBIE KAY

10 9 8 7 6 5 4 3 2 1

TABLE OF CONTENTS

Dedication - 6

Playlist - 7

Prologue - 9

One - 10

Two - 18

Three - 25

Four - 36

Five - 46

Six - 56

Seven - 68

Eight - 81

Nine - 91

Ten - 99

Eleven - 109

Twelve - 118

Thirteen - 130

Fourteen - 140

Fifteen - 154

Sixteen - 168

Seventeen - 177

Eighteen - 186

Nineteen - 193

Epilogue - 201

Acknowledgements - 203

About The Author - 204

OTHER WORKS BY COLBIE KAY

Satan's Sinners M.C. Series

City Lights (Book 1)
Quiet Country (Book 2)

Coming Soon

Saving Grace
Double Crossed

DEDICATION

*I dedicate this book to my husband.
Thank you for supporting me in this new journey I am taking and letting me vent whenever I needed it.*

Also to my readers thank you for falling in love with my characters and loving them like I do.

QUIET COUNTRY

PLAYLIST

TAKE YOUR TIME- *Sam Hunt*
WRONG SIDE OF HEAVEN- *Five Finger Death Punch*
FREE FALLIN'- *Tom Petty*
POST TO BE- *Omarion with Chris Brown and Jhene Aiko*
OR NAH- *The Weeknd with Ty Dolla $ign*
SEX THERAPY- *Robin Thicke*
LEAVE THE NIGHT ON- *Sam Hunt*
SUGAR- *Maroon 5*
FOUR FIVE SECONDS- *Rihanna with Kanye West and Paul McCartney*
OVER MY HEAD- *The Fray*
SEX IS GOOD- *Saving Abel*
THE DOPE SHOW- *Marilyn Manson*
THIS MEANS WAR- *Avenged Sevenfold*
JEALOUS REMIX- *Nick Jonas with Tinashe*
SIMPLE MAN- *Lynard Skynard*
EVERY ROSE HAS IT'S THORN- *Poison*
NOVEMBER RAIN- *Guns N' Roses*
PATIENCE- *Guns N' Roses*
DREAMING OF YOU- *Salena*
CHASING CARS- *Snow Patrol*
JUICY- *Pretty Ricky*
SEE YOU AGAIN-
KNOCKIN' ON HEAVEN'S DOOR- *Guns N' Roses*
DOWN WITH THE SICKNESS- *Disturbed*
FAR AWAY- *Nickleback*
EIGHTEEN DAYS- *Saving Able*
PUSH- *Nick Jonas*
CHAINS REMIX- *Nick Jonas with Jhene Aiko*
SCRATCHIN' ME UP- *Trey Songz*

COLBIE KAY

EARNED IT- *The Weeknd*
OFTEN- *The Weeknd*
CRAZY BITCH- *Buck Cherry*
A SKY FULL OF STARS- *Cold Play*
LOVE ME LIKE YOU DO- *Elle Goulding*
LOVE YOU LIKE THAT- *Canaan Smith*
MOTIVATION- *Kelly Rowlands*
BAD GIRL- *Marilyn Manson with Avril Lavigne*
TAINTED LOVE- *Marilyn Manson*
RUNNIN' OUTTA MOONLIGHT- *Randy Houser*
ADDICTED- *Saving Able*
PONY- *Cover by Far*

PROLOGUE

Bear

After everything that's happened in my life, I live for me. I ride when I want, fuck when I want, basically I do what I want when I fucking want. That is until I met her. I swore after my parents I would never fall in love. I never wanted the responsibility of what goes along with love. It's me and my brothers, and it was that way for years until I met her. The club, that's what was important until I met her. Now I'm chasing after this woman. I swear I don't know if she wants to love me or hate me. Shit, I don't blame her for hating me, I can be hard as fuck to handle. But I'm out to get what I want and what I want is her. I'm ready to break all my rules for her. Is she ready to break all her walls for me?

Jacey

I may come across as a bitch, but that's just to protect myself. My life was always planned out for me. I'm beginning to realize everything I was raised to believe may all be lies, and I've set out to find the truth. During that journey I fell for a man. A man I was never supposed to fall for. He goes against everything in that plan. I don't want to get hurt. If I let him have all of me, he will destroy me. This man sees who I really am. Can I let myself trust him, believe in him, and love him? Can I let him know all my secrets and everything I ran from, find out who I really am underneath?

It's crazy how one night could change your whole life. The night when Zoey almost died brought us all together. After that night, all of our lives were changed forever.

Here is our story.

ONE

Bear

I'm the Enforcer for the Satan's Sinners, which means I'm the muscle of the club. Don't get me wrong, all of us can handle our own in a fight, that's not what I'm talking about. I'm the biggest son of a bitch of all the Satan's Sinners, and no one would wanna fuck with me, so they call on me if someone needs to be scared or beaten within an inch of their life. I get the job done. Every. Single. Time. I know the limits, how much pain someone can endure before they black out or die, and I know when to stop it, if I want to. It wasn't always like that though.

The Satan's Sinners, along with the Cobras' MC, our allies, have been having problems with an Italian mob family. The Gremaldi's are trying to take both clubs down so they can take over. They've already caused us to lose one brother, Ripper, who was my best friend, my brother in and out of the club. Even though he wasn't blood, it didn't matter, he was my family. Now if shit doesn't start happening with this Italian business, I'm gonna start cracking skulls. Believe me, I can do it.

Hanger has invited the president of the Cobras to join us for church today. Since both clubs are involved in this shit with the Italians, Hanger usually goes to Snake. After they talk business, Hanger comes back, calls church, and then informs the rest of us what's happening, but today's different. Crazy Girl, Hanger's Ol' Lady, is getting further along in her pregnancy, so he doesn't feel right about leaving her, which is completely understandable. If anything happened to that girl it would kill him. They have been through their fair share of shit, enough to last a fucking lifetime. If Crazy Girl was any regular civilian, she would have died the night Hanger found her. She's not though, she was made for club life. The girl is strong, she is a fighter and fucking perfect for Hanger.

Her best friend Jacey is a different story. While she is strong and a fighter, the two girls are incomparable. Jacey is fucking intense, fucked in the head at times, and causes me a whole lot of problems. At the same time, she is fucking beautiful with a hot little body. The girl has perfect handfuls of tit and ass, along with a pussy made of platinum. Swear to

QUIET COUNTRY

Christ, just thinking about her has my cock straining in my jeans. If we didn't have church, I'd go back to my room right now and beat off to the thought of her.

Ever since that first night, all I think about is how good she felt. Being balls deep inside that wet little cunt while it was gripping me so fucking tight as she screamed out my name with her sweet release. I haven't seen her in fucking months, don't matter though, I have it drilled in my memory. I've jerked myself off to the thought of her a thousand times. Shit, even when I have a biker whore's mouth wrapped around my cock, I'm thinking of Jacey when I get off. It's not just that though, this girl has me so twisted up inside. I can't get it undone no matter what I do. Somewhere along the way I developed feelings for her, which never happens. I don't let it.

Taking our seats, Hanger starts the meeting. With our brother Writer, he has to sign while he speaks because Writer is deaf.

"Alright guys, you all know Snake," he says while looking around the room.

"We need to discuss when we wanna take those fuckers out."

Gunner, our Vice President, chimes in.

"I say we go in right now."

Since Ripper died, nobody has been thinking clearly. It would be fucking stupid to risk everything. We gotta be smart about it. I speak up. "We can't just go in right now, Gunner. We gotta get the other chapters out here first and then we do it. The more guys we have, the better and easier it'll go over."

Then Hanger booms, *"Quiet down! I wanna give it some time. Why don't we let things settle down more so they'll think we aren't gonna retaliate against them? I can't leave Crazy Girl right now. I say, let's give it six months and hit 'em when they least expect it."*

Snake opens his mouth, "Hanger, I don't think we have another six months. My club can't take much more of a hit and I don't think yours can either. What if you sat this one out, get Texas and Oklahoma here, your brothers come with mine, and we all take 'em out?"

Hanger hesitates. *"I don't know, Snake. I mean, don't you think I should be there?"*

"Nah, Prez, we know what you got goin' on with Crazy Girl," Gunner says,"so let us do this. I'll take lead with our guys."

I know Hanger hates this, but he also knows it's gotta be done. Hanger looks around, seeing we're all okay with it.

"*Alright, Gunner. If you're sure about this, I'll let you start handlin' it.*"

With a smile on his face, Gunner responds, "You got it, Prez."

"Okay. So is that everything?"

Everyone gives a nod, and with that, Hanger ends church.

"*Let's get the fuck outta here.*"

It's about fucking time for shit to get figured out.

We all file out behind Hanger and Snake, when I hear Hanger ask Jacey what she's doing here. I've heard fuck all from her in months, now she just shows back up. I push my way through the guys until I'm next to Hanger and Snake. Fuck, she's even more beautiful than I remember.

I hear Snake whisper Jacey's name. The only thing going through my head right now is, what the fuck? Then this motherfucker mumbles it's you, like he knows her, as he walks up closer, staring at her the whole time. It's like I'm in a really bad episode of The Twilight Zone. Did she fuck Snake too? I look at her, my anger bubbling to the surface.

She's shaking her head, looking at Crazy Girl.

"Oh my God, I can't do this! I gotta go. Zoey, I'll see you later."

I can see her panic as she goes to get up. I've never moved so fast in my life as I did right then, grabbing ahold of her arm to stop her from leaving. I look between her and Snake.

"Snake, how the fuck you know Jacey?"

"Umm...I think she should tell you that," he says, still staring at her. I'm fucking seeing red. I need answers. I turn my attention back on her.

"The fuck you here for? How you know Snake?"

"I came to see you, to talk to you. There's something I need to tell you."

"You wanna talk to me now? It's been months since I've seen or heard from you."

I'm staring her dead in the eyes. I'm done with her disappearing act, leaving then showing back up when it's convenient for her.

"Please. Bear, just...I have so much I need to explain to you."

She gets up, turning towards me, and that's when I see her huge fucking belly. She has my shirt on? It's the one she had to get from me the night I ripped hers apart. She never gave it back, and now she wears it here to cover her very pregnant fucking belly.

WHAT THE FUCKING HELL?

What I thought was rage before was nothing compared to what I feel right now. Right now, there is no name for it. I can feel the veins in my neck protruding. I feel like a wild animal being set loose to kill its prey.

Did Snake get her pregnant? I wanna start ripping shit apart, and fucking kill him. If I don't get some goddamn answers, that might be exactly what fucking happens.

"The Fuck!?" I yell, feeling my face heat up from the rage coming off of me.

She starts begging, "Bear, listen. Please, just listen to me?"

I always loved hearing her beg, until now. I don't wanna hear a goddamn thing this bitch has to say. She sure as fuck is gonna listen to me though.

"No. You fuckin' listen!" I scream at her. "I don't see you for how fuckin' long? Then you come back here fuckin' lookin' like this."

I motion with my hands to her body. "With my goddamn shirt on?!"

Her eyes fill with tears. Before she looked panicked, but now when she looks up to me, I see nothing but sadness on her beautiful face. As furious as I am at her right now, it rips my heart out to see her like this. Looking into her eyes, I see fear. Out of all the emotions I've seen from her, I've never seen this kind of fear. I can't let my anger go though. "Bear..."

I can't help the words that come outta my mouth before she gets to finish.

"Who have you been fuckin' Jacey? Huh? Who'd you let up in that sweet pussy of yours? Wait! Hold the fuck on! How the fuck do you know Snake? Did he do this to you?"

She takes a few quick steps up to me and before I can stop it, her hand connects with my cheek. My head snaps to the side. Fuck, she hits hard. I move my face back, staring her down. I probably deserved that.

Snake pipes up, "Bear, why don't you calm down?" If my focus wasn't solely on her, he'd be a dead man.

I catch Hanger saying, "You need to stay out of this, Snake."

"OH! MY! FUCKING! GOD!" Jacey starts to scream, her face scrunching up like she's in pain. She doubles over, grabbing her stomach. I can't do anything but just stare at her. I don't want her to be in pain. I don't know what to do with all these emotions that I'm feeling. Then Crazy Girl is there. She asks, "What's wrong Jacey?"

"It hurts! God, it hurts so fucking bad! I think my water just broke!"

Did she just say her water broke? We all look down, and sure enough there's a puddle of fluid on the floor. That's fucking disgusting. The prospects will be cleaning that shit up.

"Oh God, Jacey. How long have you been having contractions?" Crazy Girl asks.

"I don't know? I started having some back pain last night, I've been hurting all day.", she answers. I can't fucking wrap my head around all this shit.

"Shit, Jacey you know you should've went to the doctor." Leave it to Crazy Girl to be calm and rational at a fucking time like this.

"I know. I wanted to come here and talk to him first." She has tears pouring down her face now, while she flicks her wrist with her finger pointing at me. I have to know the answer to my next question.

"Jacey, just tell me who the fuckin' father is." I might just go kill the fucker. I was not prepared at all for her answer.

"You! Bear, it's your baby! STUPID!"

The fuck she just say? Now, I have a whole new set of emotions taking over, pushing the anger down, along with more fucking questions.

"What?! How?" I ask, dumbfounded. We always use a condom. I'm thinking back over all the times we fucked. Ah shit, there was the time it broke. Fuck me.

"I haven't been with anyone, but you! This is your baby! GOD YOU ARE SO FUCKING STUPID!" She screams, her face contorting, and she doubles over again in pain.

"FUCK!" she screams. I'm gonna chalk that up to the pain.

She tries to control her breathing. My list of questions for her just keeps fucking growing. It's never ending with this woman.

"Why would you keep this from me?" I turn my attention to Crazy Girl. "And you!" I point at her. "This is what you were hiding?"

"I'm so sorry, Bear. I was just trying to do what she wanted. I kept telling her over and over again to tell you. I'm sorry," she pleads. I'll deal with that shit later. Now I wonder, did Hanger know?

"Don't you dare blame Zoey for this! It was my fault! I didn't want to tell you," she spits.

"We'll deal with that in time." I look to Hanger, "Did you know Prez?"

"That you were the father, no." I give him a nod. He knew she was pregnant though. Getting back to her and my questions, I ask, "Jacey, how do you know Snake?"

"I can't deal with that shit right now, Bear! I'm in labor! I promise I will tell you everything, just not right now. Please!"

I'll let it all go until my baby is born. "I'm done with the games, Jacey. I'm done with your fuckin' lies. Why the fuck did you keep it from me?"

"Because I'm fucking scared, Bear."

She starts sobbing even harder, her body shaking. I take the steps to get next to her, watching out so I don't step in the mess on the floor. I can feel her walls breaking, and I wrap her up in my arms.

"Hell, Lil Mama. What are you so scared of? Don't you know I would've been there with you through this?" She puts her head against my chest, holding her stomach.

"I'm scared of what I feel for you and all this shit." She moves a hand around the club and all of us.

"I've seen what people go through, and with everything I've been told…"

"I don't know what that has to do with us or any of this. But, Lil Mama, you think this doesn't scare the fuck outta me too? I've never had feelings for a woman before, this shit's all new to me. I'm still fuckin' furious with you for keepin' this from me. We have a lot of talkin' to do, but right now you gotta have my baby. Let's get you to the hospital."

"I'm not gonna make it to the goddamn hospital now! I gotta have this baby here," she informs everyone.

Well hell. Shocked, and sure my eyes are about to pop outta my fucking head, "What?"

She looks around and asks, "Doc, can you deliver the baby? I need you to do it. The contractions are really close and I feel like I need to push!"

He walks up. "Alright, Jacey, let's get you to Bear's room."

He goes to take her hand, but I slap his away. Grabbing it myself, we head to my room. Just then, I realize he is gonna have to be between her legs, and that's not happening.

"Doc, you are NOT puttin' your head anywhere near my woman's pussy!" I can hear all the guys laughing, but fuck them, they wouldn't like that shit either. She glares and points her finger at me.

"First of all, I'm not your fucking woman! And second, yes he is! You don't know how to fucking deliver a baby! He's getting it outta me NOW!" Okay, she may have a point.

"Fuck, your still tryin' to be fuckin' difficult about this?"

Once we're in my room with the door shut, Doc looks at me.

"I need you to get a bowl of warm water, some towels, and a trash bag."

I get all the towels in my room, but it's not enough, so I collect more from the other guys' rooms. I run into the kitchen, searching for a trash bag. I find one and shove it in my pocket as I open up the cabinets. I grab the biggest bowl I can find and fill it up with warm water. After I get everything together, I rush back to my room, trying not to spill the water or drop the towels. I can hear her screaming in pain. I wanna take it from her, but I can't.

I'm still trying to wrap my head around everything that's fucking happened in the last hour. I'm going to be a father, what do I do with that? Fuck, I didn't even have time to prepare for this shit. I never wanted kids. Adjusting the bowl and towels in one arm, I open my door with my free hand. I walk in, shut the door with my foot, and see Jacey on my bed with her pants off. I sit all the stuff by Doc, then take a seat next to her on the bed, holding her hand in mine.

"Okay, Bear, I waited until you got back for this. I gotta look and see if she's ready to push," he informs me. I give him a tight nod and look at her. She's squeezing my hand so hard I think she might break it. Labor must give women super strength.

He lifts up my shirt, spreads her legs wide, looks down at her pussy and then looks up to me. "Okay, Jacey. I see the head. On your next contraction, I want you to push with everything you've got. I'll count to ten then take a breather. Then you do it again."

"I know what to do! I'm a goddamn doctor!" she screams. I suppress the laugh that wants to come out because even in so much pain, she still has her attitude.

"Sorry, let's do this," he tells her. During her first push, she informed me of how much she hates me and wants to kill me.

During the second push, she blamed me for getting her into this situation and swore she was never going to fuck me again.

During the third push, she said she was going to cut my dick off and shove it down my throat. Then my baby boy was out.

He was silent and for the first time in my life, I was scared. A few seconds later, he let out the loudest high pitched squeal I've ever heard and it was fucking music to my ears. I released the breath I didn't know I was holding, while tears fall from my eyes. I look down and see Jacey crying as well. I brush away the hair plastered to her forehead and give her a kiss. It took forty-five minutes to change my entire outlook on life. I now have this little person that comes before anything and everything else.

"You did great, Lil Mama," I praised her, with my forehead against hers.

"I'm so goddamn proud of you."

Looking in my eyes, she responds, "Thank you and I'm sorry for the shit I said. I didn't mean it." I smile at her.

"I would hope you didn't mean it. I like my cock."

My comment makes all of us laugh. Shit, I forgot Doc was in here, he was so quiet while cleaning the baby and wrapping him up in some towels.

"Here is your son," he says proudly, holding his arms out and handing the baby to Lil Mama.

"Thank you so much Doc. I don't know what I would have done if you wouldn't have been here," she states, while putting the baby against her chest.

"I'm glad I was here too. This'll be one experience I'll never forget." He looks at me. "Congratulations brother."

"Thanks Doc, for everything," I tell him, having a new kind of respect for my brother.

"We need to get her to the hospital now," he says as he puts the afterbirth in the trash bag.

"Will you go tell the guys, so we can get them loaded in a cage?" I ask. He nods, while standing to leave the room.

Once he's gone, I look at my son. "Jacey, he is beautiful. Fuckin' perfect."

She smiles at me and replies, "We did good making this one, didn't we?"

"Yeah, we did." I give her a tender kiss on the lips and kiss my boy on the forehead. When Doc returns, he helps me get her out with the trash bag, while she carries the baby. Once we're all loaded up, we head to the hospital. When we get on the highway I call, letting the emergency staff know we're on the way, so they're ready for us.

I start thinking back to the first day we met and all that has happened over the last nine months.

TWO

PAST

Bear

It's Saturday afternoon when Hanger calls me into his office.
"What's up, Prez?"
"What you got going on tonight?" he asks.
"Nothin', why? You need somethin'?" I'm curious as to why he would wanna know.
"Yeah, Crazy Girl is wanting to go clubbin' tonight with her friend, and with everything that's going on with her ex, I need you there. I want one of us with each girl at all times. Writer will be on Ever, and Chatty and Ripper'll be there too."
"Yeah, okay. I can do that," I reply.
Ever is Crazy Girl's twin sister. One look from her and Writer was in love. He's still a prospect, but a damn good brother all the same. He's deaf and didn't even know sign language until Crazy Girl came here. We all just wrote shit down for him and he'd write back, that's how he got his name. It just so happens that Ever is deaf as well. She's a fucking sweet as hell girl, a little shyer than her sister, but perfect for Writer. Before her, he just kinda stuck to himself, but she pulled him out of his shell.
My other brother going with us, Ripper, I've know for a long time. He's treasurer for the Sinners. His ol' lady, Chatty, came along about five years ago and my god, the woman can talk. She took on the mother role of the club, taking care of all us guys, giving her opinion when she thinks you need it.
"Alright, meet us here tonight," Hanger instructs. I give him a nod before turning to walk out. Crazy Girl's only been here for about a month, but from day one she did something to Hanger. He quit fucking with the whores as soon as he brought her back. In fact, he hasn't even looked at other chicks since she's been here. It doesn't make much sense to me how he could be a one woman man, just like that.

I've got a few hours to kill, so I go behind the bar counter to the bin we collect empty bottles and cans for target practice in. I grab armfuls of the sticky containers and head out back to set them up, each at a different distances.

I pull out my 1911 glock and start shooting until I've busted every bottle and demolished every can. After I'm tired of shooting, I clean up my mess and decide to go for a ride. I can't help but wonder what Crazy Girl's friend is gonna be like.

Is she gonna be like Crazy Girl, sweet as fuck with a laid back personality, or will she be a raging bitch and ugly as shit? Hanger got fucking lucky with her, this life isn't for everyone. It takes a special kinda woman to stand by a man who lives a life like ours.

Living in the MC world isn't the same as living a normal, civilian life. They're sitting pretty compared to us. Our members follow a specific set of rules, and when shit needs to be settled, we handle it ourselves instead of calling the cops. Things get crazy and dangerous, so my brothers and I live it up day to day, our futures aren't guaranteed. I couldn't even imagine being with the same girl all the fucking time. I like a different girl every night, and I like a few different girls at the same time even fucking better.

I check my watch and see that it's time to head back. Once I'm inside the clubhouse, I head straight for my room to get ready for tonight when I see Morgan, twirling a curly lock of red head around her little finger. "Hey, Bear. What're you doing?" She uses that voice she thinks is sexy, her green eyes turned up to me.

Growing impatient, I snap, "I gotta get ready."

"Ready for what?" Now she's just being a nosy little bitch.

"Why you questionin' me? It ain't none of your fuckin' business." I continue to walk by her when she grabs my arm. She just made a big mistake. I turn back to her, gripping her wrist tightly in my hand. I raise an eyebrow at her in question.

"I just thought we could have some fun," she pouts, pushing her huge fake tits together. They're too big for her tiny body, but God, my cock loves to fuck them. I don't have time for this, looks like it's time for me to shut this shit down.

"Some fun, huh?" I chuckle. "You like havin' my cock down your throat, do you?" I run a finger down her cheek.

"You know I do," she replies, as I throw her hand off me.

"Listen up. I come to you when I want it, not the other way around. You're the whore here, not me. You service me when I want it. Now move along, I don't have time for your shit. Got me?"

I hear her apologizing as I make my way to my room. I shut the door behind me, and head to the shower. As the warm water runs down my body, I find myself still thinking about how this night's gonna go. When I get out, I dry off and put on my usual black jeans, white beater, cut, and black boots. Shutting the door behind me, I make my way to the bar, and see the other guys are already here waiting.

"They here yet?" I ask, looking around.

Hanger replies, "Yeah, they're in my room gettin' ready. I want you to be prepared. You're gonna like this one, Brother."

I give him a curious look. What the fuck is that supposed to mean? Before I get a chance to ask, the girls walk out from the hallway. Hanger and Ripper look over. I tap Writer on his shoulder to let him know they came out. My gaze instantly goes to the sexy little brunette, and I can't take my eyes off her. I've never seen a woman as sexy as she is in my entire fucking life. This can't be the friend, because if it is, I'm in so much fucking trouble.

This isn't gonna turn out well for me at all. I can already feel it. I start at her feet and move my way up. She's wearing silver heels with a dress so tight, it could be a second skin. It doesn't cover much, ending just below her sexy round ass and leaving one shoulder bare. My cock twitches at seeing her smooth, tan skin. She's naturally fucking beautiful, so she's not wearing a lot of makeup, unlike the whores around here who paint layers of the shit on.

Those fucking eyes, goddamn, she has them outlined in bold black, making them stand out. Her long brown hair's pulled back into a tight ponytail, showing off her huge hoop earrings. She seems to be about the same height as Crazy Girl, so I'm guessing without the fuck-me-heels she would be about 5'4". She has nicely toned legs, which tells me she works out to keep that hot little body in shape. I'd like to give her a fucking work out. Damn, I can't help but to think how good it would feel to have those legs wrapped around me. Or twist that ponytail around my hand, pulling her head back, as I pound into her from behind.

Crazy Girl introduces us, bringing me back from the thoughts I'm having. She's looking at me just as intensely when I walk up to her.

"Hi Jacey, it's nice to meet you."

I give her a sexy grin, putting on the polite act. I'll do whatever it takes to get what I want, which means her underneath me, taking my cock by the end of the night.

"It's nice to meet you too, Bear," she says, smiling back at me. Her cheeks turn a beautiful light shade of pink. Is she blushing?

QUIET COUNTRY

"No need to blush, Lil Mama. You ready to go? Have you ever ridden on a bike before?" I give her a genuine smile this time.

"Yes, I'm ready and no, I haven't been on the back of a bike." A strange look crosses her face and in an instant it's gone and replaced with the sexiest grin I've ever seen. Goddamn this woman.

"You look really nice," I observe, while having not-so-nice thoughts.

"Thanks, you too," she responds, working those eyes over my body.

After the girls get their jeans on, I lead her outside to my bike, and hand her a helmet to put on. I help her with it, then get on my bike while instructing her how to hold onto me. When she's situated and ready to go, I straddle my bike and feel her arms reach around me. She's sitting too far back. I need to feel her right up against me, so I reach behind me and hook both hands under her knees, pulling her as close to my back as I can before we take off. Her grip tightens a little when I speed up, just the way I want it to.

We find a parking spot and climb off my bike. She takes off her jeans before we meet up with everyone else. Making our way inside, I can see why the place is called Insanity. We barely find a table, the place is so fucking packed, and as the girls sit down, I ask Jacey what she wants to drink.

"I want a Rum and Coke with two slices of lime. And can you make sure it's coconut rum, please," she tells me in a prim tone. She knows exactly what she wants.

"I'll be right back."

Being a big fucking dude pays off when you're in a club or a bar. People tend to move the fuck outta my way when they see me coming, so I'm back with our drinks in no time flat.

"How'd you like the ride?" I ask her, practically yelling to be heard over the music.

"It was fun!" she exclaims, a big smile covering her gorgeous face. "It felt so freeing, being out in the open, the wind hitting you. God, I love the speed and adrenaline. I love it!"

Fuck, that's exactly what it feels like for me. I try to ignore the semi-hard on I've had since I laid eyes on this woman. I've never let a chick on my bike before and I never would've thought she'd feel that way about the ride.

"What kind of bike is it?" she asks, surprising the fuck outta me. I swear this girl keeps getting sexier by the second. Never has a chick wanted to know about my bike.

"She's a 2011 Victory Judge," I answer, and she gives a small nod.

"You've got a really pretty name, Jacey. What's your last name, if you don't mind me asking?"

"It's Thomas, and thank you, Bear. I would ask what your real name is, but something tells me you won't tell," she says, looking at me. She's right, and it makes me laugh because who the fuck is this chick?

"You're right, I wouldn't," I tell her, seeing that blush taking over again. She looks so fucking cute when the pink shows on her cheeks.

"How old are you, Jacey Thomas?" I ask, her first and last name rolling off my tongue.

"I'm twenty-six. What about you, Bear?"

"Well I'm thirty, a little bit older than you. What do you do for a living?"

Usually, I don't give a fuck about the chick I'm gonna be with for the night, but this one I want to get to know, and whether that's because of Crazy Girl or the fact I find her intriguing, I'm not quite sure.

"I'm a doctor. I own the clinic that Zoey works at. I'd ask you, but I think I know the answer," she chuckles, and I give her a curious look.

"What is that supposed to mean?" I ask, feeling a little defensive. Her eyes grow large.

"I'm sorry. I didn't mean to offend you," she counters. "I just...well, you're big and have all that muscle. I just figured you did something for the club."

"It's fine, and yea, I do do something for the club," I tell her.

"I run a garage in town, although it's owned by the club. I'm a mechanic." There's that blush again and I crack a smile at her.

The girls decide to go out on the dance floor, so us guys stay at the table, being mindful that we can still see them. Ripper looks over at me with a smile on his face. "So what'd you think about that one?"

"Brother, I have no fuckin' idea yet, but she's sexy as hell."

We both start laughing. *Sam Hunt's Take Your Time* comes on, and Hanger gets up to dance with Crazy Girl. The other girls come back to the table and sit down.

"What kind of music you like, Lil Mama?"

"I love all kinds, I have a passion for it, actually. I didn't have much to do growing up, so I turned to music." I bust out laughing. She glares at me and asks, "What's so funny?"

"I wasn't expecting you to say that, at all." We smile at each other.

"Try me. Name a song," she dares, looking sure of herself.

Thinking hard, I say, "Alright. *The Wrong Side of Heaven.*"

"Come on, you can do better than that! *Five Finger Death Punch.* It's on the album The Wrong Side of Heaven and the Righteous Side of Hell Volume One, which was released July 30th, 2013."

"Holy shit!" I exclaim, shocked as shit that she would know all of that. I give her another song. *"Free Fallin'?"*

"Tom Petty, of course, from the album *Full Moon Fever*, released October 27, 1989. It's one of the greatest songs he ever did." She looks at me with the biggest smile on her face.

"That's fuckin' amazing. Why are you a doctor?" The smile falls from her pretty face and she doesn't answer, just gets a faraway look in her eyes for a moment before she shakes it away. Trying to lighten the mood, I ask "You got any more talents?" Her lips twitch, the corners turning upward. The smile returns like nothing ever happened.

"I guess you'll just have to wait and see," she answers in a sexy purr as *Post To Be by Omarion, Chris Brown, and Jhene Aiko* starts booming over the speakers. I'm glad this club plays a variety of music, I wanna find out just how good she can work those hips.

I grab her hand, and leaning into her ear, I whisper, "Dance with me?" I linger, my mouth still near her ear.

"Yeah, okay," she breathes back to me.

I lead her onto the dance floor, away from everyone. Finding a dark corner, I pull her into me and spin her around so her back is pressing against my torso. I put one of my arms around her chest and roll my hips into her ass while she mimics my movements against my growing cock. I lean into her ear. "You're a good dancer, Lil Mama."

Turning her head, she says, "So are you. Where did you learn to dance like this?"

"Now's not the right time for that discussion."

I chuckle and give her a kiss on the shell of her ear. Jacey shivers against me, so I lightly run a hand down her arm, feeling the goose bumps form. Yeah, I've got this thing when it comes to women, I just can't help the way their bodies respond to me.

Once the song is over, I spin her around as *Or Nah by Ty Dolla $ign, The Weeknd, Wiz Kahlifa, and DJ Mustard* starts to play. I back her up against the wall, running my hands down her body. I start grinding into her, my hip pressing into her pussy. There's not an inch of space between us, and her breathing becomes shallow and quick.

She's getting turned on and I'm right there with her. We're moving together to the sound of the music, getting lost in each other's presence. Everything melts away in that moment so it's just the pounding rhythm and us in the darkness. Dancing with her like this, I'm fully hard now, almost painfully so. We gotta stop before I have her against the wall with my cock buried deep inside of her.

I whisper in her ear that we should go back to the table, my voice husky and unfamiliar to me. All she can do is nod her cute little head. We make our way back, and the other girls wanna dance again, so I take my seat while she goes with them to do her thing. Not long after they have been out there, I see a guy walk up to the girls. He grabs Crazy Girl by the hips and in a flash Hanger is there. Once he takes care of that asshole, all goes back to normal. After awhile, everyone, except Ever and Jacey, decide to leave the club, which means Writer and I are here to stay for a bit longer. Fuck yeah, I'm gonna have to take her home.

We keep dancing and drinking, letting the music hypnotize us. Without anymore drama, it's an all-around good time, and Ever and Writer have been in their own world, doing their own thing. I've had Jacey to myself damn near this whole night. Usually, I would be bored with a woman by now, but she intrigues the fuck outta me. I wanna keep the mood light, so I ask the question that's been on my mind. "So what are these other talents you got?"

She chuckles, and says, "I know about cars."

"What you mean?" I ask, cocking my eyebrow at her, I'm really fucking curious now.

"You haven't seen my car yet."

"No I haven't."

"You will understand more when you see her. She's my baby." She's spiking my interest. What kinda car could this girl have?

Ever and Jacey are ready to go. We all wave goodbye as we leave the strobing lights and head back out into the night to the bikes. The girls slip on their jeans, and before getting back on my bike, Jacey lightly runs her finger across the paint. "This really is a beautiful bike," she says while looking at me under those long lashes of hers.

"You need to get on my bike right now, Lil Mama," I instruct her, hardening my tone towards her. .

Her eyes widen as she asks, "Why?"

"Because if you don't," I start, looking her right in the eyes so she knows I'm not fucking around, "I'll have you bent over this beautiful bike with my cock inside you before you even realize what's happenin'."

She gives me a nod, hops on, and gives the directions to her place. We pull up to an apartment building, and she takes the helmet off and stands beside me. The words that come outta her mouth next are the ones I've been dying to hear all night long. They have my jeans growing just a little bit tighter.

"Do you wanna come in?"

THREE

Jacey

I can't believe I just asked him to come up to my apartment. I'm very private about my life, so this is way beyond the limits of my comfort zone. Zoey's the only other person that's ever been inside my place, but I just couldn't help it. Goddammit, he has me so worked up, the way he danced with me or when he would randomly kiss me. God, even his voice has me turned on. I've danced with guys since I started going out to clubs, but no one has ever made me feel like this. I never allow them close enough to take me home or ask questions about me, until tonight. What the hell am I thinking? He is going to say yes and it's too late to back out now. Would I really want to back out anyway? Looking at him, I think not.

I watch the smile spread across his face. "Yeah, I'll come in."

Shit. Shit. Shit. What do I do now? I'll just act like I know what the hell I'm doing, make him think I've done this before.

"Alright then, let's go," I reply, giving him that sexy smile from earlier. We walk up the stairs to my apartment, and my hands shake as I pull my keys from my purse. I feel him reach around me, steadying my hand, then taking the keys from me.

"Here, let me do it," he says, his hot breath hitting my neck. "Are you sure about this?" he whispers in my ear.

"Yeah, I'm sure, just a little nervous," I say, as goosebumps cover my skin. I shiver from being so close to him.

"Nothin' to be nervous about, Lil Mama. We aren't gonna do anything you don't wanna do." I give him a nod just as my door opens. Once inside, he shuts the door behind him and locks it.

"Would you like something to drink?" I offer while I'm pulling off my heels, my voice shaking. His stare bores into me, and when I look up, his eyes are dark and lustful.

"C'mere," he instructs.

I walk over to Bear and he grabs my waist, pulling me close to him. He's fucking huge compared to me, at least a foot taller, and I feel like I could get lost in his embrace. His bulging muscles are covered in tattoos and it makes my mouth water. His black hair is just the right length for me to run my hands through, to grip onto while he does dirty things to my body. He hasn't shaved in a few days, and it only enhances his stunning brown eyes. Those eyes are hypnotic, so clear that I feel like I could see straight into his soul. He is sex, sin, and everything I know I should stay the hell away from.

His cut says "Enforcer", so I know he's the muscle of the club. Bear's always watching what's going on around him, always mindful of everyone and everything all the time. He's got a look of business in his eyes, even when he seems to be having fun, so he can tell me he all he wants that he's a mechanic, but I know he does bad things for that motorcycle club.

I told Zoey once what my type was, even though I really had no idea. I told her I liked tall, dark haired men with muscles and tattoos. I guess it was the girl talk, but I just wanted to feel like I fit in for once, and I never would've thought for one second that there would actually be a man who'd fit my fantasies. There's a lot Zoey doesn't know about me, and if I can help it, it'll stay that way. Not just for her, but for everyone.

"Hey, you okay? You still with me?" he asks, bringing me back in the moment. I realize he has my cheeks in his hands, making me look at him.

"Yes, sorry." I smile, reassuring him that I'm still here.

"Are you sure this is okay?" He's being so nice, this isn't how my mother said they were.

"Yes, I promise."

I look up at him, stand on my tippy toes, and bring my hands up to his hair. I run my fingers through it, grabbing with both hands, and bring his face to mine like I've been wanting to. He grunts in pleasure, crushing his mouth into mine. I have no idea what to do, so I follow his lead. Feeling him trying to gain access into my mouth, I part my lips and let him explore. His tongue touches then slowly rubs against mine, setting my body on fire.

Something inside of me comes alive with this kiss, and it's not enough, so I deepen it. He's moving his pelvis in a slow, grinding motion, moving me with him. His hands grip my thighs, picking me up effortlessly. Once he's back upright, I instinctively wrap my legs around his tight, firm waist. While deep in the kiss, I grip the leather from Bear's cut, pulling him closer and taking it off at the same time, when he suddenly breaks away.

"Be careful with my cut," he tells me as he moves us over to the couch. Shifting me from arm to arm, I manage to slide it off his broad shoulders and gently move it down his arms, laying it on the side of the couch.

"Where's your room?" he asks, his voice deeper than normal.

"Door on the left."

Bear takes one hand, putting it behind my head and grabs at my hair tie, letting my dark hair fall down around us. He grabs a handful at the nape of my neck, crushing our mouths back together. By the time we reach my bedroom, I have his beater off, and his jeans are undone, sliding down his thick, strong thighs. He has managed to get my dress bunched around my waist. I wasn't wearing a bra, and the air feels chilled on my naked breasts. Once inside my room, he kicks the door shut with his foot and sits me back on my feet as he helps me take my jeans off. My legs feel like Jell-O from being so worked up, no bullshit. He kicks off his boots, jeans, and boxer briefs in one swift motion.

Holy mother of God, Bear is muscled perfection. I want to lick him, run my tongue all over his tattooed body, that's how perfect he is. I take him in, all of him. When I see what he's working with, I think I might have a goddamn stroke. I know I'm a doctor, but that's the biggest cock I've ever seen. I hope to hell it fits without ripping me apart. He sees me looking, gawking actually, and gives me a cocky smile. That's when I feel my face heat up. Why do I keep blushing? I've blushed more tonight then I have in my entire life.

He pulls my dress down the length of my body, and when it hits the floor, I step out of it. While gripping the thin straps of my panties, he looks up at me. He must sense something because he asks if this is okay.

"It's more than okay," I say, giving my approval.

He goes to his knees on the floor, peppering kisses all over my thighs as my panties get ripped from my body. Running his rough calloused hands to the backs of my thighs, he starts to stand back up, taking me with him. I wrap my legs tight around his waist so that my pussy is directly over his rock-hard erection. His hands cup my ass as he rubs me along his length. The constant friction to my clit and the way he is kissing and biting at my neck makes me throw my head back as pleasure takes over my body. A soft moan escapes my lips.

"I want more of those sexy little noises. Let me hear you Lil Mama."

Oh God, his words, his voice, everything about this man has me on the cusp of an earth shattering orgasm. I lift my head back up and lay it between his shoulder and neck, then I bite down. He lets out a low growl of approval. All of a sudden, he gets my legs unhooked from behind him and throws me up in the air and catches me. With my legs around his shoulders, he starts walking until my back is braced against the wall, my bare pussy is in his face. I feel his tongue lap at me, licking and sucking at my most private place.

"Oh fuck. That feels incredible," I tell him as my moans grow louder, urging him on. He gives no mercy on my pussy, working his tongue harder, faster, and latching onto my clit. My hips buck against his face.

"Fuck yeah, Lil Mama. You taste fuckin' amazing."

"Oh God," my only response as he devours me.

He stops licking and tells me, "I know I'm a god and I'll be yours anytime you want." He's a cocky bastard, but fuck, he makes my body feel glorious.

I feel him smile against me before he goes back to working me over. God, this is amazing. I can't take it anymore. My body releases into an explosion. Grabbing handfuls of his hair, I pull him further into me. My whole body is shaking as I come undone, screaming out his name. That was way better than anything I could ever give myself with my little green machine. Yes, that's what I call my little green bullet.

"Yeah, Lil Mama, that's it. Let go."

Bear slides me back down around his waist and carries me to the bed. I'm dizzy with lust and want for this man. He lays me on the bed as he stands at the side, staring me down. He goes to his jeans, getting out a condom, then walks back to the edge of the bed to continue his exploration of my body.

"You are one gorgeous woman, Jacey Thomas."

He pulls his phone out and then I hear music start. Oh my god. It's *Sex Therapy by Robin Thicke*. This man knows exactly what the fuck he's doing.

I sit up and scoot to where he's at as he tosses the phone down on my nightstand. I run my nails down his defined pecs and abs, feeling him, treasuring him. He looks down at me, watching as I take one of my hands and wrap it around his long, wide shaft. Moving my hand up and down, I never break eye contact. I take him into my mouth, moving down as far as I can, which doesn't feel very far. It's not my fault, the dude is packing something massive.

I do my best at taking him in until I can feel him hit the back of my throat, while my other hand massages his balls. He lets out a fierce growl as he pulls me away from him and throws me back onto the bed. Bear opens the wrapper, puts the condom on, and then is on top of me, all in an instant. His mouth descends to mine, kissing me hard again, when I feel him thrust inside. In one hard push, he did it. He took my virginity. He is going to hate me when this is over, right now, I don't care, he's got me so turned on. I always thought it was supposed to hurt but it wasn't painful, a little uncomfortable maybe, a lot of pressure definitely. I pull my head back from the kiss.

"Bear, wait." He stills inside of me.

Looking down at me, his brows furrowed, he asks, "Are you okay? What's wrong?"

"I'm fine. I just need a second. You're really big." I pant.

"Yeah, you're really fuckin' tight. Are you sure you wanna do this? We can still stop." He says, concern lacing his voice. He stays still until the pain stops, and then pleasure starts to take over.

"We are not stopping. I want you, I want this. You can move now." No going back now.

"Are you sure?" he questions, seeing if I'm telling the truth.

"Yes, I want you to move." Getting frustrated and proving to him I'm fine, I start moving my hips. Finally he starts matching my movements, slowly picking up more speed. This is so much better than anything I could've ever imagined.

"You're so fuckin' tight Jacey. You feel so damn good. So good, baby," he tells me while rolling his hips, bringing his head down to my breasts. He's running his tongue around one nipple, sucking it into his mouth and flicking his tongue against my skin. Letting it go with a pop, he moves to the other, repeating his actions. My nipples are so hard now and my breasts feel so full, it's almost painful, which turns me on even more.

"Oh God!" I yell out.

"Call out whatever you want baby. Tell me what you need." He rolls his hips, hitting my g-spot.

"Yes! Right there! I'm gonna cum again!" I scream out.

"You wanna cum again?" he asks, a smile taking over his face as I look at him.

"Yes!"

"Beg for it." he commands. I push my head back into the pillow so I can see him better. He's serious.

"No," I say, shaking my head. I don't think this is how it's supposed to go.

He stops moving and looks down at me. "You want to cum, beg for it."

"I'm not begging." He thrusts once and stops.

"Let me hear it," he says as he rubs on my g-spot. "Let me give you what your body craves." Oh god, it's too much, I can't hold out any longer. I need this.

"Please Bear! Please let me cum!" I shout, surrendering to my body's needs. He slams into me, thrusting harder than he was before. I match him, throwing my hips up, seeking the release that's just out of my reach.

"Fuck yeah, cum now Lil Mama!" A few more hits and I feel the warm sensation throughout my body. I'm screaming out his name again. Not long after, he's right there with me and I feel him pulsing inside me. He growls into the crook of my neck. "Jacey."

He rolls to the side, taking me with him as we catch our breath. Once our breathing evens out, he unwraps his arms from around me. I automatically miss the warmth of him as he pulls out of me and gets up. He walks into the bathroom, and I prepare myself for the backlash of what I just did. He comes back immediately, turning the light on. Bear asks, worried, "Jacey, why the fuck is there blood on the condom?" I lower my head, feeling my face turn red from embarrassment. I try to cover my face with my arms, but he's there in an instant grabbing them, keeping me from hiding. He puts them over my head as he hovers over me. "Jacey, answer me now! Why the fuck does the goddamn condom have blood on it?" He looks down at the bed. "It's on your sheets too." I try giving him my most innocent look.

"Well, because umm…I might have..." He's glaring at me now, waiting for my response.

"You might have what?" he asks, raising his voice.

I let out a breath. "Do not get loud with me!"

"I'm sorry. Okay? Just tell me what is going on. Did I hurt you? I told you we could've stopped." Concern coming back.

"No you didn't hurt me. As I was saying, I may have been a virgin." I wince as soon as I say it, and squeeze my eyes closed. I wait for it. He's quiet for a minute, so I barely open one eye, just enough so I can see him and here it comes. Oh shit! It's gonna be bad, his nostrils are flaring, his face is red. He looks like one of those raging bulls.

"The fuck? You were a virgin? Why the fuck didn't you tell me?" Letting go of my hands, he sits back on the bed and starts pulling at his hair.

"I'm sorry I just…I didn't want to stop and I thought you would," I say, trying to explain but I don't think he understands.

"Jesus Christ, Jacey! Damn right, I would of stopped! Outta all the goddamn women I've ever been with, I never taken somebody's virginity, never wanted to."

"Yeah, well, um, thanks for that. Didn't really need to know you're a man-whore."

"Well, shit! What do you fuckin' expect? We barely know each other! I thought we both had done this before," he says, as he pulls the condom off. "Goddamn it! Fuck! The condom broke. Fuck! What the hell is going on? Never had one break before! Fuck, I've never been with anybody else without one, I swear! Shit!" He's starting to freak out so I know I need to stay calm.

"It's okay, Bear. I'm on the pill. You know, I've never been with anybody else either," I tell him, hoping it will make the situation better. It's done and over now. There's no going back, so why freak out about it?

"No, it's not fuckin' okay, Jacey! You were a fuckin' virgin. Why wouldn't you fuckin' tell me that? Fuck, Jacey. Why would you do this?" I don't think I've ever heard someone say the word "fuck" so much at one time. This is so not good.

"Because Bear! You were the first guy that's ever turned my body on and I knew you wouldn't wanna do it if you knew," I try to explain further, but he's not getting it.

"Fuck no, I wouldn't have. Shit. Jacey, I fuckin' took it from you!"

"Bear, I let you. It's fine! You didn't even know."

"It's not fine! Why would you wanna give it to a guy like me? I'm not the good guy, Jacey. That's who you should've given it to. How is that even possible for me to be the only one? You're fuckin' beautiful. You could've had anybody, I promise you that."

"I didn't want anybody else! Tonight, I wanted you."

"Jacey, you don't even know me. Fuck, this is so fucked! This shouldn't have happened." He regrets it. Out of all the things I thought would happen, I didn't think he'd be sorry he was with me.

"Then go! Just fucking get out!"

"Jacey…"

"No, get the fuck out of my house!" He grabs his clothes and leaves. As I lay here, under my covers, I hear my mother's voice in my head.

"Jacey, you see those men over there? They are trash. Do you understand me? They will use you, then throw you away. You will marry money, don't ever make my mistakes."

"But Daddy..."

"No, Jacey. You do not ever bring your father up again. He never wanted either of us. Forget him."

Coming back to reality, I think about what happened. People may not understand how I would just let my virginity go like that. It's pretty simple really. I'm twenty-six and I don't trust people, nor do I let anyone close enough. I wasn't holding onto it for marriage or anything like that, it wasn't something I was cherishing. I just wanted to find the guy who could turn me on and hold my interest for more than five fucking minutes. Doesn't hurt that he is the sexiest man I've ever seen and I've been getting myself off to thoughts of a man like him for years.

I fall asleep, dreaming about my father from when I was six years old.

My momma opens the front door, hard. She looks around outside until she finds me. "Jacey get your ass in here."

I stop playing and run inside. "What Momma?"

"Don't 'what' me, you little shit! Tell your father good-bye, we are leaving."

No, she's gonna take me. I don't want to go, so I start crying and begging. I run over to my Daddy and grab his legs, holding on as tight as my little arms can.

"No, Momma! Please! I don't wanna go. I wanna stay with Daddy, please!"

She grabs my arms roughly, yanking me from him. I start crying harder. I don't wanna leave my Daddy. I love him. "Just let me say bye to my daughter! Give me one goddamn minute with her before you fuckin' take her from me!" He pulls me back and gets down on his knees, cupping my cheeks with his hands. "I love you, baby girl. You're my Princess, you always will be. Daddy will always love you."

"Daddy, I don't wanna go with her. I wanna stay with you." I see a tear leak from his eye. My Daddy is strong, he's not supposed to cry.

"I know you do, Princess, but you have to go with your Momma, but you always remember what I said."

"I love you, Daddy." I hang my head.

"I love you too Princess." He kisses me on the forehead before he stands up and my Momma takes my arm. Right before she shuts the door, she turns.

"You remember what I told you. You try and come for her and I will bring you down."

Then I hear my Daddy tell her, "You will pay for this one day. I'll fuckin' make sure of it."

She already had our stuff in the car. She shoves me in the back seat, goes around, starts to drive and we drive for a long time.

I wake up in a dead sweat, just like every other time. I go to my bathroom, turning the water on, and I get in the hot shower, trying to clear my head. I go back and lay in my bed, tossing and turning, trying to get back to sleep. The worst thing about the dream is I don't know if it is real or not. Did my father really love me or was my mother right? Did he never want me?

QUIET COUNTRY

    The next morning, I wake up and I'm sore from the night before. It's a damn good feeling though, because it was the best night of my life until it all went horribly wrong. Thank God Ever took me to the clubhouse so I don't have to go back to get my car and face him. When I get up, I check my phone and see a message from Zoey asking if I want to go shopping. Hanging my head in defeat, I text her yes, so I guess I'll be seeing him after all. Trekking my way to my room, I shower and get ready. I obviously wasn't thinking this through properly, and could use some good retail therapy after what happened last night. What if I do see his stupid ass? I'll just have to ignore him. I know, real grown up, but fuck! The asshole regrets being with me. I can be childish if I want to. Who gives a fuck anyway, right? Not me.

    When I pull up to the clubhouse, I park and see that Ever is just getting here too. I'm so glad I don't have to walk in alone. The four of us girls all hug, then decide where we're all going to go. A guy named Ghost will be going with us today, so when we're ready to leave, he leads us to his white 2012 GMC Acadia. Man, this thing is clean. Once we're all in, our first stop is the bank. Zoey checks the joint account, and sure enough, that son of a bitch cleaned her out. Thankfully, I had told her when she started working with me that she needed to have a secret account and all that money was still there.

    The next stop is the mall, which is one of my favorite places to go because I love shopping. With everything that happened last night, I may go overboard. I bought something from all the stores we went to. The next place we hit is the phone store, so Zoey can get a new phone. After all, our numbers are programmed. Then we go to Victoria's Secret and I get some new bra and panty sets. I can't help but to think of Bear. I don't know why, since I'm sure he hates me. Zoey walks up, holding some demi bras and thongs that she's going to get, and my eyes almost pop out of my head, along with her sister's. Chatty doesn't look surprised at all, but she doesn't know Zoey like we do. I've never seen her get anything like this. Normally, it's just regular granny-panty, cotton, boring shit, but this stuff is sexy. She's picked some silky and some lacy, a colorful array of lingerie. She's going to make Hanger's mouth water when he sees her in this. Even though I never had a man, I always bought myself sexy bras and panties. They make me feel good and I had hopes that one day somebody would see them. Guess I took care of that last night, but he won't be seeing anymore after the way he acted.

Chatty exclaims, "Crazy Girl, he's gonna love that shit!" She's got that right, I think to myself. I really like Chatty, she fits in well with us. She can have fun and shop like we do, and I think we added another girl into our little circle that's already not easy to get into. I'm happy Zoey made a friend after everything that happened with her ex.

We're all hungry so we pick a little deli to go to. While we're eating, Zoey fills us in on what happened with her and Hanger. I feel her eyes on me as she asks, *"Jacey, what happened after you and Bear left?"* The good thing about Zoey is when Ever is around she signs, but at the same time she speaks, so everyone knows what's being said. I feel my face heat up. Being the private person that I am, and with how things turned out, there's no way I'm telling her anything.

"Nothing. He took me home. That's it." By the look on her face, she knows there's more to it. One of the things I love about Zoey, though, is she won't push it. She then turns to Ever, and questions her. *"What about you?"*

"What about me? You know nothing happened, I still live with Mom and Dad. He kissed me goodnight, and it was amazing, the best kiss I've ever had. I need to move out!"

We all start laughing, then she continues, *"I really like him, and when we hung out that one night at the clubhouse, we went to his room. We talked all night, but he never tried anything, then last night he took me home so obviously nothing could happen. I'll either go to the club more or move. We text a lot, have been since that first night."*

Zoey replies, *"Okay, I really like Bear and Writer. So maybe you guys should hang out at the clubhouse tonight, see what happens?"*

I don't know if I should. I don't even know if he'll want to see me after what happened, but fuck it. What's the worst that can happen? I'm ignoring him anyway, right?

"Well, aren't you just the little match maker?" Chatty asks, while laughing.

"I can't help it! I want the people I love to be just as happy as I am," Zoey says, with a smile and a shrug of her shoulder, "If we're partying at the clubhouse, we need to get some guy attention. We need to look hot, like, hotter than last night at the club."

Chatty speaks up. "I know just the place!"

When we get back to the car, Chatty tells Ghost where to go, and I see him turn bright red. For him to be blushing, I wonder where the fuck we're going. As soon as we pull up, I know exactly where we are. I may or may not have made a trip here before to help myself out. Zoey doesn't know though, so she asks, *"Umm…Chatty? Where are we?"*

"We're at a sex shop, Crazy Girl," she proudly states, with a grin on her face.

"WHAT?! Why are we at a sex shop?"

I knew the freak out was going to come, and I have to roll my lips in to keep from laughing. This is so out of her comfort zone, and I can't help but smile. When she looks at me, I just shrug my shoulders. Then Chatty says, "We want to get the guys attention, this is the way to do it."

When we walk in, the first room is filled with sexy clothes and shoes. The back room is where they keep all the toys, but I think today we'll all be staying in front. When Chatty and Ever are done picking out some shit, I look over and see a girl talking to Zoey and she doesn't look happy.

Not too long after Zoey comes back over, she asks if we're ready to leave. On the way to the registers, she explains, *"I just ran into Jasmine."* We check out and we head back to the clubhouse. I ask her who the girl was and she simply says she's a club whore. I can tell she doesn't want to talk about it, so I leave it alone, as my nerves take over.

I'm nervous as fuck to see him again.

FOUR

Bear

I left Jacey's apartment as quick as I could, I got the hell outta there. I don't know what the fuck just happened. I never expected her to be a fucking virgin. For fucksake, she's twenty-six years old! Who the fuck is a virgin at that age? I've never taken somebody's virginity, never wanted to, just like I told her. Why would she just give it up to somebody she didn't even know? To say I was the only guy that's ever turned her on, where the fuck did this girl come from? Maybe the alcohol had something to do with it.

I storm into the clubhouse and go straight to my room, laying in bed for most of the night and thinking it over. I should've realized something was up when she didn't really know what to do when I kissed her. She was nervous when we got to her place, and if she had done this a lot, she wouldn't have been. It also explains the blushing. Why couldn't I have just paid attention, instead of letting my cock lead me into this clusterfuck? But I lied to her when I told her it should never have happened.

It felt so good, unbelievably good. I can still feel her wet cunt strangling my cock. Goddamn, she was so fucking tight, clenching and throbbing around me. Fuck, I can still taste her in my mouth, so sweet and salty. God. Outta all the women I've been with, it has never been like that. Her cunt, her smell, her taste, and her mouth, all of it bliss, total fucking perfection.

I didn't lie when I said I'm not the good guy. It just goes to show, because I'd do it all over again without a second thought, just to feel her wrapped around me again. I overreacted, I know that, but it took me by surprise. Now I gotta figure out how to fix it, and I don't know what the hell I'm gonna do. She probably never wants to see me again, but I gotta talk to her about what happened. Once I fix it, I can get in that pussy again. I'll show her just what she's been missing out on.

QUIET COUNTRY

When I wake up the next day, I head to church, taking my seat at the table. Gunner and Writer are already here. Once everybody finally arrives, Hanger lets us know that Ghost'll be going with the girls shopping. That pisses me off, not because I don't trust him, of course I trust him. It's that I really need to see her and talk to her. I wish it was me going instead. I'm not the only one bothered by this, Writer is too. He's got it bad for Ever. Hanger sees my expression and asks, "Bear, you got something to say?"

I cross my arms over my chest. "I'm not happy about him bein' the one to go with them, but it's your decision. You're the president. Can you at least keep us informed with everywhere they go?"

"You're right, it is my decision. We need someone to be in the background and not stick out. We all know that Ghost is the one to do that and he'll keep them safe. I'm trusting him with Crazy Girl. He'll inform me wherever they go, and I'll keep you updated."

Goddamn it, I know he's right but I keep the scowl on my face and give him a tight nod. Hanger then asks where Romeo is, and Gunner informs him that he's gonna be late. I don't really give a shit about any of this right now, so I let my mind drift to Jacey. I wonder if she's okay, if she hates me, and if she'll even want to see or talk to me again.

I come back to reality when I hear the words Ol' Lady, and II know that Hanger is talking about Crazy Girl. He'd be stupid not to make her his Ol' Lady. I hear him ask, "What, Hacker?"

Hacker replies, "Well, I never thought I'd see the day when the biggest asshole of us all would settle down." He's chuckling.

Hanger responds, "What can I say? She did something to me, brother." A slow smile spreads across his face.

I chime in. "I bet she did." I practically whisper it, so Hanger doesn't know that I said it. That's what the fucker gets for pissing me off. I drop my head with a smile on my face. Gunner speaks up. "What she did was come in here and take you by the balls, you pussy-whipped motherfucker." We all start laughing.

Hanger shakes his head. "Yeah, well wait til this shit happens to you, and it will happen. I'm gonna sit back and give you fuckers shit then." Everyone pipes us, saying 'not happenin'' and 'no fuckin' way'.

Romeo walks in. Hanger's pissed that he's late, but gives him the okay to stay. Romeo starts filling us in on some chick named Giovanna and the restaurant. We get the conformation that it's for sure the Italians taking from us, and he wants to bring this girl into the club, even though her family's the enemy. He must have lost his goddamn mind, getting everyone riled up, and being stupid enough to say shit about Hanger bringing Crazy Girl to the club. Romeo shouldn't have done that shit. Hanger jumps outta his seat, I think he is gonna fucking throttle Romeo, but Gunner holds him back. Once that's settled, we get to business, and by now I'm ready to get the fuck outta this room. I can't get her off my mind. Why am I still worried about it when Jacey told me to get the fuck out? Hanger goes over everything about Crazy Girl's ex and what he wants to do. His phone goes off, and I see a look on his face that I don't like. I start to panic, thinking something has happened to the girls, so I yell, "What's wrong?"

He replies, "Nothing, the girls are fine. They'll be back soon. They went to the mall, had lunch, and they have one more stop to make before they come here."

"Are you sure they're fine? Because the look on your face is sayin' somethin' different."

"They're fine, and you know I would tell you if they weren't. Now, write it down for Writer so he can relax." Writer's watching me as I write down what Hanger said and I see him settle back down. Yeah, he was just as worried as me. Hanger goes over everything one more time and then we're finally dismissed. I head back to my room, sit down on my bed, and continue to think about what's gonna happen the next time I see her.

About half an hour later, I make my way into the bar and grab two fingers of Wild Turkey. That's when I see the girls walk in. Hanger takes Crazy Girl to their room, Chatty finds Ripper, and Ever goes with Writer. That leaves just Jacey sitting at the bar by herself. I down my Wild Turkey, hissing out a breath as it burns my throat. I walk up to her, she looks so fucking adorable, and I can tell she's uncomfortable sitting here. She doesn't see me walk up because she has her head down, playing with the straw in her drink. It's not until I get right up to her that she looks up at me with those big beautiful eyes. I've never seen anything like 'em, they're two different colors. One is light brown with a little blue-green in it and the other eye is the opposite: the blue-green predominant, with just a little light brown flecked in. Even in shorts and a T-shirt, she's sexy, and she stands out from the girls that normally hang around here. They all dress skanky, showing off all the goods in the hopes that one of us will be fucking 'em later. She's not like that though, it's a big fucking turn on.

"Hey, Lil Mama, can we talk for a minute?" She turns on the stool as she throws her hand on her hip and glares at me.

"What do you want to talk about, Bear?" she asks, venom thick in her voice.

I lower my voice. "Don't you think we should talk about last night?"

"Why would I want to do that? You made it clear how you felt about it." Shit, her attitude is making me hard. Women don't give me attitude, they just do what I want, but I'm liking this feisty little one.

"You're the one that kicked me out. Now come the fuck on and let's go have a talk."

"Don't tell me to 'come the fuck on'. Who the fuck do you think you are?"

I lean into her, putting my mouth to her ear. She tries to move, but I place my hand on the back of her head. As I lightly grab a handful of her soft brown hair to keep her in place, I whisper, "I think I'm the one that had my cock so deep inside you that you were screaming my name. I also think I'm the one that gave you two orgasms that made you come completely undone, and it was the sexiest fuckin' thing I've ever seen. Now, I wanna talk, so come talk to me." I pull back to look at her. With her eyes closed, she nods her head and I take her hand, pulling her to my room, shutting the door behind us. She leans up against the wall and I stand in front of her. "Jacey, about last night...I'm sorry for getting pissed."

She's lost the attitude, saying, "It's okay Bear. I understand why you were."

"I just don't get why you didn't tell me."

"I already told you: you're the only one that has ever affected me like that, and I knew you wouldn't want to go through with it if you knew the truth."

I take a couple steps so I'm right in front of her, bracing one arm on the wall and placing my knee between her legs, I spread them open while I lean into her. "Are you affected right now?" I run a finger down her cheek, pressing my thigh against her, putting pressure on her pussy. Watching her eyes flutter.

She lets out a breathy "Yeah."

"Good, because I want you again. I get what I want, Lil Mama, and I want my cock pushin' in that tight little pussy. Can't quit thinkin' about how good you felt underneath me." That's when I hear Hanger asking where she is. Jacey pushes on my chest, trying to recover from my words. I back away so she can open the door and walk out.

"Lil Mama."

She turns and gives me a heart stopping smile. "Yeah?"
I smile back. "I don't regret it, not for a second."
"Me either Bear." With that she walks out.

I walk out to the bar a while later, and stand to the side in the shadows, watching my surroundings. I hear the girls coming down the hallway, focusing on that spot until I see her. She's fucking stunning, everything about her is unlike anything I've ever seen before. She almost looks exotic, with her long dark hair, her soft tan skin, and those fucking eyes. Everything about her is just fucking beautiful. She's wearing tight black jeans with a shiny top that looks too big for her because it's hanging off one shoulder. Fuck, seeing her bare skin, I wanna put my face in the crook of her neck and smell the strawberry scent that I know she'll be enveloped in. My jeans are growing tighter by the second just thinking about what I'll be doing to her later. I know I'm a cocky bastard.

The fuck-me-heels she's got on make her legs look like they could go on forever. I want those heels digging into my back, while she's crying out from the pleasure I'll be giving her. I stay back watching and let her have her fun. Crazy Girl introduces her to all my brothers. She's dancing, talking with the other girl, and it looks like she's having a good time, when I see one of the hang-arounds walk up to her. We call him 'Twitch' because he's spun the fuck out, and he reminds me of my mother in a way. He tries to talk to her, but she automatically blows him off. Good girl.

I get her favorite drink, a Rum and Coke with lime, and when I turn back around, another hang-around has come up to her. This time it's Justin. He's clean cut, with a nice job in town. No one would know he's on drugs unless they saw him here, he hides that shit well. He looks like the type of guy she needs to be with, but just the thought of that twists me up inside. She doesn't blow him off like the other one and starts laughing at something he said. Nope, don't like that at all. It's time for me to make my presence known.

"Hey Bear," the douche lord says.

"Hey Dustin. It's time for you to leave." I see her body stiffen and as she turns to face me, I place the Rum and Coke in her hand.

"It's Justin, and we were just talking," he replied.

"I don't give two fucks what you were doing. I suggest that if you ever wanna step foot in this clubhouse again, you'll leave right the fuck now." Justin doesn't give it a second thought as he hurries away. Pussy.

Sam Hunt's Leave The Night On starts playing right when Jacey says, "Bear, what the fuck are you doing?" Oh yeah, she's pissed now. Her arms are crossed over her chest, still clutching her drink, pushing up her ample tits. Her eyes narrow as she glares at me. I'm irate, so I question, "Do you want him now?"

"I didn't fucking say that, did I? You can't just come over here and scare off somebody because they're talking to me."

"No, you didn't say that," I answer, feeling out of sorts because I shouldn't care. I point to her. "You can't just come in my clubhouse, chattin' people up either."

"He came up to me," she says, pointing right back at me. "You can't tell me what to do." She downs her Rum and Coke, slamming the glass on the table. She's making me fucking crazy.

"I sure as fuck can, when it was my cock in you last night."

"If you're going to try to be a controlling asshole, then that was the first and last time your cock will get anywhere near me."

"It's not being controlling. It's showin' who the fuck you belong to." Where the fuck is this shit coming from?

"You did not just fucking say that to me," she says, getting pissed all over again, throwing her hand back on that hip.

"Yeah, I did. What are you gonna do about it, Princess?" After I say that, I see her face change to reflect an emotion I'm not sure of, maybe sadness. Then she goes off.

"Oh my god! Do NOT call me that, you fucking piece of shit! You don't know anything about me. I don't belong to you and I never will."

"Oh really? Are you sure about that?" Suddenly, we hear yelling and look over.

"Shit, Zoey just got in a fight!" Jacey hollers, as she runs over. When I walk up behind her, I hear her asking if Crazy Girl's okay, then Hanger takes his woman off to their room.

"You ready to finish our conversation now?" I ask from behind her.

She spins on me, narrowing her eyes. "There isn't anything left to say, Bear."

"Oh Lil Mama, there's a whole lot left to say." I give her a devilish grin.

"No, there's not. You think you're gonna control me, own me, and it's not happening. So, I'm just going to go home." She's got another thing coming if she thinks she's really leaving.

"You're not going anywhere." Before she can answer, I bend down grab her by her thighs, fireman style, carrying her to my room, all while she's screaming at me.

"Put me down, you son of a bitch!" She starts slapping and hitting my back. I just chuckle and everyone else is laughing too.

"No can do, Lil Mama, you're comin' with me," I reprimand her with a good hard slap to her ass. She lets out a moan. I guess somebody likes to get spanked, making my cock twitch at the thought of turning her ass red. Once we're in my room, I turn to face the door, slam it shut, and flip the lock. I let her down onto her feet.

"Bear, just let me go," she whines.

"No can do, Lil Mama. I'm gonna show you who you belong to here. Don't think I didn't hear that moan come outta you when I smacked your ass." I close the space that's between us as she steps back until she's up against the wall. I lean over her, putting my mouth to her ear. "You know you want me, for me to make you feel good. You wanna feel me deep inside you again, don't you?"

"Hmm" I know I got her right where I want her. Fuck yeah! I bring my face up and look to see her head against the wall, eyes closed. I put my mouth to her ear again.

"How wet are you for me? I bet you're soaked just from thinkin' about last night, and maybe from that little smack I gave you." I take one of her hands, placing it over my jeans on my rock hard cock. "Feel what you do to me." I let her hand go, but she doesn't move it off of me. "Turn around and put your hands on the wall, Lil Mama." I demand her to do as I say, and she listens with no hesitation, knowing the pleasure I can bring to her. "Good girl. Do not fuckin' move 'em. Got me?" I reach around her and undo her jeans, pulling them down.

"Okay," she answers, on a whisper.

I remove her fuck-me-heels long enough to get her jeans off. I slip them back on her feet before standing and pulling her shirt over her head. That leaves her standing before me in just her black strapless bra, matching lace panties and the heels. "You're the most beautiful fuckin' woman I've ever seen," I say, watching her head drop down. God damn, she is sexy. I undo her bra, letting it fall to the floor. Then I bend down, removing her panties so she is completely bare to me. I stand back up and lean over her again, giving her another slap just to see how she'll react. Her hands form into fists as a moan escapes her lips. I move her hair off her neck and place soft kisses against her skin. Letting another moan release, she tilts her head to the side giving me better access.

"You like pain, Lil Mama?" I ask, as I run my hands around to her stomach, letting them move over her body, feeling her softness.

"Seems so. I don't know what I like."

"Guess we'll be findin' out." I pull her back to me so her back is to my front. She lets her head fall back onto my chest as I massage her perfectly sized tits in my hands. I take my thumbs and fingers, rolling and pulling at her hard little nipples, harder than I normally would, but I've never had a woman so responsive to pain. Her moans grow louder as she reaches back, gripping onto my jeans. I start to caress her skin as I move one hand down between her tits to her stomach, giving her nipple a pull every so often with my other hand. My hand caresses her, landing on her beautiful pussy. I run my finger through her slit just to see if I was right, and I was because she's fucking soaked.

"You're soaked just like I knew you would be, Baby. You like this?" I whisper, feather light against her ear.

"Uh- huh," she says, nodding.

"Tell me what I wanna hear," I instruct, as I give her a slap on her pussy.

"Oh god. Bear, please," she begs.

"Mmm, I like you begging. Do you wanna cum?" I ask as I push a finger inside of her tight little cunt.

"Yes, please." I then put a second finger inside of her, stretching her open to fit my size. I start finger fucking her, curling them inside, rubbing on her g-spot. Jacey's moans are so loud, I'm sure everyone can hear her outside. I feel her start to clench around my fingers and I stop.

"Bear. Oh my god, please don't stop!" That begging again. I love it!

"Tell me what I wanna hear, Lil Mama, then you can cum." She knows I want her to tell me she belongs to me here.

"No, I'm not saying it."

"You will, Baby. Believe me, before this is all said and done, you will tell me. For now, just agree you won't fuck anybody else." I'm not gonna push her anymore.

"Bear, I'm not one of your whores here. So no, I won't be fucking anybody else. What about you?"

"Way I see it, we've got a good thing goin'. No need to go get somethin' else," I assure her. It's true, as long as I got this perfect girl, why would I need something else?

I take my thumb and rub her clit, sticking two fingers back inside her. I take her over the edge, her body convulsing against me, she's moaning out my name. God damn, I love hearing that. I hold onto her until she comes back down from the high I just gave her. I turn her around and lean her against the wall. I let Jacey watch as I stick my fingers in my mouth, sucking off her arousal. "So fuckin' sweet, I love your taste."

"God, Bear. What are you doing to me?"

"Nothin' but good things," I reply as I let her go to take my shirt off and undo the button on my jeans. I pull the zipper down, grabbing a condom from my pocket before letting them fall to the ground. I pull my boxer briefs off and stand in front of her. She is watching my every move. "You like this Lil Mama? You like what you see?"

"This is so wrong, but yeah, you're fucking sexy as hell."

I keep eye contact with her as I take the condom, rip it open with my teeth, and slide it in place. "I don't know why you say this is wrong, but I'm glad you like what you see." I bend and grab onto her thighs, lifting her up so she straddles my waist, and kiss her. She opens for me automatically. I touch my tongue with hers, deepening the kiss. I lean her against the wall, bracing her weight between the wall and one arm. With my free hand, I grab my rock hard cock, put it at her opening and push in until I'm balls deep. I stay there, letting her adjust to my size. "Fuck, Baby, you're so tight."

"Move, Bear. Fuck me." I start a slow pace, pumping into her, and she's moving her hips to match me, then I start to go faster. "Harder!" she yells. Giving her what she wants, I pick up my pace, hitting her g-spot again, the sounds coming out of her mouth growing louder. "Fuck! Bear, this feels so good!"

"I know, Lil Mama. Fuck, you're so wet." I pull her to me and away from the wall, rolling my hips, pushing her up and down on me.

"Faster please, harder and faster!" Shit, I start going like a crazy man thrusting into her. I've never gone this hard or fast and it's fucking amazing, this woman is amazing. "Oh! God! I'm gonna cum! Fuck don't stop!" That gets me on the edge as I continue slamming into her soaked cunt.

"Let go, Baby. I got you."

A few more hits to her spot and she's throbbing around me. It's so fucking good. This is what I wanted to feel again, her clutching and tightening around me.

"That's it. I feel you squeezing me. So fuckin' good, and tight. Let me hear you, Lil Mama."

Her orgasm takes over and she claws at my back, biting and sucking on my neck. Her screams fill the room as she calls out my name. It's so fucking sexy when she comes, taking me over with her. I feel the buildup of my release, my balls tighten up, and I'm letting go inside her sweet cunt.

"Fuckin' hell, Lil Mama," I moan, my mouth in the crook of her neck, coming harder than I think I ever have in my entire life.

With us both sated, I tighten my arms around her waist and Jacey holds onto me as tight as she can. Something twists inside of me, I don't know what it is, and I don't know if I like it. I walk us over to my bed, where I lay her down, pulling out on the way. Making my way to the bathroom, I could give two fucks if any of my brothers see me. The whores already have so it doesn't matter, but nobody's in the hall. I pull the condom off, throw it away, and grab a washcloth, cleaning myself up. I grab another one, getting it wet under the hot water. I open the bathroom door and head back to my room, but when I open the door, Jacey is gone.

"Goddammit!" I say under my breath, while running my hand over my face. I take the rag back to the bathroom.

What the fuck just happened? I think to myself as I go back to an empty bed, lying down, and lighting up a cigarette.

FIVE

Bear

It's been a couple of days since Jacey fucking dipped out on me and I can't figure out why she ran. Shit, I thought we had come to an agreement, that was until I walked out of the bathroom and saw my bed empty. I don't know what the fuck is wrong with that woman. Her mood swings are starting to give me fucking whiplash. She's pissed at me one minute, but when I tell her the things I want to do to her, her body can't help but respond to me. I just need to figure out how to get her head and body on the same page. There's only one person I can talk to about this mess, and he won't give me shit, plus he has some experience with insane women. I knock on his door and when he opens up, I greet him. "Hey, Rip."

"Bear, hey brother. What's up?" He moves, opening the door wide for me to enter.

"Does Hanger need somethin'?"

I run my hands over my face, sit down in a chair, and shake my head no. He takes a seat on the bed, and starts laughing.

"What's so fuckin' funny?" I ask, giving him a hard look.

"That girl got you all twisted up, doesn't she?" he asks.

Trying to be casual, I reply, "What are you talking about?"

"I know that fuckin' look, brother. I had the same one when I met Chat, you remember?"

I put my elbows on my knees, and leaning forward, I drop my head to run my fingers through my hair.

"I swear to Christ, this girl is fuckin' insane." He just laughs. I'm glad he thinks this shit is a fuckin' joke.

"What happened?" he asks.

"We've fucked a couple of times, then she gets this fuckin' attitude. It's hot as hell, don't get me wrong, but it pisses me off at the same time."

"Brother, it sounds like you've got your hands full," he says.

"You remember what it was like with me and Chat? I was crazy about her from the first time I looked at her, but I had to work for it.

She made me chase her ass for a good long time before I got her to cave."

"Yeah, Ripper, I do. I don't know what to fuckin' do with her. Usually I don't give a fuck, but she dipped out on me, and I haven't seen her since. It's not the same as with you guys, though. I'm not tryin' to make her my Ol' Lady. I just wanna keep gettin' my dick wet."

"She got under your skin is what she did! And we'll see 'bout the Ol' Lady part. Bear, I've known you since you were a young shit. You've never come to me 'bout a damn girl before, so that's gotta count for somethin' Brother. You got her number, call her."

I look at him like he's fucking stupid.

"Don't you fuckin' think if I had her number, I would've fuckin' done that already? God, I just don't understand her ass."

"We're men! We'll never understand what goes through a woman's head. You know where she lives?"

"Yeah, I took her home that first night."

"So go to her place. If she isn't there, wait." He shrugs his shoulders like it's so fuckin' easy.

"Alright, Brother. Thanks."

"No problem."

I go by the garage to get some work done, then go check and make sure everything is good with the cabin before heading to her place.

I go to her door and knock, but nobody answers, so I go to my bike, lean up against it, and light up a cigarette. I inhale and slowly blow smoke outta my mouth. I see a black 2014 Stingray with 5-split spoke chrome aluminum wheels. When it pulls under the light in the parking space, I can see the gray glitter over coat and red brake calipers and hear the stereo blasting *Sugar by Maroon 5*.

The windows aren't tinted enough for me not to see that it's her. Fuck me, that's a beautiful car, she wasn't lying when she said she knew about cars. I throw the smoke down and grind it into the cement to kill the fire. I walk up to Jacey's car once she's parked and open her door. I glance inside and see that she's got carbon flash black and red leather interior, six speed with paddle shifter and competition sport bucket seats. Fuck, her whole damn car is fucking custom and just as sexy as she is. I look at her and she's looking up at me with wide eyes, her mouth hanging open, so I give her a grin.

"This yours, Lil Mama? Sexy car for a sexy woman. I guess you do know about cars."

She huffs out a breath., "Bear, what the fuck are you doing here?"

"We need to talk, Jacey."

"No, we don't."

"Yes, we fuckin' do. Woman, I've been waitin' for you. I'm not leavin' til we clear up a few things," I tell her, and I'm not taking any bullshit.

"Fine, come on." I let her lead me to her apartment. She's lets us both in, and I lock the door behind me. Jacey drops her purse and keys on the table and she turns to see me standing there, legs spread, arms crossed over my chest, a pissed off look on my face. "Don't look at me like that! You didn't need to come over here in the first fucking place."

"Why don't you tell me why you dipped out on me the other night?"

"Because you like to have me say shit like 'I fucking belong to you' and I don't fucking belong to you. It's sex, Bear, that's it," she tells me, but I don't believe it.

"I call bullshit, Lil Mama. I think you got scared."

"Scared of what? We fucked, and it was done so it was time for me to go," she says casually.

"Right. It might just be fuckin' but that doesn't give you reason to bounce out. Your body calls to me, it obeys me. Your head needs to get on track with that."

"You need to go." She's getting defensive again, I can tell by the look in her eyes and the way she stands.

"I'm not going anywhere yet."

"Bear, please. I'm tired. I don't wanna do this."

"Well, you're gonna do it, because you're not gonna pull that shit on me again. Got me?"

"I can leave whenever I want." I drop my hands and walk over to her, backing her up to the table.

"You can," I nuzzle my nose in her hair, smelling her scent. "You can leave whenever you want, but tell me when you're leaving. Don't just dip out like that. When you're at the club, you belong to me. It's for your protection. If they know you're with me, they won't fuck with you, and if you go around messin' with different guys at the club, they'll mistake you for a whore."

She puts her hands on my chest, gripping my beater in her hands. "I'm sorry I did that. It just freaked me the fuck out, you saying I belong to you," she says, as I bend and grip her thighs, picking her up. I sit her on the table, spreading her legs with my hips so I can get in between them, placing my hands on her cheeks to make sure she looks at me.

"I didn't mean to scare you. I was pissed because that hang-around was comin' on to you."

"I can handle myself, Bear. I would've told him to leave me alone. I was trying to be nice and talk to him."

"Jacey, you're not that nice," I smirk at her and she is pursing her lips trying not to laugh. "Promise me you won't leave like that again."

"I promise. I'm sorry, I shouldn't have done that."

"Damn right. Now I want your phone number." I pull out my phone and she rattles the numbers off then I put it back in my pocket.

"So, will you tell me why it scared you so much?"

"No, I don't wanna talk about it."

"Alright, I'll let it go for now, but eventually you are gonna have to open up."

"Bear, there are things in my past that I'll never talk about. Can we just keep doing what we have been?"

"Yeah, we can do that." For now, I think to myself. I bring her face to mine, put my lips to hers. I give her a slow tender kiss, sliding my tongue along hers. Every other time we've kissed it's always been hard, rough, and hungry. I want this one to be different. Even though I can feel my dick twitching, we are not doing this tonight. I pull away from her mouth before I really want to. She's trying to catch her breath, and slowly opens her eyes to look at me. "Alright, Lil Mama, it's time for me to go."

"You can't go now. Not after a kiss like that."

I give her a smile. "Yeah, I can. It's getting late and you need rest. You gotta work in the morning. I'll call you soon." I give her one last kiss on her mouth, then forehead. Making my way to the door I turn. "Goodnight, Lil Mama."

She gives me a soul shattering smile. "Goodnight, Bear."

With that, I lock the door, shut it behind me, and head back to the clubhouse.

Jacey

This last week has been hard for me. I used to go running to clear my head, now all I think about is Bear. I've done a lot of thinking since he came to my apartment. I know I shouldn't have dipped out on him, it was a bitch move, but I had to get out of there. I threw my clothes on and ran like my ass was on fire. I couldn't get my mother's voice out of my head. *"Jacey, guys like your father, they try to own you. They think you belong to them. They will use you and abuse you, then throw you out once they are done. You will marry rich, honey. You will marry a doctor or a lawyer, not scum like that."*

I blasted *Four Five Seconds by Kanye West, Rihanna, and Paul McCartney* as loud as my speakers would go, just trying to get her out of my head. She's a monster. That night I fell asleep and had another dream about my father. It's happening more now since I met Bear and I've never had this one before.

"Daddy, will you tell me a story?"

"Yeah. Lay down and I'll tuck you in. Once upon a time there was a Princess. She was favored in her father's Kingdom. All the boys wanted to marry the Princess, but the King wouldn't let them. Every boy feared the King, only the boy that would be allowed to marry the Princess would have to stand up to the King. He would be strong, that way the King knew his Princess would be taken care of and protected. Goodnight Princess. Always remember Daddy loves you."

Now all this shit with the dreams and Bear is getting to me. It scares me. I like to be in control of shit, he takes that control away. My body loves it, but my mind is completely opposed. My mind thinks he's going to do to me what my mother says my father did to her. I don't want that, but then the dreams are showing me that my father wasn't a bad man. I just don't know what to do or what to believe.

Bear pisses me off because he makes me feel things I shouldn't. I don't want to belong to him and I don't want to have a life with the club. I don't know how Zoey does it. She just takes everything in stride, but I can't do that, I'm not that person. When I choose to be with someone it'll be when I'm ready to settle down, get married, and have a family, and certainly not with the same type of guy my mother told me to stay away from.

He's a fucking biker for Godsake.

He lives in that fucking clubhouse, with a bunch of other bikers and whores.

What kind of life would that be?

My mother's voice comes into my head, *"They are not the type to settle down and be with one woman. They don't fall in love and they have no respect for women."*

No, I'll be marrying into money. I'll find me a doctor or lawyer, just like my mother said. Bear fucks with my head so much though. When he's there, I don't want him to be, and when he's not, I miss him. I miss the feel of him, I miss looking at him, and mostly I miss what he does to my body. God, it's so damn confusing, the way he left me, with a throbbing fire between my legs. He's never kissed me like that, and it took my breath away. I'm about to close up the clinic for the night when my phone rings. "Hello?"

"Lil Mama." God, his voice! It's so rough, so rugged.

"Hey Bear." I try to sound cool and calm even though I know it came out a little shaky.

"I'm outside."

"What? Why?"

"You've got five minutes to get your ass out here and on my bike."

I can't help the smile forming on my face. "Umm... You can't just tell me what to do."

"Are you trying to fight with me?"

"Maybe." I know he can hear the teasing tone of my voice.

"Make that three minutes. If you're not out here, I'll come get you and paddle that sexy ass. Got me?"

"Maybe I want you to paddle my ass."

"You're runnin' outta time."

"Fine." I hang up and hurry to get everything locked up. I get outside and see him just like he was at my apartment. He's leaning up against his bike, one hand on it with the other holding onto a cigarette. The smoke rolls from his mouth. "You know those things are addictive. You should quit!" I yell out to him as I walk.

"Seems to me they're not the only thing that's addictive, but I'm not quittin' those either anytime soon." He gives me that sexy smile of his and it makes me grin.

I continue checking him out on my way over. Bear has on his usual black leather boots, dark but worn jeans, and a white beater with his cut. He's perfection to look at, tall and muscled like nothing I've ever seen, dark hair I like running my fingers through, and bearded. God, just thinking about having him between my legs has me getting turned on. I remember his facial hair rubbing against my inner thighs and I'm feeling a fire build within me, a dull ache forming. I get to him and I see the smile still on his face, right along with mine. He holds out a helmet for me and I put it on, then climb on the back of his bike.

We ride for about forty-five minutes until we are back in the city and he takes us to a little diner called Ma and Pop's Place, where he parks the bike. We both dismount, and I take the helmet off and ask, "What are we doing here?"

"Thought you might be hungry. This place has the best food

around." He takes my hand and leads me inside. It's a small place, quiet, and it looks like one of those fifties styled diners. He leads us over to the booth ushering me in on one side, him taking a seat across from me. The waitress comes over and gives us both big smiles. She's an older lady with graying hair, but bright piercing blue eyes. "Hey Bear. How you doing?"

"I'm good, Ma. How're you?"

"Oh, honey, you know, the usual. Working too much, but I can't get Pop away from this place."

"Yeah, I know. I don't think you ever will."

"You want your usual, Honey?"

"Yeah." He looks to me. "What would you like?"

"I'll just have the same." Ma nods her head and walks away. "So you come here often?"

"Yeah. I like it here, been comin' here since I was thirteen."

"So, what did we order anyway?" I ask, curious now.

He chuckles, but responds, "Burger, fries, and Cokes." Just then Ma brings over our drinks. She sets them down with straws, giving me a warm smile before she walks away.

"What made you start coming here?" I ask.

"I had a good life, until it went to shit. Found this place one day, didn't have enough money to pay, but they fed me. Been comin' ever since. I love 'em like they're family."

"What about your family, do you have any?"

"Nope, just my brothers at the club, that's it. Enough 'bout me, what's your story?"

I drop my head, taking a drink then playing with the straw. "There's not much to tell."

"For some reason, I doubt that. Have you always lived in Kansas?"

"No. I did when I was little, then my mother moved me away. I decided to come back."

"Why did you come back?"

"I don't really want to talk about it."

"Why did you become a doctor?"

Ma drops our food on the table and this burger's the biggest I've ever seen. "Bear, I can't eat all this." With wide eyes, I look at him grinning.

Not dropping it, he asks again, "Why did you become a doctor?"

"My mother pushed me to become one. That's enough, let's eat."

We stop talking so we can eat. By the time I'm completely full, I've only finished half the burger and some fries, while Bear ate everything.

He gets up, drops a fifty on the table, and holds his hand out to me. I take it and before we walk out Ma says, "You be sure and bring her back."

"I'll try, Ma." He gives her a smile over his shoulder, then we're back at his bike, and he takes me back to my car. Why can't this just be easy? I've had so much fun with him and I don't want it to end. He pulls to a stop, parks, then helps me off his bike. I hand him the helmet back.

"You want to come over? This has been fun, I'm not ready for it to end," I tell him, it's just what I was thinking.

"Yeah, I can do that. It has been fun, huh? I'll follow you." I unlock my car door, get in, and drive to my apartment complex. We walk up together, holding hands as I unlock my door and he shuts and locks it behind him.

"You want to watch a movie?" I ask, seeing him give me that fucking grin again.

"What you got?"

I point to my collection. "They're over there. You can pick something or order one, it doesn't matter. I'm going to take a quick shower. I'll be right back." I go into my bedroom, picking a pair of pajama pants and a tank top, then head into my bathroom and run the water. I pull my hair out of its ponytail, get undressed, and climb in, letting the hot water fall down my body. It feels so good. Suddenly, I hear the bathroom door open. Bear steps in the shower with me, condom already on, burning me with his stare.

"You are, fuckin' hands down, the most stunning woman I have ever seen."

I smile. "You're pretty fucking stunning yourself." He is, I can't express it enough, with all his tattoos and muscles, that massive cock standing at attention. He comes close to me, placing one hand on the back of my head, gripping my hair. He leans down, bringing his lips to mine, seeking an opening. I willingly give him what he wants, parting my lips and allowing him access. He tries doing the sweet soft kissing, but it's not enough for me. I deepen the kiss, wrapping my arms around his neck, pulling him closer to me. I let out a quiet moan into his mouth as he stands straight up, taking me with him. I wrap my legs around his waist, feeling the head of his cock at my opening.

He breaks away from the kiss.

"This is gonna be hard and fast, Lil Mama. I've been wantin' you since the last time I was here."

I give him a nod and crush my mouth back to his. He sits me back on my feet, turning me to face the wall.

"Bend over, spread your legs."

I do what he wants.

"Hands on the wall."

In one quick thrust, he's all the way in. I can't help but let out a loud moan as I hear him growl. He has one hand holding my hip while the other is pulling my hair as he pushes into me. He was right, he wasn't going to be easy, and I'm loving every single second of it. I can feel him hitting my spot every time he thrusts into me.

"Fuck, Bear! Pull my hair harder!"

He picks up even more speed, causing my orgasm to build and my head to snap back.

"Oh shit! Oh God, I'm gonna cum! Harder goddamn it!" He does as asked, giving me everything I need.

"Fuckin' hell Lil Mama, you feel good. So fuckin' good."

Then I'm screaming out my release, and he pulls me back on him with a few more hard, deep thrusts. I feel him let go inside me, growling out my name. After we get our breath back, he gently pulls me up. I might have bruises from his grip, but sweet baby Jesus, that was amazing. We wash ourselves off and get out. Once we're dried off and dressed, me in my pjs, him just in his boxer briefs, we go into the living room and he starts a movie. Bear sits on the couch and I lay down with my head in his lap. He runs his fingers through my wet hair, putting me to sleep.

I had the best night's sleep I've ever had last night. I'm kind of disappointed that Bear wasn't here when I woke up. He must have put me to bed before he left, but I can still smell his scent lingering on my sheets. It's comforting and for some reason, makes me feel safe. He always has this hint of motor oil, cigarette smoke, and leather mixed in with his cologne. It reminds me of my father, which takes me back to when I was twelve years old.

I had been living in California for the last six years. That's where my mother took me when she left my father. My mother and father were never married, so she didn't have to worry about getting a divorce or anything. She could just pick up and move on, which she did. Two years ago, she married a man that I hate. He has a lot of money and that's why she married him. He wants to act like he's my father and wants for me to call him dad. I can't do that, I have a dad. Everyday my memories of him fade, regardless of how hard I try to hold on. I'm trying so hard to remember what he said to me the day my mother took me away. He told me I was his Princess and that he would always love me. If he loved me, why hasn't he come for me? Why would he let me stay with her?

"Jacey, are you paying attention?"

"Mom, I really want to go outside and play."

"I said you are not going outside. Future doctors don't have time to play. Besides no daughter of mine will be playing with filth."

"What if I don't want to be a doctor? You don't even know those kids, the houses around here are too nice to have filth."

She takes another sip of her wine. "Are you questioning me, you little bitch?"

The tears threaten to fall, but I hold them back, I'm not giving her the satisfaction of seeing me break. "Why'd you even take me? Why couldn't you just let me stay with my Dad?" I feel the sting from her slap and I cup my cheek. She bends down so she's eye level with me and I try not to gag from the smell of alcohol on her breath.

"You listen to me, you ungrateful little shit. Your father never wanted you. He never wanted either of us. You should be grateful I took you away. I could have left you there to be trash like him."

"He wasn't trash, Mom, and as hard as you've tried to take my memories, I'll never forget his face. I'll never forget his smell and what he was wearing that day."

The tears are falling now. I step away from her and run to my room, locking the door. I turn on some music, it's all I have. I'm not allowed to have friends, she keeps me inside the house at all times, unless I'm at school, and the kids at think I'm mean because I don't play with them. They don't understand that she won't let me. I just want to be like all the other kids.

My mother has always drank as far back as I can remember, but it's gotten worse, and she's nothing but a drunk now. I look in the mirror, seeing my red cheek. I go into my bathroom, wet a washcloth with cold water, and place it against my burning skin. Walking to my bedroom window, I look out and watch the kids outside play and ride their bikes.

I come back from my memories and see the note Bear wrote.

> Lil Mama, I had to go.
> I'll call you soon.
>   - Bear

It puts a smile on my face to see what he left me. I get up and start my routine for the day. I run, shower, drink my coffee, and eat. Arriving at the clinic by eight A.M., I see my first patients are the Johnson family. Mrs. Johnson must be Wonder Woman, I swear, taking on six little boys all ages, from ten to two. When I get done for the day, I'll pack up and head home to my lonely apartment, sit at my desk and look up my father once again.

SIX

Bear

Once a week, the Sinners come together with the Cobras at their compound and have a fight night. We get one of our guys and one of theirs and bet on a winner. Hanger used to come until he saved Crazy Girl, but now he sticks close to her, thinking this would be too much after what she's been through. I missed last week's fights because I was at the club, watching over Jacey, but I'm not missing this week's. I walk up to Hunter, he'll be our fighter this week.

"Brother, who you fighting tonight?"

"Dodger, I think."

"Good match up," I tell him. "Make sure you avoid that right hook."

"Yeah, thanks Bear. Are you going tonight?"

"Fuck yeah! I wouldn't miss this one, it looks like it's gonna be a good fight." I give him a pat on the back as I walk over to the bar to get a shot.

A few hours later, we all get on our bikes and head out. When we get to the compound, we have to wait for a prospect to let us through the gate. We park our bikes and walk into the clubhouse. All my brothers and I order our choice of poison and go our separate ways. We're not the only ones who come out to watch the fights: civilians, hang-arounds, and whores like to partake as well. The only reason civilians get to watch is because most of them are high society with high amounts of cash to throw away. They place bets, and they like to see the bloodshed, which in turn gets you more money if you play your cards right. Who's gonna turn down fast cash, I sure in the fuck am not. I love my money and the more I can get, the happier I am. If the civilians can't make the minimum bet, they can't watch. We do the fights to get some aggression out, and they take place in the back of the clubhouse. There's no cage or ring, we just make a circle around the fighters. They go bare knuckle until someone either taps out or gets knocked the fuck out. I look over, see Deuce, Snake's VP, and walk over to him. "You takin' the bets tonight?"

"Bear, good to see you man! You know it. You missed last week's. It was a great fight."

"You too! Yeah, had shit to do. Heard Hacker fucked your boy up pretty good. What's the number tonight?"

"Yeah he did. Five large."

Giving a whistle I say, "Alright, five on Hunter." I pull my money out and hand it to him.

"Good luck," he says as I'm walking away.

I find Hunter and give him some tips. "Watch his right hook, and that fucker is fast on his feet, but he's got a jaw made of glass. If you can land a solid, he'll go down. Protect your face and body, he likes to do combos."

"Thanks, Brother."

"No problem. I got a good chunk of change ridin' on you tonight."

With that I walk off and take my place in the front row of the circle. Everyone makes room to let the guys through.

Snake comes in. "Alright, boys, you know the rules. Fight goes on until someone taps or is knocked out." They both give nods.

"Fight!" Snake moves to join the crowd. Hunter and Dodger circle each other. Dodger comes in first, trying to put all his weight into a single punch. Hunter goes left, avoids the hit. Dodger throws a punch into Hunter's stomach, and he stumbles back with the force, but recovers quickly. Dodger comes in with quick jabs to the nose, making it bloody. Hunter moves to the right then he sees his opening, throwing a hard punch to Dodger's face and connecting with his jaw, just like I told him. Dodger goes down, but he's not out yet. Hunter jumps on him, throwing fist after fist and blood's flying everywhere. Dodger tries to get Hunter off, but it doesn't work. Hunter is quick with his fists, and Dodger finally quits defending himself, he's out. Storm, the Cobras' Sergeant At Arms, comes in, calling the fight. I walk up to Deuce to get my money and when he hands it to me, I fan through it. A good thirteen g's I made in a couple of minutes.

After the guys get cleaned up, the music starts booming throughout the clubhouse and everybody gathers inside to celebrate or sulk. Getting drink after drink, I look around the room, watching the guys from both clubs start picking their whore for the night. Others get on the pool tables for a game, betting more money. The one thing this clubhouse has that we don't is a stripper pole. One of their girls jumps on the little make shift stage and starts dancing. Some of the Cobras got their Ol' Ladies here, so they're keeping them close, dancing or just talking with others. It's a good time, but I don't wanna see any of this shit. I'm missing Jacey. I go sit at the bar, order another drink, and pull my phone out, writing her a text. I'm a little fucked up when I press send.

> **Bear: Got a song for you.**
> **Jacey: What's that?**
> **Bear: The Fray, Over My Head.**
> **Jacey: U trying 2 tell me something?**
> **Bear: Just thinkin' bout u.**

Deuce walks up to where I'm sitting at the bar, and takes a seat next to me. "You made a good bit of cash tonight." I look at him, not hearing what he said.

"Huh?"

"I said you made a good bit of cash tonight. What pussy has you all spaced out like that?"

"You watch what you say. She's not like the whores 'round here."

"So it is a chick?" He chuckles. "Only a man in love would look and act like that."

"Act like what?"

"Defendin' her, keepin' you in your phone. You got a faraway look to ya."

"It's not love, we're just fuckin'. Besides, I've only known her for a week."

"Yeah, you keep tellin' yourself that, doesn't matter how long you've known her. So who is she?"

"Hanger's Ol' Lady's best friend. Her name's Jacey."

He gets a strange look on his face. "Jacey, huh? Been a long time since I heard that name."

"What's that fuckin' mean?"

"Shit, nothin' man. Have a good night. My son Crawler's over there, gotta go." He gets up and walks away, and I leave not too long after that. When I get back to the clubhouse, I can't quit thinking about what Deuce said, so I pull my phone out and text her again.

> **Bear: Hey u know anybody from the Cobras?**
> **Jacey: It's the middle of the night.**
> **Bear: Answer.**
> **Jacey: Idk don't think so.**
> **Bear: K nite.**

Jacey: Nite.

Over the next couple of weeks, I haven't seen Jacey. I've been working on my truck a lot and dealing with club shit. We text a lot and when I sent her that song, I guess it started something. Now about every night we send a different one to each other, and she sends me her's first tonight.

Jacey: Saving Abel's Sex Is Good.
Bear: U trying to tell me something now?
Jacey: Can't sleep.
Bear: Is that an invite?
Jacey: Kinda, miss u.
Bear: I know I'll be over in a lil.
Jacey: I'll leave the door unlocked.

An hour later, I park my bike next to her car and walk up to her door. Turning the knob, I find it unlocked just like she said. Shutting and locking it behind me, I walk to her bedroom. She must have fallen asleep waiting for me. I see her breathing is even and shallow, so I take everything off except my boxer briefs and climb in beside her. I've never slept in a bed with a woman, it's always been just us fucking and then she or I left. Tonight I'll give her one of my firsts that's still intact. I pull her to me, place her head on my chest and get her arm around me. I stare at the ceiling and run my hand through her long brown hair until my eyes get heavy and I fall asleep.

Since the night I stayed with her, we've been seeing more of each other. She's wanted to keep what we're doing a secret, and I've went along with it until now. I'm done with that shit. I want her to be mine and I want every fucking body to know it. Today is the Fourth of July BBQ that Chatty wanted to have, and Crazy Girl is helping her set up everything. She is gonna make one fine First Lady, but my eyes wander to my Lil Mama. She's feisty and stubborn as hell. She has me all twisted up and I don't think I can get her out of my system even if I wanted to. We text constantly and I see her when time allows it. The pussy is unreal, I've never had anything like it. She's just fucking perfect, and I want her to be mine, but I don't know how she is gonna take that. The fireworks are about to start when she walks up to me. "Hey, Bear."

"Lil Mama."

"You want me to watch the fireworks with you?" she asks, with that beautiful smile.

"Yeah, Lil Mama. I gotta ask you somethin'." She gets this nervous look on her face, the smile fading, as she gives me a tight nod. "We've been doin' this back and forth shit for a while. We kept quiet but I don't want to anymore. Will you be mine? Let me call you mine and let everybody know?"

She starts frantically shaking her head no. "I can't do that Bear. I already told you, I like what we're doing. Don't try to change it on me now. Why can't you just fucking let it be?"

"Goddamn it, Jacey, because I've got real feelings for you! I don't want it to stay that way because you aren't just a fuck to me anymore!"

"Jesus, Bear. I can't! I thought you understood that."

"So what is this, just a good fuck until some fancy ass prick comes along that you think is better for your princess ass?" I'm getting pissed. What the fuck is her deal?

"Bear, I've told you! Don't call me a fucking princess! Goddamn you!"

"No, you know what Jacey? Fuck it! I'm done!" I can't. I can't do this with her anymore.

"Bear!"

"No, Jacey, take your fuckin' princess ass somewhere else! I said I was done."

"You want it to be like that, then fine! Fuck it." With that, she walks away and I go into the clubhouse, to my room. Fuck, she pisses me off. She gets to me like nobody ever has, and I know she feels the same way I do. When we're outside of the clubhouse she shows it, but once we are here, her guard goes up. She builds walls that I can't fucking break down. I can't do this shit with her anymore. I've never been like this with a woman, and this is why I never wanted love or relationship bullshit.

Chatty had Hanger call in a couple of our other chapters for the BBQ. It was a good thing too because now that we're all together we can discuss this Grimaldi shit. After church this morning, we went to the Cobras' compound to let them know the plan so far for the Italians. When we got back to the clubhouse, I went straight to my room, slamming the door shut. I'm still fucking pissed at Jacey, and everybody knows to leave me the fuck alone, they just don't know why. I pull out my phone and see my light flashing, letting me know I have a new text. It's from Jacey, saying she's sorry so I text back.

> **Bear: Yeah 4 what?**
> **Jacey: For making you feel like you aren't good enough.**
> **Bear: I don't get it.**
> **Jacey: Get what?**
> **Bear: Why you close up at the clubhouse why you're so guarded.**
> **Jacey: I can't talk about it.**
> **Bear: Fuck Jacey!**
> **Jacey: There are things I just won't talk about.**
> **Bear: You got to eventually Lil Mama or they will destroy you.**
> **Jacey: I just can't gotta go.**

With that I close my eyes and fall asleep, exhausted from the day and that psycho ass woman.

One week later, I fucking miss her. God dammit, I can't fucking help it. I told her I was done, but I swear to Christ, her pussy is platinum. Making myself look like a fucking pussy, I head to her apartment, and I know she's here because her car was in the parking lot. I knock on her door, and when she opens it, fuck me, she looks good. She has on fucking tiny blue sleep shorts, paired with a thin blue and white tank. She narrows her eyes at me. "What are you doing here?"

"I wanted to see you," I say, giving her a half grin.

"You said you were done."

"I know." I walk up to her, backing her into the apartment. When we are far enough inside, I close the door and flip the lock.

"You shouldn't be here."

"I had to see you." I grip her waist, bringing her hard and fast against my body. I take my free hand, putting my finger under her chin to bring her face up to mine. "Couldn't stay away," I tell her. Her eyes close and her breath deepens, so I take full advantage and bring my lips to hers, giving her a slow tender kiss, tangling our tongues together. I lift her up and carry her to the dining room table, sitting her down on top of it.

"Bear, we can't do this," she says, trying to fight against it.

"I gotta have you, Lil Mama. Gotta get in that sweet cunt. Can't think of nothin' else." I pull at the bottom of her top and bring it over her head. "Lift up." She does as she's asked, giving up the fight because she can't resist me either. "Good girl," I say, as I pull down her shorts. I lean in, licking at the skin of her neck, she tastes so fucking good, always smelling like fucking strawberries. I reach around and undo her bra, releasing her perfect full tits, and take one hard nipple into my mouth, flicking and sucking it. I move over to the other, showing it the same attention. She lets out a moan and it makes my cock harder than it already was. Hearing the little sounds coming from her is so fucking sexy, it drives me insane. I kiss down her belly, ripping her lace panties from her body. "I'm gonna taste this sweet cunt of yours now." I grip her thighs, bringing her to the edge of the table, and I drop to my knees so her pussy is right in front of my face. Needing just that one taste, I lean in giving her one good stroke of my tongue front to back. I run my hands from her ankles to her thighs, placing my fingers on her lower lips, and spreading her wide open for me. Before I start slowly lapping at her, torturing her by barely letting her feel my tongue, I lay it flat against her cunt, and put just the right amount of pressure to have her begging for what she wants.

"Bear, please," she begs.

"Tell me what you need," I say against her hot slick pussy.

"I need more. Please give me more."

"Who's the one that makes you feel good? Who's the only one to give you what you need?"

"You, Bear," she starts panting. "Only you. Please make me cum." That's exactly what I wanted to hear. Applying the pressure she needs, I lick her clit until I have her body shaking. "Bear, yes!" I place two fingers inside her, curling them, rubbing her g-spot. My other hand runs up her body until I'm pinching and pulling at her hard little nipple. Giving it to her just the way she likes, she starts thrashing on the table. I feel her tighten around my fingers, I know she's close. I keep licking her, but pull my fingers out. I stick my pinky inside her, letting it get wet, then pulling it out. I let her nipple go, bringing my hand back down to her pussy spreading her open once again. I softly put pressure on her asshole, making slow circles with my wet finger. Her moans grow louder then I slowly start to push in as I see her tense up. "Bear?" she questions.

"Trust me, baby, it's gonna feel good. Just relax."

She does as told, so I go back to licking and sucking on her clit. I slowly keep pushing in further with my little finger, and Jacey starts screaming in pleasure, just like I knew she would. She goes back to thrashing on the table, she's close, and I continue working her clit some more. I slide two fingers into her pussy, working them in and out of her, along with my pinky in her ass.

"Jacey, let go Baby. I got you." Soon she's clawing at my arms, and arching her back.

"Fuck, Bear! Oh! God! Yes!" I don't give her time to come back down.

I get my jeans down around my ankles, slide a condom on, and line up to her, pushing hard and fast into her tight wet heat, hitting her sweet spot inside that lights her on fire. I'm pounding into her when she sits up, taking my cut and beater off. She starts kissing my chest.

"Lil Mama, you grippin' me so fuckin' tight. You're close again, I feel it. Fuckin' let go."

She does exactly that as she bites down on my chest, claws at my arms, and calls out my name as she comes again. I'm right behind her, grunting and growling out her name into the hair that's covering her neck. I pull out, and go to her bathroom to clean myself off with a warm washcloth then I run one under hot water for her. At least I know she can't dip out when we're at her place. I carry the washcloth to her, and she's laying on the table still trying to catch her breath. I run it between her legs, cleaning her up. She has an unusual look on her face. "Jacey, what's wrong?"

"Huh? What? Oh nothing." She gives me a lazy smile, but I know it's fake.

"Jacey, talk to me."

"There's nothing to talk about."

"Then why do you seem distracted?"

"Bear, it's just work. I'm fine."

"What the fuck ever." Why does she always have to do this bullshit?

"Are you fucking kidding? Don't 'what the fuck ever' me." She points to me saying, "You are the one that came over here."

"I swear to Christ, there is somethin' seriously wrong with you. You're fucked in the head."

"It's time for you to leave." What the fuck is wrong with this goddamn woman?

"You wanna be like that, fine." I shake my head at her.

QUIET COUNTRY

"I came over here because I fuckin' missed you, god-dammit. Keep runnin' Jacey! It's what your good at, right? I hope you find what you're lookin' for and he can treat you like the little fuckin' princess that you are."

I get my clothes back on, continuing, "You are un-fuckin'-believable! You play all these games! What is it, 'let Bear make me cum then I'll throw him out like the trash I think he is'? You have no fuckin' idea who I am Jacey."

I see tears slide from her eyes, but I can't bring myself to care right now. I slam her door shut and don't look back.

A couple of days after I left Jacey's apartment, I'm out in the garage at the clubhouse putting new custom head lights in my '87 Chevy pickup. I got Marilyn Manson's *The Dope Show* playing. I have my head under the hood when I feel hands slide up my bare back. I know those fucking hands and they're not the ones I wanna be feeling. I turn around, and sure enough, it's Morgan.

"What do you want?"

"I wanna show you a good time. You've been out here working so hard on your truck," she purrs at me, trying to be sexy, but it's not, not anymore.

"I don't have time for you, go on back to the clubhouse."

She runs her hands up my chest. "Come on, Bear. I miss you. First Hanger, now you? Just let me give you a little something." Her hands are at my jeans, trying to undo them, when I hear her.

"What the fuck is this!?" I push Morgan off of me and turn to Jacey.

"I can explain, it's not what it looks like," I tell her, trying to defend myself.

"Oh yeah?! I think it's exactly what it looks like. And fuck you very much for that." She flips me the bird, then turns to leave.

"Jacey! Wait!" I yell after her.

"Fuck you, Bear!" she screams back over her shoulder.

I turn and look at Morgan.

"You go take your fuckin' ass back to the clubhouse, and don't ever fuckin' pull that bullshit again. Got me?" She gives me a nod and runs away.

Jacey's already in her car, pulling out and driving away like a bat outta hell, throwing gravel everywhere. Fuck, I gotta make this right. What the hell was she doing here anyway? I jump on my bike and head to her apartment.

When I get to her door, I hear banging noises and she's booming *This Means War by Avenged Sevenfold*. Shit, this is gonna be bad. She didn't shut the door all the way when she got home, so I slowly open it and go inside. I see her breathing heavily and she looks more pissed off then I've ever seen her. She must clean when she's angry because she's scrubbing her table so fucking hard I think she might take the varnish off. I don't understand why she's pissed, she's the one that keeps saying she doesn't have feelings for me.

"Jacey, let me explain." She looks up at me, taking the cleaner in her hand and chucking it at me. I dodge just in time as it almost hit me in the forehead. Damn, she's got good aim. She goes into the kitchen, and stupid me follows behind her. I see her grabbing dishes out of her dishwasher and putting them away.

"There's nothing to explain," she says, shrugging her shoulder.

"You didn't see what you think you did." She turns on me and starts throwing fucking plates. I have to dodge left and right so I don't get hit, and she keeps them coming.

"Oh, I know what I saw." When she runs out of plates in the dishwasher, she opens the cabinet and starts throwing those. "Get out! Get out of my fucking apartment, you goddamn asshole!"

"Jacey, let me fuckin' explain."

"There is nothing for you to explain! I already said that, dickface! We got into a fight, you had a whore there, you were about to fuck her, end of story!"

"You're wrong, Lil Mama," I say, shaking my head at her.

"I'm not! This is what you do," she pants at me, hands free of dishes finally. "You lie and you cheat." What in the actual fuck is going on?

"Lil Mama." Her expression softens at the use of her nickname. "I wasn't gonna do anything with her. I told her to get off me. I was about to push her away when you came in."

"Why should I believe you? It's not even really cheating, we aren't together. So you wouldn't even consider it cheating!" she says, as she throws her arms up in the air.

"Did I ask you not to fuck anybody else?" She nods.

"Did I tell you we had a good thing and I wasn't lookin' to find somethin' else?" She gives me another nod.

"You need to trust me, Jacey. I've told you how I feel, you're the one that won't admit your fuckin' feelings. You wanna know what I think about every day?" She gives another nod.

I slowly start walking over to her as I say, "I think about you, Lil Mama. I think about how beautiful you are, how perfect you are. I think about how good you feel when I'm deep inside you, about your taste on my lips, and your smell in my nose. I think about all the ways I wanna make you come, and how goddamn gorgeous you are when I do. I think about when the next time I get to be with you again is. That, Lil Mama, is what I think about every goddamn second of the day. Those club whores, or any other woman, will never measure up to you. I don't lie and I won't fuckin' cheat. Got me?" I see the tears roll down her face and I place my thumbs on the bottom of her cheeks, slowly wiping them away.

"I got you." Her voice sounds so small. "I didn't like seeing that. I wish I could give myself to you. Bear, I really do."

"Hey, let's not worry about that right now. Why did you come over?"

"Because, I was going to apologize to you for the other night. I don't know what's wrong with me. I'm always making you feel like shit, then turn right around saying I'm sorry."

"I don't know what's wrong with you either," I tell her as we both let out a small laugh.

"I gotta get back to the clubhouse." I give her a kiss on her lips and she deepens it. She moves over to my neck, kissing, licking, nibbling, and sucking at it. I do the same to hers, as my hand runs up under her shirt, feeling her smooth skin while I work my way up to her tit, massaging it. She breaks from my neck and pushes at my chest.

"You said you had to leave. You can go now. I've got a mess to clean up." I give her a curious look and she has the most evil smile on her face.

"Alright, I'll text you."

"Yeah, you do that." She's acting fucking strange, but I give her one last kiss on the mouth and forehead, then head back to finish working on my truck. The whole way there I Thank God that shit got fixed. Fucking whores need to learn their place before they're all out like Jasmine's dumb ass.

Once I get done with my truck for the night, I go in the clubhouse and the guys all look at me, then burst out laughing. The fuck is going on? I go to my room to grab some clean clothes and head into one of the main bathrooms. I'm about to take my clothes off when I see what the fuck they were laughing at. I grab my phone out of my pocket.

```
Bear: You branded me?
Jacey: Nope, I don't know what you
are talking about :)
Bear: You are not fuckin' funny.
Jacey: Just giving a warning to
the whores.
Bear: You're jealous!
Jacey: NO!!
Bear: Yeah you are!
Jacey: Fine maybe a lil :p
Bear: Got a song for you. Nick
Jonas remix of Jealous :)
Jacey: Haha u got jokes.
Bear: Nite Lil Mama.
Jacey: Nite Bear.
```

I put my phone down and get in the shower. My cock is hard as hell from being around her. I have to rub one out, then another before my dick starts going down. She infuriates me a lot, yet she makes me feel so many other things. Tonight just proved she has feelings, I just have to get her to admit it. When I'm outta the shower, I head back to my room, lay down, and try coming up with a plan to get my woman.

SEVEN

Jacey

It's been about a month since the BBQ and a week since I last saw Bear. Zoey came back to work two weeks ago and found out she was pregnant. Before I went to the clubhouse to the BBQ, I realized I had missed my period and had been feeling sick.

I had all the symptoms, leading me to believe I might be pregnant too, so I went to the clinic and did a test on myself. That was the longest few minutes of my life, waiting to find out if I was going to be a mom. Sure enough, it came out positive and I about lost my shit, so I took two more. Yep, they were all positive.

God, how could I be so fucking stupid? It fucking figures, that's just my luck. Then my mind wanders to Bear, and oh God, how would he feel about a baby? How could he support a baby? He doesn't even have a fucking house! I'm sure as hell not going to let my baby live in a motorcycle clubhouse, so my only option was to start a fight with him, make him mad enough so he'll be done with me for real this time. I'll raise this baby on my own and he'll never have to find out.

The only problem I have is that I like Bear, but he goes against the big picture of my future. Actually, it isn't even my plan to begin with. I may be twenty-six years old but I'm still living the life my mother wanted for me. According to her, I was supposed to find a rich guy and marry him, not end up knocked up by a biker.

No matter how hard I've tried, I can't deny my feelings for Bear, and when they interfere with what I'm supposed to be doing, that's when I start feeling bad. I message him and apologize, then when he thinks everything is good and fine, I get in my head again. I end up going 'Crazy Bitch' on him and I know he thinks I'm insane.

When I went over there and saw him with that whore, it made me go psycho on his ass because I hated seeing another woman touching him. When it comes to Bear, my head, heart, and body are all fighting against each other. I wish it was easy to shut off the heart, then all of this wouldn't be a problem.

He's messaged me a few times asking if I want to go eat or go for a ride, but I've been telling him that I'm busy. After a few attempts, he quit asking and I haven't heard from him and I certainly haven't reached out either. I think he's leaving it up to me now, whether or not we see each other. That's fine with me because I'm trying my best to keep distance between us.

Since Zoey and I are both pregnant, that's all we've been talking about in and out of work. It's fun having someone to talk pregnancy with: the morning sickness, which isn't exclusively morning, being tired all the time, mood swings. Neither of us are showing yet, but when we do, you bet your ass we'll be complaining about getting fat. We talk about all the good things too. She's so happy to be pregnant and I'm getting there too. I recommended my doctor to her. I see Dr. Greene and she's amazing. She was my attending physician when I was doing my residency.

When it's time to close up for the night, we go to the front and see that Andrew's there with that bitch Jasmine. No, this can't be happening, they can't be here. I try to get the door locked quickly, but he's too fast. He throws the door open, pushing me back and out of the way. I look to Zoey, and she's just standing there in shock when I notice he has a gun. He points the muzzle back and forth between the two of us: first her, then me and back to her again. Andrew tells us to go into one of the exam rooms, and not wanting to get hurt, we do as asked. When we get into the cramped space, he tells us to sit down. I'm so fucking scared and I know Zoey is too, especially after everything he had done to her over the years that she was with him. This is not good. Once we sit, I grab her, bringing her close to me so we can huddle together.

Jasmine starts laughing and it's evil and sickening to hear, it makes my stomach turn. I thought I was crazy, but I don't have shit on this bitch. This fucking whore is the epitome of crazy. "So you thought what happened at the club was the end of it? You were wrong, so very wrong. I told you then that you couldn't just come in there and take over."

"I didn't just come there, Hanger brought me there. I didn't do anything to you that you didn't deserve!" she asserts.

I can tell Jasmine is getting angry, her face is turning red and her breathing becomes heavy, then she screams, "You didn't do anything? You didn't fucking do anything wrong? You took him from me, you made him leave me! You took everything! The club, Hanger, everything! You fucking little bitch!"

"That's enough!" Andrew yells, and it gets deathly quiet. He points the gun at my best friend. "Okay, Zoey, you're coming back home with me, so Jasmine," he turns to her, " you can have your life back." The black haired whore plasters a satisfied smile on her face. I look to Zoey and she's frantically shaking her head back and forth.

"No, Andrew, I'm not. I'm staying with Hanger."

"You've had your fun, now you are coming home with me. You're mine, Zoey, and that's the end of it."

"I'm not yours, not anymore. You think this has been fun for me? You almost killed me!" she shrieks.

"I see you've forgotten who you obey. I guess I'll have to remind you. Jacey, let go of her."

"No, I'm not letting go." He points the gun at me, then the tears I have been holding back break free, cascading down my face.

"No, Andrew. Oh God, please! Just leave us alone!" Zoey cries to him. He walks over to us and grabs her arm, yanking her away from me. "Don't do this, Andrew, please! Hanger will kill you if you hurt me." She begs as the tears run down her face. We'll be goddamn lucky to make it out alive.

"You think I'm scared of your little no good boyfriend?" I see him lift his leg, bringing it behind him, and we both scream NO! at the same time, but he doesn't listen. Zoey tries to cover her stomach to protect the baby, but it doesn't help. Andrew put all of his weight behind that kick. She falls over, lying on the floor in a fetal position. She holds her stomach screaming in pain, screaming how bad it hurts.

I hear Jasmine laugh. "Look at that! Not so tough now, are you bitch? Look at how much pain she's in! This is so funny! Look how good you did, Andrew!" I go to reach for her, but he knocks my hands away with his foot. I look up at him, narrow my eyes and scream, "She's fucking pregnant!" I don't hear her crying for help anymore and when I look over, I see blood all around her. Zoey's unconscious now. Oh God no! She's losing the baby.

Andrew asks, "What do you mean she is pregnant?"

"Just what I said you motherfucker! She's pregnant, carrying a life! A life that you killed!"

"She let that piece of shit inside of her? Well fuck, she's tainted now." He raises his gun to her. Oh god, he's going to kill her! I start crying even harder, begging him not to. He gives me an evil smile, pulling back the trigger, when I see Bam Bam come running in and jump in front of her just as I hear the BOOM of the gun ring out. I bring my legs up, putting my forehead against my knees. I cover my ears with my hands, and start screaming. I can't believe this is fucking happening. Even over my screaming, and through my hands, I hear another gunshot. My head snaps up just as I see Jasmine fall to the floor, blood dripping from her forehead, pooling around her. Strong arms wrap around me and I don't stop screaming until I realize it's Bear holding me. Thank god!

I wrap my arms around him as tight as I can and lay my head on his chest. I'm crying even harder, because he came for me. He whispers in my ear, "Lil Mama, I got you. It's ok. Shh… Baby, are you alright? I won't let anything happen to you. I promise. Are you hurt?" I shake my head no. "Good, I'm gonna take care of you. Nothing can hurt you now. Believe me baby, it's all gonna be fine. You are gonna be fine, Jacey. We are gonna handle this, but you don't tell anybody what happened, okay?" I nod, then ask, "What's going to happen to Andrew?"

"Hanger's gonna kill him, Jacey." I look up to him as he cups my cheek in his large hand.

"That's what we do, Lil Mama. We protect what's ours. He won't be able to hurt her again. Shit, he won't hurt anybody again for that matter." I nod and lay my head back against his chest.

Just letting him hold me makes me feel warm, safe, and protected for the first time that I can remember, and it's real. Watching Hanger hold Zoey while punching Andrew, I finally get it now. I get how she fell in love with him, along with the other brothers. I get now what she means to Hanger. I understand the love they have for each other, and it's unlike anything I've ever seen.

Could I have the same if I just open up and let Bear in? I don't think I can do that. Bear picks me up as we hear the ambulance coming and carries me outside.

"Do you have your keys?"

"Yeah, they're in my pocket."

"Well give 'em to me," he says, as he holds his hand out.

"Oh no fucking way. You are not driving my baby."

"Yes, I am. You don't need to drive right now. Hand them over and get in the fuckin' car."

"Fine, but you hurt her in any way, I will castrate you."

"Your precious car will be fine."

I climb into the passenger seat and he takes me straight to the hospital. After he parks, I head to the doors but I have to turn around. I can't go in there yet. I walk right back to Bear's open arms. He must have known I wasn't ready because he got out of the car as well, but he wasn't going in.

I gaze up at him as I tell him, "I have to stay out here for a while. I'm scared to go in there and see her."

He doesn't say anything in return, just keeps me wrapped up in his big frame, and I lay my head on his chest, relaxing into his embrace while he rubs my back. He doesn't try to move, he just keeps soothing and comforting me. I don't know how long we've been out here, but when I finally get the courage to go in, I see her family standing outside of her room.

The E.R. must've been quick with getting her taken care of. Most of the time it takes hours before you get a room, but I'm sure Hanger probably had something to do with that. After I give all her family hugs, I see Hanger coming out of her room to tell us we can go in, and he's not looking too good.

As we all walk in, I see her sleeping on the hospital bed, hooked up to monitors, and it hurts to take in. I've been against the club and what they do all this time, but in this moment right here, I hope they make that son of a bitch suffer for what he did.

When Dr. Greene comes in and tells all of us that she lost the baby, it's devastating. We all cry for her and Hanger losing what they wanted so badly. Christ, she didn't even get to tell her family she was pregnant. She wanted to wait just a couple more weeks to be in the 'safe zone'.

Hanger comes back in, asking me what happened tonight with a look of determination set on his face. When I tell him, my hand instantly goes to my stomach, and I see the strange look he gives me, but he looks resolved, like he knows what he'll do to that piece of shit. It won't be pretty or quick.

Hanger's going to make Andrew pay with a slow painful death, I just know it because the look in his eyes says it all. It's time for all of us to go and give Hanger time alone with Zoey. He needs to tell her what happened with their baby, and they need their time to mourn.

When I get outside, Bear is there, leaning up against my car smoking a cigarette. I walk up to him. "Thank you for everything. You didn't have to wait."

"Don't thank me, Lil Mama. I wanna be the one that's there for you, and the way I see it, I need a ride back to my bike." I guess he's right. I didn't even think about that.

"How is she?" He jerks his chin towards the hospital.

"She was asleep, but she lost the baby."

"Fuck. Nobody even knew she was pregnant."

"Yeah, she wanted to wait a couple more weeks until they told everyone. I only knew because I did the test for her."

"Are you going to be okay to drive home?"

"Yeah, I'll be fine. Let me take you to your bike."

We get back to his bike, and before he can get out I grab his hand, stopping him.
    "Bear, will you come over? I don't want to be alone."
    "Yeah, I can do that." I give him a nod.
    He gets out, goes to his bike, and then follows me to my apartment. We get parked at my complex, and he gets off his bike to come and open the door for me. He helps me out of my car, then puts his arm around my shoulders. I keep thinking about what would've happened if they didn't get there in time. I'm so glad he's here giving me the support to keep me on my feet as we walk inside my apartment. I hand him my keys to let us in and just like every time, he shuts and locks the door. Bear leads me over to the couch, sitting me down before he walks down the hall towards the bathroom. A little while later he comes back, puts his hands out to help me up, then walks me back to where he was. He lit candles and ran a bubble bath for me.
    "I'm gonna take care of you, Lil Mama. Get in." He helps me out of my clothes and into the tub.
    I watch him the whole time as he undresses then gets in behind me, and when he's completely in the tub, he pulls me against him. He puts soap into his palms, then starts to wash my body, massaging my back and shoulders. We don't talk, but it's not an uncomfortable silence. Really there aren't any words that need to be said, this isn't the time to talk about us and we both know it. He washes my hair and helps me out of the bath, then dries me off. I've never had anybody take care of me like this and it's nice. After I'm dry, he doesn't bother with clothes, just picks me up and carries me to my bed. Bear lays me under the covers then crawls in behind me, bringing my back as close to him as he can get. Feeling his warmth and having him running his hand through my hair, it doesn't take long for me to fall asleep.

    It's been a few days since the incident at the clinic and Zoey's still in the hospital. I knock on the room door and she tells me to come in. Seeing that Hanger is with her and hasn't left her makes me feel good. I don't understand though, how can these guys be the way they are, but my father be such a bad man. It makes me wonder if my mother was telling the truth or if she just hated him that much.

He stands up. "I'll give you guys some time to talk." He leans down, giving Zoey a kiss before making his way out, and I sit down in the chair he was using.

"Zoey, are you doing okay?"

She takes my hand in hers. "Yeah, I'm okay. How are you doing?"

"I'm okay, I'm so sorry about the baby. I didn't know how you would handle that."

"I'm sorry too. We'll have another one eventually. I can't let it destroy me though, because if I do Andrew wins, and I can't let that happen. I wouldn't be able to get through any of this if it wasn't for Hanger."

"You really love him, don't you? I think I get it now."

"Yeah, I really do. You could have this to, you know. Have you told him yet?"

"No, not with Bear I couldn't. And no, I haven't told him. I can't. You don't understand."

"I don't understand because you won't let me. Jacey, you gotta open up let me in, shit, let Bear in."

"I can't do that. I wish I could, but I just can't." Hanger walks back in. "I'm gonna go. I'll see you later. Hanger, take care of her for me." I give her a kiss on her forehead and leave. I know she's right, but I can't bring myself to do it.

Bear

The morning after the incident at the clinic, I left before Jacey woke up. She was vulnerable that night and all I wanted to do was take care of her. She doesn't let me do it often, so those are moments that I cherish. For some reason, she feels like she has to keep up with the tough persona. She doesn't understand that with me she doesn't have to, I would be there through anything with her. I gotta figure out a way to break down Jacey's walls, so I go find the one person I can talk to: Ripper. He's the only one that can give me advice, the only one who knows what's gone down with us. He's been there with Chatty, having to chase her until she finally gave in. The only one who seems to have gotten it simple with these damn women is Hanger. He got it so easy with Crazy Girl and sometimes I wish Jacey could be like that, but then she wouldn't be the woman I fell for.

I find Ripper in the bar, so I order a shot of Wild Turkey, down it, and then look at him.

"You got a minute?" I ask.

"Yeah. You wanna go outside?"

"What's goin' on?" He questions once we are sat down at one of the picnic tables.

"I need some advice."

"Jacey?" he asks, knowing exactly what it is.

"Yeah. She's so fuckin' difficult. She has all these fuckin' walls up and I can't break 'em down. One minute she's pissed at me, then she's not. She lets me take care of her when she needs it, but it doesn't last. What the fuck do I do?" I grip my hair in my hands, pulling at it with my elbows on the table.

"Are you in love with her?" He asks, just like it's no big deal.

"Fuck, Brother. I don't think so. I feel somethin' for her though, I know that."

"You need to figure that out first: if you love her. Is she even worth all the trouble?"

"How'd you know with Chatty?"

"Brother, that woman gave me a run for my money, but I knew without a doubt that she was it. From the first time I laid eyes on her, she was the one for me. I had to work for her, had to chase her until she wanted to be caught, and once I caught her, I vowed I would make her happy every day until my last breath."

"So, I just keep doing what I'm doing?" I ask, getting frustrated because this is no fucking help.

He chuckles before saying, "Yeah, Brother. Give her time, she'll break eventually. When she does, all you gotta do is be there to pick up all the pieces. You need to figure out if she's really worth it or not, and if not, chalk it up to a good time and move the fuck on. But if you are in love with the girl, just be there when she needs you. Not all of us can get it as easy as Hanger. He's got a special one there."

"Thanks Ripper."

"No problem, Brother." He looks off into the distance.

"Can you promise me something?"

"Yeah, whatever you need."

"With all this shit goin' on with the Gremaldi's, none of us are guaranteed to come out. I need you to promise me that if I don't, Chatty'll go on and be happy," he says, staring me in the eyes which shows me he's dead serious.

QUIET COUNTRY

"Don't talk like that Ripper, we're all gonna be fine," I tell him as his stare turns hard. Out of all my brothers, Ripper is the one I refuse to think about losing.

"Bear, you know this life. You know a lot of us don't get long and we're never promised the next day. I need to know that she'll be happy if I'm not here. I can't go into this thinkin' she would never get over me. Chatty's young, she's got so much life ahead of her. Just promise me that you'll see to it that she's happy and lives her life."

"I promise." He gives me a nod, gets up, and walks away.

Chatty is everything to him. I know it had to be hard for him to say that and it goes to show how serious this Italian shit is. I decide I'm gonna text Jacey.

Bear: U busy?
Jacey: No what's up?
Bear: I'll be there in 20.
Jacey: Why?
Bear: Just be ready.

I pull up and she's waiting outside for me. After she gets in, I start pulling away. "Why'd you come get me?" she asks nervously, a curious look on her face.

"Had to take this cage for a test drive and I wanted you with me."

"I love this truck. What's wrong with it? Why do you have to test drive it?"

"You know I've been working on it for a while. I put on new headers, a lift, and just rebuilt the transmission. I want to make sure she's runnin' right." She settles back into the seat, holding onto her stomach. "You alright, you're not sick are you?"

"I'm fine. This is a great song," she states, switching the subject. *Simple Man by Lynyrd Skynard* is playing on the radio.

"Yeah, my parents loved rock. My momma used to sing this song to me. Hey, are you comin' to the patch party for Writer and Bam Bam?"

"Yeah, Zoey wants me to. Do you like a lot of older rock?"

I pull up to a pond by the cabin outside of town and park the truck. It looks like it's going to rain, and that's the other reason I picked her up in a cage. I don't like to be in 'em often, I don't like feeling trapped. "Some, my parents mainly listened to it. When I'm ridin' in a cage, I like to just drive. The music brings back memories of better times."

"I'm going out of town this weekend," she says, holding her head down, playing with her fingers.

"Why?" She has me curious and a little worried with the way she's acting.

"There's a car show in Tulsa. I put my car in different ones, plus it gives me reason to check out the other cars people have."

"You really know that much about cars?"

"Yes, it was something I was interested in, kinda like music. Why are we stopping?" She looks at me with sad eyes.

"I wanna talk. C'mon get out." I've backed in so the bed of my truck is facing the pond. Off in the distance, you can see my cabin and this pond is part of my property, but she doesn't need to know that right now. I lead her to the bed of my truck, let the tailgate down, and hop up to sit down. I take her hand, bringing her between my legs, and turn her around. I put my hands on her waist, lifting her onto the tailgate with me, her back to my front. Resting my chin on the top of her head, for a few minutes we both look out to the water. I decide to be the first one to speak. "Jacey, what's wrong?"

"Nothing, I told you I was fine." That defensiveness is back when she answers.

"You're not. You gotta let somebody in, Lil Mama."

"Why are you doing this? Why can't you just let this shit go?"

I start to feel light raindrops hitting me. "I can't because I've got feelings for you, Jacey, and I know you feel the same way."

She pulls away from me, hops off the tailgate, and starts walking off.

"You don't mean that, and I don't. You're wrong, you don't even know me!" she all but yells at me. About that time the rain really starts coming down. I run up to her and grab her arm, spinning her around, making her look at me. I've never seen Jacey look more beautiful -- her hair is lying flat to her head, soaking wet strands sticking to her face, and her makeup leaves black streaks down her cheeks.

"Quit runnin' from me, goddammit! Fuck! All you gotta do is let me in, shit. Why can't you just admit that you have feelings for me? Why do you have to play all these fuckin' games? I don't know shit because you won't fuckin' tell me!"

She screams back at me. "I can't Bear! I've told you that! I don't even know what to believe anymore. You make me think everything I know is wrong. This isn't the life I was supposed to have! I can't do this, we can't do this anymore. We were just supposed to be fucking!"

"It's passed the just fuckin' stage! That shit passed a long time ago Jacey, and you fuckin' know it."

"No! Not for me, it didn't. I wanna go home! Take me home now."

QUIET COUNTRY

"This is the last fuckin' time, you remember this. I bet you think about me just as much as I think about you. I bet when you try and move on from me, you can't do it because you're gonna wish it was me. Just like I would with you, just like I try to do. I can tell you however many times I fuckin' want this will be the last time, but we both know I can't fuckin' leave you alone, no matter how hard I try." Gripping my hair in frustration I continue on. "Why do you have to do this to me, play these fuckin' games, and lie to me?" I point at her. "I bet when you go to let another man inside you, you're gonna wish it was my cock, just like no matter what pussy I'm in, it'll always be yours I'm thinkin' about."

"How do you know I haven't already been with someone else?"

That right there, that did it. That was like a punch to my fucking gut. Is she fucking serious right now?

"C'mon." I walk back to my truck, get in, and wait for her. No words are spoken and the stereo pumps out *Poison and Guns N' Roses* all the way back. I drop her off and go back to the clubhouse, thinking the whole time about the last thing she said to me. I hope to god she hasn't been with someone else.

The patch party is in full effect and everyone is fucked up from playing one of Crazy Girl's drinking games. I have been watching Jacey all night since she got here, noticing she hasn't had one drop of alcohol, which isn't like her. She looks different too, like she has a glow to her. I don't know what it is, but she looks even more beautiful than she normally does. I see that hang-around Justin walk up to her and she looks happy to see him. I should just let it go, move the fuck on, and let her be with somebody she thinks is better for her than me. Nope, I can't do that and this is so fucked, I don't know why I keep doing this to myself. That's my fucking woman he's talking to. I walk up to them, staring him down.

"What did I tell you the last time you were talking to her?" I say while tilting my chin towards her.

"I'm sorry, I was just saying hi."

"It's a little late for sorry. You should've stayed away from what's mine, asshole, like I fuckin' told you." I bring my fist back and throw my punch, connecting right with his jaw. He just got knocked the fuck out with one hit. Fucking pussy.

I grab her arm and start towards my room. She's screaming for me to let go, but I'm not listening to shit she has to say right now. Once I get us in my room, I slam the door shut. Taking her by the arms, pinning her against the wall, I put one of my legs between hers, spreading them. I put both my arms on each side of her, caging her in.

"Tell me you haven't been with somebody else. For once in your goddamn life, tell me the fuckin' truth, that you haven't been with someone else!"

"I haven't Bear, I swear! I was just mad, I'm sorry. You're the only one." Thank fuck for that.

I lean in, putting my mouth to her ear. "I have decided that me bein' the nice guy isn't workin' anymore. So this is what it is. You're mine, you belong to me. I claim you, Jacey Thomas, and there's not a goddamn thing you can do about it."

I start kissing her neck, sucking her skin into my mouth, and she tilts her head to the side, giving me better access. Losing her fight against me, I brand her for everyone to see.

"I'm not, Bear," says in a low moan.

"You think it's still up for discussion? You think you still have a choice?"

"I do. I decide what I want."

"You don't. You're wrong. This is a done deal."

I take her away from the wall and walk her over to the bed, pushing her down. She halfheartedly tries to crawl up to get away from me, but that's not gonna work either. I grab her ankles and pull her back to me.

"Why you runnin', Lil Mama?" I straddle her on the bed, bringing my body over hers.

Leaning my head down, I put my mouth to hers and she resists for about half a second, before her lips are opening to give me the access I crave. Jacey grabs the bottom of my beater, pulling it up and over my head, breaking me from the kiss. I pull her up in a sitting position so I can pull her shirt off, along with her bra. She undoes my jeans, pushing them and my boxer briefs down my legs. When we are both free of all clothing, I start giving her kisses down her body. I stop at her nipples, showing them some attention, then work my way down to her stomach. I hear her making soft little sounds, so I lean back to look up into her eyes.

"Your body can't say no to me," I tell her while giving her a sexy grin.

"I love how responsive it is. I bet you're soakin' wet for me and I haven't even really touched you yet."

"Well you need to get to touching because you are driving me fucking crazy!"

"Yes ma'am." I salute while she laughs. I get back to business working my way back down her body, spreading her legs wide. "I was right, you're fuckin' soaked, and your pretty pink cunt is glistening' for me."

I put my mouth to her and her body jerks. I need her still so I place a hand on her stomach, but she reaches down, moving my hand to her hip. I noticed she's gained some weight so maybe that's why she moved my hand. I won't say anything though, that'll ruin what's about to happen. I run my tongue up and down her pussy, tasting her, drinking her in. I spread her open, finding her clit, flicking it with my tongue, and sucking it into my mouth. I push two fingers inside, curling them to find her sweet spot, and her back arches, body tenses up. She starts tightening around my fingers then she screams her release and calls out my name. She needed that release, she came quickly, but that doesn't bother me because it gets me closer to taking my cock home.

Grabbing a condom and putting it on, I climb up over her body, line myself up to her opening, and push inside with one swift motion. I know exactly where to hit to throw her into another orgasm, and that's what I do. Sure enough, when I pick up speed, her moans grow louder and she starts matching me thrust for thrust. Scraping her nails up and down my back, sucking and biting at my neck, she screams out, "Bear, Oh! Fuck! Yes! I fucking love... your cock, you feel so good!" I still for a minute to look down at her, she still has her eyes closed. I don't think she realizes what she was about to say. I start backing up, moving in and out of her for a few more strokes until I find my own release. I fucking love how wild she gets! Rolling to the side, I bring her with me and we lay there, silent until I ask, "Will you stay?" I light up a cigarette.

"Bear, I can't." I put one arm behind my head and give her a nod. She gets up and as she's getting dressed, she looks to me. "Hasn't anybody ever told you those are bad for you?"

"I think I've heard that somewhere before. Seems they aren't the only thing that's bad for me." Giving her a smile, I hold my smoke out towards her.

"These, Lil Mama, will not be the death of me." She smiles back at me, continuing to get dressed. Jacey's always giving me shit about smoking, but she'll kill me before these do. I watch her walk out, thinking back to when I told her she could leave whenever she wanted. I meant it back then, but maybe I should start chaining her up so she can't.

COLBIE KAY

EIGHT

Jacey

I can't believe I almost told him I loved him. What else could I do but say I loved his cock? I mean, that's true, right? Once I get home, I grab my phone to make my weekly call to my mother, I've got to let her know I'm still alive. Of course she picks up. I always dread these calls.

"Hi honey. How are you?"

"I'm fine, Mother."

"Jacey, you don't sound fine. What's wrong with you? It sounds like you have a bit of an attitude today."

"Yes, Mother, I do. You wanna know what's wrong with me? Let's talk about Dad."

"No, we are not talking about your father."

"I think it's time we did."

"I'm not doing this with you, Jacey."

"Just tell me why you did it," I plead.

"Why I did what? Give you a better life."

"No mom! Why did you take me away? Why did you make me forget him?"

"Your father is a sorry excuse for a man. He is nothing but trash. He abused me and cheated on me. That is why I did it. I wanted better for you."

"Yeah, well that worked out so well for me didn't it?"

"What is that supposed to mean? I gave you a great life."

"Mom, you married a man I hate and I ran across the country to get away. I did everything I was supposed to do to become a doctor. I had no life growing up, I had no friends. Then, the first chance I get at a life, I end up pregnant. Not just pregnant, but by a man you would think is trash. You have me so fucked in the head that I can't even be with him because I'm scared he will be like my father! And I don't even know if my father was a bad man!"

"You're pregnant?"

"Yes, I am and I can't even tell the father because he doesn't fit into this life you made me believe that I should live. Christ, I live how many fucking miles away from you and you still run my goddamn life?"

"I'm coming to you. I'll be there in two weeks."

"No."

"Jacey Marie, do not argue with me. I'm coming in two weeks end of discussion, goodbye." I hear the dial tone. Fuck my life! That is just fucking great! As if my life couldn't get worse, now add my mother into the mix. FUCK! I don't need this shit.

The weekend before my mother is supposed to show up, I got a call from Zoey. She asked me to come over and stay the weekend with her because the guys would be gone for a few days. I agreed, because after this I'm not going to be seeing her much anymore. I have to let her know that I won't be coming back to the club. I'm starting to show and the last thing I need right now is for Bear to find out. While I'm about to pack my stuff to take over, I hear a knock at my door. I open it and find Bear standing there, looking sexy as hell leaning against the frame.

"What're you doing here?"

"It's good to see you too, Lil Mama." He gives me a slow, sexy smile and I return it with one of my own.

"It's just that Zoey called and said you guys were going on a run. I thought you'd already be gone."

"Did you really think I'd leave without saying goodbye?" Bear grips my hip with his big hand, bringing me to him, out of my apartment and onto the stoop. He leans down, taking my mouth with his and exploring with his tongue. He's always leaving me breathless and panting for more after one of these kisses. He pulls away, looking in my eyes, as I try to ignore the need I feel throbbing between my legs. He moves his mouth over to my neck, brushing my hair out of the way with his fingers. He peppers kisses at the shell of my ear, tucking my hair behind it, whispering, "I'll be back in a few days, Lil Mama, then I'm comin' for you." He continues kissing down my neck, and he doesn't give me time to respond as he leaves me standing there dazed and him walking away, composed as always. When I finally pull myself together, I yell, "Be safe!" He turns with a smile and a wink, then says, "Always." I go back inside, pack my stuff, and head over to the clubhouse. Chatty and Ever are already there when I arrive. "Alright, ladies, this first round is for the guys to have safe travels. I usually do this by myself, but now I have all of you, so let's fuckin' party!" Chatty exclaims, and we all laugh. "What'll it be ladies?" She turns to Zoey, who tells her what she and Ever want. When she looks at me, I tell her just water. She narrows her eyes at me, then puts a hand on her hip.

"Alright, what gives with you?" Zoey looks between the both of us with big eyes.

"Nothing. What are you talking about?"

"Girl, you know damn good and well what I'm talking about. You haven't had alcohol for months. If I didn't know better, I'd say you're pregnant. You know, as ladies to this club, we gotta stick together." I see Zoey signing to Ever, and all I can do is drop my head.

"I'm not part of the club, Chatty."

"You and Ever may not wear the property patches, but you two are as close as it gets. Let's go sit down. I don't think we'll be livin' it up tonight." We all make our way to the couches..

"Let me tell you girls something," Chatty starts, sounding beyond her age.

"I've been an Ol' Lady for the last five years. I didn't make it easy on Ripper, he had to work for it. I didn't wanna belong to anybody, be anyone's property, and I didn't understand it until Ripper explained it to me. You girls need to realize that these guys live in their own world. They're a family, they live by their own rules, and when you become an Ol' Lady, it's about respect. If anyone fucks with you, the whole fucking club will bring them down. When they ask you to be their Ol' Lady, it's a privilege.

It's an honor, for them it's even more than being married. Zoey knew what the deal was when Hanger asked her because I told her. I have known these guys for a long time and never seen Writer or Bear the way they are with you two. They may not have asked you to be their Ol' Ladies yet, but them claiming you as their women is more than any of those fuckin' whores will ever get. Those whores are nothing but biker groupies, here to give up services to the guys."

She looks right at me.

"Jacey, I don't know if you know this, but Ripper is the one that brought Bear to this club. He was just a boy then. He thinks of Ripper as a brother outside of the club as well as inside. He's gone to Ripper and talked to him about you. You got that boy all twisted up and at this point, he doesn't know his ass from his head."

We've never talked about how he became part of the club, so it surprises me.

"I didn't know that he knew any of the guys before he was here."

"Okay, this is all I'm gonna say to you about this and then it's time to have fun. I like you, Jacey. I really do, but I'm tired of seeing Bear all messed up over you. After this weekend, you need to go home and figure out what you want. Stop playing this back and forth shit with his head and heart. Don't come back if he's not it for you, tell him straight out you're done, don't sugar coat it. If he is what you want, then you come back, do the right thing and fix this."

"I understand, Chatty, thanks for that."

Then I look to Zoey.

"How would you feel about not going back to the clinic?"

"I don't know. I mean, I loved working there, but after what happened...I'm not sure I really want to go back."

"I agree. I'm thinking of putting the building up for sale. I didn't want to leave you without a job, so I wanted to talk about it first."

"Yeah, let me talk to Hanger."

"Sounds good." I'm worn out. I tell everyone goodnight and make my way to Bear's bedroom. I curl up in his bed, smelling his sheets, and I cocoon myself in. After all the time that has passed, this is the first night I've laid in his bed for anything other than fucking. I think over everything, how we feel about each other, how we text a lot and still send the songs at night. When my car won in the show, he was the one I text to let know. I can't keep the thoughts away that he's not it for me, he's not right for the plan my mother had for me, the one I still plan on following through with. How can I do that though when my body can't say no to him, my heart can't be away from him? It's time I start pulling away. He'll move on and be the perfect guy for someone else. Even thinking about it has my heart hurting. I fall asleep to memories and the smell of him. It's the first time that I've dreamt of something other than my mother or father.

The next day, everything went by without a hitch. We ate pizza, watched movies, and listened to music. I have to get my place in order before my mother gets here, so I left early that night, but before I left I told Zoey I wouldn't be back. She's not happy about it, but she understands. As I walk into my apartment, I send Bear a text, letting him know not to come over. I can't let him come over to be berated by my God awful mother. Later that night, she's at my door, starting in on me as soon as I open it.

"Hello Jacey. How's my pregnant unwed daughter?"

"Mom, don't. I'm not doing this, and you didn't need to come here."

She ignores me as she pushes her way into my apartment. "Why don't you tell me about this man?"

"Mom, I don't want to talk about it with you."

"Well we are going to talk about it."

I know she's not going to let it go. "Fine, what do you want to know?"

"What does he do for a living? Is he a doctor, does he have a high paying job?"

"No, he's not a doctor. Did you not hear a thing I said when we were on the phone?"

"Well to be honest, no. I was surprised by the whole 'you being pregnant' part."

"Christ, mom. Not everything is about money." She always thinks that and I hate it. She gets me so angry.

"Well... when do I get to meet him?"

"Oh, no. You aren't meeting him," I tell her as I shake my head no. "You're not going to belittle the father of my child."

"Why would I do that? He is the father of my grandchild, after all."

"Because mother, you made me grow up hating my father with everything you've ever said about him. I can't even have a normal relationship with my baby's father because I grew up knowing I had to live a certain life. You have me so fucked in the head, I think my baby's father is going to be just like mine."

"Everything I have ever said about your father is the truth. Why would you put the two in the same category? You would not have gone against me and ruined your life."

"Oh, but that's exactly what I did Mom! I'm going to bed. You can sleep on the couch." I walk away, feeling defeated.

"If you really did that, then you are packing up your stuff and moving back to California!" she yells at me.

Turning back around, I point my finger angrily at her. "I'm not a fucking child, I'm twenty-six goddamn years old! It's about time I figure out what the fuck I want! You're not running my life anymore, mother! I'm not going anywhere. Have a goodnight!" I walk to my room, slamming the door shut and wishing Bear was here so I could see him. I don't know if I should though, with what Chatty said and now my mother, but I need his comfort right now and the best I can get is a text.

```
Jacey: R u headed back in a.m.?
Bear: Yeah. How r u?
Jacey: exhausted :(
Bear: what's wrong?
Jacey: My mom is a fucking Bitch.
```

> Bear: Sorry baby wish I could c u.
> Jacey: Me 2 I can send pic.
> Bear: yeah do that! I will 2.
> Jacey: Sexy pic no shirt all muscle and tats :)
> Bear: Urs 2 just in a pink bra. Huh?
> Jacey: Yep gotta give u something to look at lol.
> Bear: Get some rest lol.
> Jacey: Selena's Dreaming Of You.
> Bear: Snow Patrol's Chasing Cars.
> Jacey: Nite Bear.
> Bear: Nite Lil Mama.

The next day I get a text from Zoey saying the guys'll be doing a striptease. I make sure it's not going to be a problem with Chatty before I agree to show up. There's no fucking way I'm missing this shit, especially when one of those guys is Bear. I told my mom I was going for a drive to get out of the apartment so she wouldn't question where I was. This is for real the last time I'll be coming back. I'm going to be really showing soon.

I park my car and make my way into the clubhouse. Zoey and Chatty have moved a couch right up front so we're going to have the best seats to this show. When all four of us girls are at the clubhouse, Zoey lets the guys know we're ready. Taking our seats on the couch, I hear the music start and it's *Juicy by Pretty Ricky*. Oh, this is going to be good! Zoey doesn't know how good Bear can dance and she's in for a surprise.

They start walking out from the hallway in sweats and beaters, forming a line in front of us. They jump into the air and when their feet hit the ground, their legs spread. Taking their hands, they pull at the sweats a bit and start grinding to the music. I've never seen the guys in anything but their shirts or beaters, jeans and cuts. I knew they were sexy, but this is a whole new type of sexiness, with all their muscles and tattoos on display. The guys put their arms behind their heads, slowly rolling their hips.

In a slow motion, they start bringing their hands down, running them along their chests and abs. All three of them hook their thumbs in their waistbands, moving their hips with the beat of the music. Working their hands slowly back up their bodies, the guys stop when they reach the neckline of the beaters, and with one tug straight down the middle, the beaters are ripped from their chests. Hunter and Hacker are good dancers, and I see what they're doing, but they have nothing on Bear, where my attention is solely at.

He's doing a damn good job at keeping my eyes glued on him. Us girls all look at each other with the same expression: mouths open, eyes big, then we turn to watch the guys again. I knew Bear could dance from our night at the club, but this is a whole new ball game. Watching him dance like this is hot, and it's turning me on more than when I danced alone with him. The ache between my legs is growing so intense I have to shift in my seat, trying to dull it down even just a little. I can feel the moisture in my panties.

The brothers fall to their knees, thrusting their hips forward. Hacker and Hunter stay back while Bear gets on his hands and knees and starts grinding the floor, sliding up in front of me. They all stand back up and drop the sweats, so now Bear is in his boxer briefs, grinding his hips in my face. Oh fuck, this is too much! He could probably make me cum just dancing like this. He straddles me on the couch, and I know my face is bright red, but I can't keep from touching him any longer. I run my hands over his thick, muscular thighs, then back to his tight ass, all while he's moving on me, rolling his hips and grinding on me. He takes one of my hands and puts it inside his boxer briefs, placing it on his rock hard erection. I can't help but squeal, "Bear! No! Do not put my hand....OH MY GOD!"

I hear everyone around us laughing, hooting and hollering.

I hear Zoey yell out, "Hey, Bear? Nice ass!"

Then I hear a loud smack. I know Hanger made her pay for that comment. I can't focus on anything but what is going on right in front of me. I didn't even realize I had started stroking up and down his length until I hear him let out a loud growl.

He pulls my hand out and lifts up a little, gripping my legs and pulls me down so I'm half on, half off the couch. He has one arm over me, gripping the couch and holding his weight, while the other hand is next to me. He grinds his hips into me, just like he would if we were fucking. I let out a soft moan and Bear whispers in my ear. "You like this Lil Mama?" I nod.

"I know you do. I can smell you, smell your arousal. You're so turned on, you're about to burst." He lifts up again, pulling me back up. I see the other guys have stopped dancing and everyone is just watching us. They sure are getting quite the show. Someone must have put the music on repeat, because it's been playing the same damn song all this time. He continues teasing me, and my body's in over drive from him dancing on me. He's bringing me to a level of turned on I've never been to.

The next thing I know, I'm being dragged to his bedroom. I can hear all the guys' catcalls but I could care less right now. The door gets slammed closed, and before I know it, I'm up against the wall with his mouth on mine. Clothes start getting ripped off, literally. Once we're both naked, I push him back. He gives me a perplexed look, but I keep pushing him until he hits the bed and falls down, then I pounce on him like a tiger finally getting her prey. I can't wait any longer, I have to have him inside of me. He grabs a condom, putting it on quickly. I line him up and slide down, until he's all the way inside of me.

"Oh fuck! Baby, you're so goddamn wet! I can feel it on my thighs, you're fuckin' drippin'!" he exclaims, as I find my rhythm and pick up speed. He reaches up and takes handfuls of my breasts.

"Swear to Christ, your tits have gotten bigger. Fuck me, you're so goddamn sexy." That urges me on.

I'm going even faster, chasing the release that's just out of my reach. Bear drops his hands to my hips, digging his fingers into my flesh. He thrusts into me, setting the pace and I let him take over. He's pounding into me so hard, I think I might have bruises from his hands and pelvis, but it feels so good.

"Bear, don't stop! I'm so close! Please, make me cum!"

He picks me up and throws me over, climbing on top of me. He grabs my hips, slamming in balls deep, hitting my g-spot every single time. I claw and scratch at his back as I throw my head back, screaming out the best orgasm I've had. I hear him yelling *fuck!* while he fills the condom with his hot seed. He falls over me, holding his weight with his arms so he doesn't crush me.

"That was fuckin' incredible."

"Yeah it was," I agree. He rolls to the side taking me with him. I lay there, running my fingertips over the tattoos on his chest while he runs his hand up and down my back, giving me kisses on the top of my head. I just have to tell him, there's no easy way to do this. I feel tears welling up in my eyes.

"Bear, we have to stop this." He pulls back to look at me.

"Stop what exactly?" He looks curious, but he knows what's coming.

"Everything we're doing. I need some time to figure some things out, plus my mom's here."

"You have got to be fuckin' kidding me!"

"Bear, please. Just give me this time."

He pushes me off him and gets up from the bed, walks over to his jeans and puts them on as he says, "Don't you worry about that Lil Mama, I'll give you all the time you need. For you to tell me this right after we got done fuckin'...you've got real shit timing." He opens the door, slamming it shut behind him, leaving me feeling more alone than I ever have. Fuck, he ripped my shirt apart. What am I going to wear? I go to his dresser and find a Sinners' shirt, putting it on before hightailing it out of there. This routine is getting so old, I have to figure out what the fuck I'm going to do, and soon.

Over the next week, I put my building up for sale. It's bitter sweet for me because this is what I wanted when I became a doctor, but now it sickens me to even see the place again, let alone having to go in and clean it all out. Zoey didn't want anything, which is understandable. I load two small boxes, one in my trunk and one in the passenger seat. Luckily, I didn't have much here worth keeping because there really wasn't much space for anything. I get back to my apartment and my mother's still there.

"Hey honey. Did you get everything?"

"Yeah."

"Well, what are you going to do now for money?"

"I don't know yet mom."

"You can't not know, Jacey. You have a baby on the way." Like I don't know this. "How do you expect to take care of a baby without a job?"

"I have my ways, Mother. Don't worry about it."

"Don't tell me not to worry! That is my grandchild! You need to start worrying about finding a husband to take care of you and this baby."

"I don't need to find a husband. I'll take care of this baby myself."

"Why don't you just go work at the hospital, find you a nice doctor?"

"I don't want a goddamn doctor, Mother! I want the father of my child, but I'm too goddamn scared to be with him. Hell, I don't even know if I want to be a doctor anymore!"

With that, I walk away and slam my bedroom door.

Why does it always have to be about money with her? She irritates the fuck out of me, and I can't deal with her anymore. Hopefully, she'll get the point that I don't want her here and don't want to talk to her. I pull my phone out, about to text Bear. I really miss him and want to talk to him, but then I decide not to. It's for the best to just let him be.

NINE

Bear

The night that Zoey made us dance for losing the bet was the last time I saw Jacey. It's been over a month and now she refuses to see me. After I walked out, I went to the bar, and not long after, she hightailed it outta there as usual. I've decided the chick is fucked up in the head. I've made my feelings clear, but she doesn't want any part of it so I'm fucking done. I don't know if she's moved on. Shit, I don't even know if she really was fucking someone else while we were together or not. She said she wasn't, but with her I never know what to believe. It'd make sense, all the back and forth she does, between wanting me and hating me. She's never gonna let me in so I'm done.

Zoey and Hanger came back that night, engaged, and while I'm happy for him, I'm pissed too. It's jealousy, I know. He got so fucking lucky with Crazy Girl, and I'm stuck wanting a woman that doesn't want me back. Her body desires me, but that's not enough anymore, I want all of her. I'm not giving in this time. I wasn't lying, I'll give her all the time she needs. I miss her crazy ass, but if Jacey wants me, she'll have to come get me.

This last month has been full of tension because of Romeo, plus we have three new prospects. Two of them came from the Oklahoma chapter and the other is fucking Anthony Gremaldi. Apparently the Oklahoma boys, Demon and Chasyr, got into some trouble over their sisters and they needed to come here to lay low. Of course, already being part of the club, they were welcomed with open arms, plus Demon was helping Hunter watch over the warehouse so we knew him beforehand. Now Anthony, aka Pretty Boy, we weren't too sure about, but he pulled through for us though. He kept his word and in the end, killed his uncle. That was the night we had to bring Crazy Girl in to help with club business. Hanger didn't like it, but just like we all knew she would, Crazy Girl agreed to help get Romeo's ass back from being held hostage by Pretty Boy's uncle. Yeah, we had to put her in a dangerous situation, but she held her own and took her first life that night. She did it to save Hanger, I think that's why she doesn't feel too much remorse for killing the cunt that played our brother.

I'm in my room when I hear gun shots. Jumping outta my bed, I grab my 1911, charging a round. I run out to the bar, where my brothers are taking cover. The whores and hang-arounds are lying on the floor too, hiding and screaming. I see Chatty on the ground covering her head, and someone has the door open so they can shoot back. I go out the back door of the clubhouse and come around the side to the front. Peeking around the corner, I see Ripper is down, I take aim and shoot, hitting the windshield of the car. I don't know how long the crossfire lasts, but I look over and see Chatty run out the door. FUCK! I scream at her, "No, Chatty! Do NOT come out!" She doesn't fucking listen, and she runs out, dropping down next to Ripper, pulling him into her arms. The shooters peel out and I run over to her. Looking down, Ripper has blood pouring from his chest and back. When he coughs, it comes from his mouth.

"No! Oh God! Fuck! Not Ripper." I say to myself. I can't believe I'm gonna lose him. She needs a few minutes with him, and I wanna give them privacy so I step back far enough where I can't hear them. I just watch them, knowing this'll be the last time they are together. After I see her kiss his lips, I know he's gone. Coming back to them, I tell her, "Chat, I need you to come with me."

"I'm not going anywhere, Bear."

"You gotta let Doc look him over."

"There's nothing to look over! He's dead!" She's sobbing and screaming at me. "My husband, your brother, is dead!"

"I know, and I don't want him to be gone either, but Doc needs to look at him."

"For what? He can't do anything."

"Chatty, please don't make me pull you from him," I beg her. This is too much, I can't fucking believe he's gone.

"You're gonna have to if you want me to leave."

Fuck me! I can't deal with this. I grab her around her waist as she clutches onto Ripper's dead body. Gunner helps me get her hands free while she's screaming, "Please! Don't take me from him!" I carry her away so the guys can take his body. She's kicking, hitting, crying, and screaming at me. I sit her down on the couch, then Gunner comes over to hold her. He pulls her tight to his chest and talks to her and I don't know if she's listening or what he's saying, but I can't deal with this shit. My best fucking friend was just shot and killed. Fuck this day! I head to my room until Hanger gets back.

When Hanger comes back, he calls church, and when it's over, I go to my room and pull out my phone. I said I wasn't gonna give in, but I fucking need her. I can't deal with being here right now.

```
Bear: I need u.
Jacey: Bear?
Bear: No 4get everything else I
need u.
Jacey: I'll be there in 20 wait
outside.
```

I walk outside and wait for her by the gate. I don't wanna be here or around anybody. I see her pull up and I go climb in the passenger side of her car. "Drive," I tell her, trying not to sound too much like an asshole.

"Where do you want to go?"

"I don't care, just drive. Get me the fuck outta here."

She drives us to the pond I had taken her to in my truck. Jacey parks and we sit there for a while, neither of us saying anything. She has the stereo playing, when *See You Again by Wiz Khalifa and Charlie Puth* comes on. She reaches out to turn it off, but I stop her. "Leave it."

"Okay." Her voice is so quiet, she knows something is wrong.

Leaning back into the seat, I rest my head on the headrest, cover my eyes with my arm, and let a few tears free. When the song ends, I turn my head to look at her the exact same moment she looks at me. Her features are so soft. God, I fucking miss her. I can't resist not touching her anymore so I take her hand in mine.

"Bear? What happened? I'm kind of freaking out here."

"I'm not trying to freak you out. You're the only person I could be around right now. Ripper got killed."

"What?" she asks and her eyes widen.

"Yeah, some shit went down with Romeo, the people retaliated against us. They came today, shot up the club, and killed Ripper."

"Oh god, Bear. I'm so sorry. Is Chatty okay? Is everybody else okay?" She pulls me to her the best she can, wrapping me up in her small arms. I lay my head on her breast, letting her comfort me for once.

"No, she lost it. Jacey, I had a good life once and if my life wouldn't have gone to shit, I would have never been part of the club. Then you would've been proud to call me your man."

"Shh…let's not do this right now. Let me just hold you," she says, her hold on me tightening.

"Jacey, I hope you figure your shit out, and decide what you want soon. I can't keep doing this. I say I'm done and then somethin' always happens. I miss the fuck outta you. All this shit fuckin' hurts, it's too much."

"I know." Still using her quiet voice, holding onto me for dear life.

"Did you know that Ripper is the reason I came to the club?"

"Yeah, Chatty told me he brought you in." Going back into my memory of that first day I was brought to the clubhouse, I just start talking.

"Yeah, I had to go into state custody. They placed me in a few different foster homes, not good ones either. The last one was with Ripper's parents. He came over one day and seen what his ol' man did to my face, and I guess he got tired of seein' me beat up every time he came over, so he took me out of there and never looked back. He was twenty-six at the time, I was sixteen. He was already a patched member, but he talked to Hanger's pop, who was president at the time. The club voted that I could live there as long as I kept my shit clean and didn't draw attention to the club. By the time I was eighteen, they were my family. They had been takin' care of me for two years by then so I decided to prospect instead of leavin'. I needed that sense of family, I longed for."

"What happened to your parents?" She seems genuinely curious about it, so I continue.

"I'll tell you what happened to my dad, but not my momma." No fucking way am I getting into what happened to my momma.

"Okay," she agrees.

I think back to that fateful night that changed my entire life. "It was a Tuesday evening, I just got done eatin' dinner at my friend's house. It wasn't quite dark yet, but the sun was goin' down. I rode into the yard at my house and parked my bicycle. I ran up the porch and turned the doorknob, throwing the door open.

"Momma, I'm home!" I yelled. She didn't answer me, which was unlike her, she always answered, and that's when I heard it. My mom was crying. I had never heard my mom cry until that day, and I knew something had to be wrong. I made my way into the living room and that's when I saw her. She was sitting on the couch with her hands covering her face, her shoulders were shaking from the force of her sobs.

I asked, "Momma, where's Dad?" She looked up to me with the saddest look on her face. I didn't understand what was happening. I saw her red, wet eyes and her tear streaked face. I could tell she had been crying for a while. She reached over to pat the cushion next to her. "Come sit down, Baby. I have to tell you something."

I sat next to her and she took my hand in hers. They were so cold and she looked into my eyes.

"Momma, what's happening? Where's Dad?" I asked again.

"Baby, there was an accident."

QUIET COUNTRY

"What do you mean an accident?"

"Oh, Honey, he was in the wrong place at the wrong time."

"What happened to Dad, Momma?"

"Your father was shot tonight. He didn't make it."

I started shaking my head no so fast, thinking it can't be real. "You said it was an accident. How is that an accident?" I asked.

"The police came over and told me that he was at a gas station in town. I guess it was being robbed. When he went to go in the store, the police told him to stay put. He listened, but I guess he went to reach for his phone and they thought he was reaching for a gun. They shot him. They were confused and didn't know how many robbers there were."

"So the police killed him? They're supposed to protect people. Momma, why would they do that? Why would they take my Dad away from me?" I could feel the tears leaking out of my eyes.

"Baby, I don't know. I am so sorry," she told me.

"I stood up and pulled my hand from hers and ran to my room. I fell onto my bed and just kept thinking I'm never gonna see my father again. He's never going to be able to go outside and throw the ball with me again. He will never be at one of my games again. The ones that are meant to serve and protect innocent people took him from me, and from my momma.'"

Oh my God. Bear, I'm so sorry." I look up at her and she has one hand covering her mouth and tears in her eyes.

"Yeah, that was a long time ago. You can take me back now."

"Okay?" I'm starting to get angry, she shouldn't be crying for me. The whole way back is silent, and once we get there, I get out without saying a word and go inside. Thank fuck they got everything cleaned up. I go to my room, lay in my bed. Seems like forever, but eventually I fall asleep.

Over the next week, things have been quiet around here. Crazy Girl has taken the place of Chatty, seeing as she won't get out of bed. I haven't heard from Jacey since that night. All the brothers are in mourning, especially me. I miss my brother, my friend. We had the funeral, and didn't use a police escort. Everyone knew who we were when they saw us coming and they showed their respect by pulling over. Chatty rode in the limo in front along with Crazy Girl. Chatty doesn't let her too far outta her reach. She's depending on her a lot and I'm thankful Crazy Girl has been there. I know right now she needs time, but I'll see to it that she follows what Ripper wanted, but I don't think she'll stick around too much longer. She has family in another state, so I see her going to them for a while. She won't be gone forever though.

All the brothers are on our bikes and the other chapters have come to give their final goodbyes to one of the best brothers we had. Chatty can't get through her eulogy so Crazy Girl steps up to help her. Hanger sang *Knockin' on Heaven's Door*, which made even the biggest of the men lose their shit. I saw Jacey standing off in the distance. She's wearing a long loose fitting black dress and it looks like she's gained some more weight. I hadn't really paid attention the night she came and got me. Jacey usually always wears clothes that show off her sexy figure, but the dress she is wearing today is big, hangs straight down. Just knowing she was there was enough for me, and she left when it was over without a word to me, or anyone else for that matter. I don't know what the hell is going on with us, but I'll leave that up to her.

After the funeral, we go back to the clubhouse and have a bonfire for Ripper. Chatty and Crazy Girl stayed inside, with Chatty going right back to bed. All the guys stood around the fire drinking beer and telling stories about Ripper from his twenty-some years as a patched brother.

About a week after the funeral, Chatty left, just like I knew she would. She didn't say goodbye to anybody except Crazy Girl, which doesn't surprise me either. Losing Ripper and then leaving all of us, it would have been too much for her. When she comes back, and one day she will, we'll be here welcoming her with open arms. She will always be a part of this family.

I spend my days going to work at the garage. Once a week, I go to the cabin to keep up on the maintenance and yard work. I don't think I'll ever live there, but I like to keep up on it, just like my dad did. I spend my nights working on my truck. I do all this shit so my mind can stay the fuck off Jacey. I've texted and called her several times, which she doesn't respond to anymore. I know something's up, and for her not to show up to Ever's graduation party isn't like her. For her to just quit answering my texts or calls isn't normal either. Fuck, for all I know, she moved the hell on. The graduation party has been going on for a few hours, and I'm pretty fucking wasted when I decide it's time to ask Crazy Girl what the fuck is going on. I walk up to her trying to stay calm, asking, "Crazy Girl, why's my Lil Mama not here?"

"Well, she said she had some shit to do." She can't even look me in the fucking eyes when she says it.

"Crazy Girl, you're lyin' to me. You know you're a shit liar. Jacey hasn't been here in months."

"Bear, I can't tell you. If she wants you to know, she will come and tell you."

This is so fucked. I should've known she wouldn't tell me shit. "I call her, she doesn't fuckin' answer, and she's stopped comin' 'round. Somebody needs to tell me what the fuck's goin' on!" I'm getting pissed because now I know she is keeping something from me. I've been sitting 'round here for months, waiting for her to make up her goddamn mind.

Hanger looks over and very calmly says to me, "Bear, you need to watch yourself. Watch how you talk to my Ol' Lady." I know I need to, but I can't bring myself to give a shit right now. I just want somebody to tell me what the fuck is going on with her.

Crazy Girl says, "Bear, I would tell you if I could, but it's not my place. You guys have got your club rules, well, us girls have our girl code. Just give her some time. I think she will come to you."

"You know what? Whatever. Fuck it. I'm so fuckin' done with this shit. I'm outta here." Fuck them and their girl code. I'm done waiting. If she can't have the fucking decency to call me and tell me about whatever is going on, I'm done with waiting. I storm out to the garage, turn on *Disturb's Down with the Sickness* and start looking at my truck. Somebody puts their hands on my back, running them up and down. Those hands, I haven't felt them in months. I turn and look down at Morgan. I haven't had pussy since I was last with Jacey and I don't want this bitch's pussy either. I'll take her mouth though.

"On your knees." She drops down, like a good little whore, with a smile on her face. I pull my cock free. It's not hard, but she can get it there.

"Put me in your mouth, suck me until I cum." She does exactly what I say.

After a few minutes, my shit's still not working. She pulls out and asks if something's wrong, her voice grates on my nerves. "No, keep suckin'."

I know what I gotta do. I think of the sexy little brunette with the two-toned eyes. In no time, I'm shooting my load into her mouth. I look down at her.

"Get the fuck up and get outta here." She stands and scurries away.

Over the next month, I'm with all the whores. I can't bring myself to fuck them, and I don't pleasure them, but I'll have them suck my cock all day long. Every single time, I think of my Lil Mama. I think I've even called out her name a few times while I was at it. I thought it was done between us. Little did I know, at the end of the month she would come back, pregnant, and my whole life was about to change once again.

TEN
PRESENT DAY
Jacey

Once the guys got us to the hospital, the baby and I were rushed to the labor and delivery unit. Dr. Greene checked us out and we were both healthy. Bear went between checking on me and checking on the baby. They had to take him to the nursery for a while to clean him up and weigh him.

Bear sits in a chair next to the bed, and I scoot to the edge, patting the bed next to me. "I don't think that's a good idea Jacey. I don't wanna hurt you."

"I'm fine. Now get up here." He comes over, carefully sitting down. I lay my head on his chest, putting my arm around his waist. He wraps me in his arms and kisses the top of my head. "I'm sorry Bear, for everything I fucked up."

"Hey, look at me." I lift my head to meet his eyes. "Yeah, you did. You really fuckin' did. I'm serious though. No more fuckin' games, no more lies, and you don't run from me anymore. This is the last time. I know I've said that a lot, but I'm serious. Don't fuck it up." I feel the tears burning my eyes, as I nod. "First, we need to name our boy," he says, with pride in his eyes. "Do you have any names picked out?"

"Depends," I say, smiling. "What's your name, Bear?"

He bursts out laughing, then replies, "We really did this wrong, didn't we?" I can't help but laugh too. "My name is Kellen Rhodes. Damn, it's been a long time since I've said my real name."

"I love it!"

He looks shocked at first and then it hits him. "Wait? You wanna name the baby after me?"

"Well, yeah. You're his father. Now if you had a horrible name, I would've had second thoughts." That makes us laugh again.

"I guess it's a good thing my parents gave me a *good* name then," he says with a smile, then it falls. "Ripper's real name was James, but I always called him Jimmy. I wanna name him after Ripper." That brings the tears back and I nod.

"We are not calling our son Jimmy, but how about Kellen James Rhodes?"

"I like it." He leans down, taking my mouth with his.

"How did you get the name *Bear*?" I wonder why I never asked before.

He starts laughing. "Well, when Ripper took me to the clubhouse that first day, I had to wait outside until the club voted if I could stay, and Ripper took me out back where Hanger and Gunner were shooting BB guns. They asked what to call me, and since Ripper called me 'Kid', I told them to call me the same thing. They both laughed and said they couldn't call me 'Kid' because I was way too big. I was always bigger than most kids my age, and Hanger took notice. He said he was gonna call me 'Bear' and it stuck."

"But when you took me to the diner, Ma called you Bear. Didn't they know you before the club? Why wouldn't they call you Kellen?"

"Yeah, at first they did. I couldn't prospect for the club then, so about six months after I was there, I got put in charge of watchin' out for Hanger and Gunner. I would take them to the diner with me. One day, Ma asked them why they call me Bear. Hanger told her that I said to call me 'Kid' and he couldn't do that, but took a look at how big I was compared to the two of them. She thought that was the funniest shit ever and it stuck with her too. What was so bad, was Hanger and Gunner were two scrawny fucks then so I looked even bigger."

The door opens and the nurse walks in holding our baby. He has a little blue hat on and is wrapped in a light blue blanket with bears on it. I can't help but chuckle that he's wrapped in bears. "Hey mom and dad, we got a healthy eight pound, twenty inch, baby boy here." She hands Kellen to me. "Do you have a name for him?"

We look to each other, smiling, and look back to her, at the same time saying, "Kellen James Rhodes." Smiling, she nods and walks back out. Bear runs out to tell all the guys, and when he comes back in, he sits next to me and stares at his son. I ask him if he wants to hold our boy.

"Yeah," he says, while smiling from ear to ear and nodding his head. I hand Kellen over. "This is unreal. I never thought I could love anyone so much. I do, Jacey, I love him. I'm gonna be the best father I can be."

"I know you will."

Once Kellen has eaten and gotten changed, we laid him in the bed they wheeled in for him. Then Bear looks to me. "I think it's time we have that talk."

"Yeah, it is," I tell him. "What do you want to know?"

"How exactly did you get pregnant?"

"Well, you remember that first time, the condom broke. Before I met you, I had been sick and was taking antibiotics. The kind I was taking made the birth control not work." I already know what his next question is going to be.

"That explains a lot," he says, smiling. "How do you know Snake?" He thinks I had sex with him and that is a disgusting thought. I look down and start fidgeting with the hospital gown. "He's my father."

"What!?" He all but shouts.

"Bear, quiet, the baby," I reprimand. "Snake is my father."

"How is that even possible?"

"I'll start from the beginning. I lived in Kansas until I was six, when my mother took me away and moved me to California. Over the years, she did her best to make me forget him, but I dream about him, and in my dreams he loves me and was a good father. My mother tells me things like he is trash and scum, that bikers try to take ownership of you, and they cheat and abuse the women they are supposed to love. She said he never wanted me, and I believed her because if he did, why didn't he come get me or at least come see me?"

He looks at me with understanding in his eyes. "That explains why you were always runnin' when I said shit like 'you were mine' and 'you belong to me'."

"Yeah. My mother is a monster. That's why I never want you to meet her. She'd be so mean and I can't let you go through that. She kept me sheltered my whole life, thinking we were better than everyone else. Hell, she wouldn't even let me play with other kids! I had to study all the time to become a doctor. That's why I love music and cars so much. She could hear the music, but could never knew about the cars, she would've flipped so I kept it a secret. I became smart, like, really fucking smart and I graduated high school when I was sixteen just so I could get away from her."

"So that's why I was the first?"

"No, my mother and father were never married. She didn't have to go through a divorce or anything like that when she took off. When I was ten, she married a guy that I absolutely hated. He wanted me to call him dad, and I just couldn't do it. The dreams kept me from that, I was hanging on to something I wanted to be real, you know? Well, as the years went on and I got older, he started looking at me differently and not in a fatherly way. The night of my graduation, something happened, and I left the next day and never went back."

Bear has a hard look on his face. "What happened Jacey?" he asks. "I know he didn't rape you, so what happened?"

"I've never told anyone this, not even my mother." He nods, encouraging me to go on. "I went to a party that night, the first one I had ever been to, and I got drunk. When I got home, he asked me come into the study, where he tried to rape me, but I stopped him by hitting him with a lamp over and over again until he got off of me. I ran into my room and locked the door. The next day, I blackmailed him. I told him I would tell my mother and the cops if he didn't give me money and pay for my schooling. I had to get out of there, and I didn't have the money to leave." His features are hard, his jaw tense. He's pissed.

"I'm so sorry that happened." He squeezes me tight in his arms, giving me a hard look, letting me know he's not happy.

"Bear, you can't do anything. He's very well known in California, and he's rich. No, you can't do anything to him."

"I'm not gonna do anything," he reassures, looking kind of scary. "How much did he give you?"

"Two and a half million."

"Holy fuck, Jacey!"

"Yeah, I used some for school, my car, and the clinic building. That's it though, the rest is in an account. I don't touch it."

"Okay, so you lost trust in people and were scared of men. That's why I was the first?"

"Yeah, I mean, I had opportunities before, but I never felt anything for them, so I couldn't do it. When I first saw you, it was like something out of my fantasies. You made me feel all sorts of things. Did you know you were my first kiss?"

That makes his smile return.

"I kinda thought so. You've made me feel all sorts of things for a while now, Lil Mama. I'm gonna have all your firsts, and you can take the ones I've got left. I wouldn't want anyone else to have them."

A smile overtakes my face. "Your firsts? Like what? Your ass?" I bust out laughing.

"Fuck no, smartass! I was talking about you bein' my first baby mama!" He smiles and my laughing stops.

"Excuse me? Listen here you prick..." He stops me from continuing.

"Jacey, I'm kidding! You're the only baby mama I want."

"You're not helping yourself, mister. I'm not your 'baby mama', I'm the mother of your child, Baby Daddy," I huff out.

"Okay, okay, Lil Mama." He throws his hands up in surrender. "I was just kidding. You could never be just my 'baby mama'. I'm serious though, whatever I have left to give is yours."

"You know you can be pretty great?"

"I know," he says, showing off that cocky smile. "So why did you come back to Kansas instead of just going to a different city in California?"

"I wanted to get as far away from my mother as I could and I know she hates Kansas. Plus, I wanted to find my father."

"I guess you accomplished that tonight."

"No, I found him a while ago, but I can't bring myself to talk to him. I'm scared he's not going to want anything to do with me, just like my mother said."

"It might be good to talk to him though. Find out how he feels."

"Yeah, I'll think about it. I've seen pictures of him on the computer and he looked happy."

"We've covered a lot, Lil Mama. Why don't you get some rest before Kellen wakes up?"

"That sounds good. Can I see your phone first?"

He hands it to me and I open up his YouTube app. I look up at him, close my eyes.

"This is from me to you." I hit play on *Nickleback's Far Away*.

We listen to the song, while he holds me close, and I finally realize that this is where I should've been the whole time. Once the song is done, he tells me to look at him so I lift my head, meeting his eyes once again.

"No more runnin', let me love you now."

"Okay, no more running and I'll try." I lay my head back down and fall asleep.

"Did you get the songs I sent you when you never answered?" I look at him once more, smiling.

"You mean *Eighteen Days by Saving Abel*, *Push* and *Chains by Nick Jonas*?"

"Ah, so you did," he chuckles.

"You know, that's three songs of his you've had me listen to. You got a thing for Nick Jonas?" I bust out laughing again.

"Shut the fuck up," he starts laughing himself. "Not my fault they're good songs and fit your ass."

"So true." I close my eyes, enjoying being back in his arms while he runs his fingers through my hair until I fall asleep.

We're exhausted. Kellen didn't sleep at all last night so we started taking shifts. I feel like a weight as been lifted off my shoulders after telling Bear everything. We can only move forward from here, and I finally feel like I'm ready to take what he has been offering for so long. It was surreal seeing my father that close. I remember every feature to his face and the way he smells: oil and leather, even after all these years. I'm not sure what will happen with my father now, but I guess time will tell.

The nurses come in to check on us, making sure we're both fine. I'm exhausted, having a baby takes a lot out of a person, and Bear sees it, so he tells me to sleep for a little while. I'm so grateful because I'm running on fumes. I'm not sure how long I slept, but when I open my eyes, Bear is holding Kellen, whispering to him. I can't hear what he's saying but just the sight forms a lump in my throat and tears well up in my eyes. Why did I have to be so fucking stupid and let him miss everything?

All the guys, plus Zoey and Ever, come to see us. The brothers congratulate us and stare at Kellen in wonderment, but don't hold him. Poor guys, they're big bad ass bikers, but scared to hold a little baby. I find it funny because when you meet them and are around them, they don't seem to be scared of anything. The girls hold Kellen though, and of course, fall in love. I can't wait for Zoey to have her babies!

I need to apologize to everyone and there's no better time than the present. "Guys, I want to tell you all how sorry I am that I really haven't given you a chance. I was holding shit against you all that had nothing to do with you. I hope you can forgive me. You're Bear's family and now Kellen's too."

"Oh, well fuck, I guess we can forgive you," Bam Bam replies with a smile.

"We never held anything against you, just treat our brother right," Hacker chimes in. I nod, tears shining in my eyes. They all come give me hugs, even the girls. When it's Doc's turn, he whispers in my ear, "He loves you Lil Mama. Treat him right, please. The love you guys could have only comes around once in a lifetime and you don't wanna lose that, believe me. Don't keep Kellen away either, he's special to me. First baby I ever delivered and I certainly won't be forgettin' that."

"I won't, I promise," I say, pulling away to look at him. "I won't ever forget it either and I can't thank you enough for delivering him." He smiles, nods and backs away. After everyone leaves and we're alone again, I look to Bear. "Will you tell me about your mom?" He comes over to sit next to me on the bed.

"The only reason I wouldn't tell you before is because I didn't know where we were going and this isn't something a lot of people know about. Really, only Ripper knew and I hope you don't have second thoughts after I tell you."

"Bear, I'm not going to. This is a new start for us, so we need to get it all out." He gives me a tight nod starting the most heartbreaking story I've ever heard.

"I told you about my father being killed when I was eleven. My parents were so happy before he died. My momma couldn't deal with the pain of losing him, so she started going out all the time, leaving me at home to fend for myself. I started noticing changes in her, and finding burnt and bent spoons, needles laying around. And guys would start coming around when she was home.

I didn't understand at first, until two years had passed since my father's death. In that two years, my mother became a heroin addict. We lost the house, we lost everything and had to move into a horrible fuckin' apartment in a shit part of town. She couldn't hold down a job at all and any money she got it would go to her addiction. But the bills still had to get paid and I needed food and clothes, so I found a group of kids to hang with and they taught me how to hustle. Being bigger than most kids my age, no questions were asked about how old I was and I don't think they would've given a shit anyway. So at thirteen, I was paying all the bills, buying groceries, and taking care of myself. When my mother needed to get high to take the pain away, I supplied her with what she needed. I would give her enough to last her a week. That was the deal, no more, no less. On the second anniversary of my father's death, I came home to find her dead. I had gotten new shit and had given her the same amount I normally did that morning, but instead of spacing it out, she did all of it in one blast. Jacey, I killed my mom." Bear's gazing out the hospital window. I put my hand on his cheek, bringing his eyes to mine.

"Baby, listen to me. You did not kill your mom. She was hurting and couldn't deal, she chose to leave you. You have to let that guilt go."

He tilts his head into my touch, closing his eyes. "Ripper used to tell me that all the time. I never believed him though. I've held onto that for so long. I knew what that shit did to people, what it did to her. Jacey, my mom was so happy before my dad died and when he was taken from us, she gave up and never returned. My mother used to be so beautiful, with her tanned skin, long brown hair, and big, bright brown eyes. She always had a smile on her face. When I found her in that kitchen chair, she had stringy greasy hair, her face was sunk in, pasty with deep black circles all around her eyes, and she had lost so much weight. She had sores all over her face and her arms. Her head was back and her eyes were open, so was her mouth, and I could see the tourniquet tied around her upper arm, the needle sticking out. I'll never forget it, how awful she looked. I remember it like it was fuckin' yesterday."

"Oh, Bear. I'm so sorry. You've been through so much."

"Yeah, well, it was all a long time ago. Just gotta keep movin' on."

"Is that why you call me Lil Mama?"

"What do you mean?"

"Well, you said she used to have tan skin and long brown hair."

"Huh… I never thought about it that way, but yeah. I guess. You do have some of the same features she had. I guess the name really does fit now that we've got Kellen." He lets out a soft chuckle and shakes his head.

"Bear, you've said to me that I wasn't proud to call you my man. That's not true. I was scared. I don't and wouldn't want anyone else. I didn't know anything you had been through. You're so strong for making it through all that."

"I meant what I said last night, Jacey. Fuck, we did this all wrong, but from this point forward, we're gonna make it right. We're gonna start from the beginnin'."

"What the hell does that mean?"

There's a knock at the door, and in comes my witch of a mother. How the hell did she find me? "It would have been nice to hear from you. I was so worried, I started calling all the hospitals around this God forsaken place until I found you." I guess that answers my question. She sees Bear and narrows her eyes. "Let me see my grandchild." I hand Kellen over to her and she looks at Bear. "You're dismissed now. You can leave."

"Bear, meet my mother." I look to him and I see he's getting pissed, nostrils flaring, face turning red. "Mom, he's not going anywhere. That is his son."

"Yes he is. Leave now. No grandchild of mine will be raised by biker trash. You will find a good man, someone who can support you and this baby." Yeah, this isn't good. He's gonna flip his shit if I don't handle this, and quickly.

"The fuck?" He sets his cold hard stare on her.

"Bear, don't. I got this." I hold out my arms. "Give me our baby." She hesitantly does and I pass him over to Bear. "Let's get something

QUIET COUNTRY

straight, Mother," I spit. "I *am* a grown ass woman. I *will* make my own goddamn decisions. I *will* do what is best for my child and that *is* having his father. You *took* me away from mine, I will *not* do that to them. You kept me sheltered my *entire* life, having no friends, studying all the time for something I didn't even really want to be. Bear has been good to me all this time, even after everything I have put him through. I'm *in love* with *him*. I *won't* let you mess this up for me, not anymore. Now, you are the one that is dismissed. Pack your shit and get out of my apartment and go home."

"You ungrateful little bitch," if looks could kill, I'd have been six feet under. "After everything I have done for you."

"Enough." Bear's voice echoes through the room.

He gently lays Kellen in his bed. Walking right up to her, rage clear on his face, he growls, "You will not disrespect my woman ever again. I could give two fucks who you are. I've been chasin' somethin' unattainable for months because of you. You will not fuck with her head any more than you already have. My baby will not be raised by another fuckin' man, and for you to even suggest some shit like that makes you the biggest fuckin' cunt I've ever met. One last thing, I do believe she told you to get the fuck out. If you need help gettin' your shit from her place, it would be an honor to call my brothers to help you. I don't believe you've met the Satan's Sinners, have you?" She shakes her head while walking to the door, fear written all over her face.

Just like that, she opens it and leaves. He turns, looking at me.

"Are you okay?"

I let out a laugh.

"Me? Yeah, I'm fine. You don't know how long I've wanted to tell her to get the fuck out. Are you okay though? I'm sorry she said that shit to you."

"No need to be sorry," he pauses. "Did you mean what you said?"

"Every word," I respond without hesitation.

"I'm movin' you into my place."

"We can't just move in together. You were just talking about starting over. And we can't move a baby to the clubhouse either."

"Not talkin' 'bout the clubhouse. You'll be livin' at my place but, I'll still stay with my brothers."

"Well, where is it?"

"Just trust me. I'll have the prospects clean out your place, and go get everything for Kellen."

"That's fine, but tell them not to do my bedroom."

"Why?"

110

"Bear, I'm being very cooperative here. Just promise me they won't go in my bedroom. I have my personal things in there. You want the guys to see the kind of bras and panties I wear?"

"Good point, I'll tell 'em. When you get out tomorrow, we'll go clean out your room."

"Okay."

"We'll do it right this time. We need to start over, see how it goes. You good with that?"

"Yeah. Let's do this shit." He bursts out laughing which causes me to laugh too.

"So, if you don't want to be a doctor, what do you wanna do?"

"I don't know yet. Take time to focus on being a mom, live my life for me and not someone else."

"Sounds good, Lil Mama."

ELEVEN

Bear

She was right, her mom is a fucking bitch. No way could I sit there, letting her talk to Jacey like that. I give two fucks who you are, no one will disrespect my woman, the mother of my child, and for her to say another man should raise my son, she must have lost her fucking mind. I could've killed her with no remorse.

After I talked to Jacey about moving in with me, I called all the guys to have 'em clear out her apartment, except her bedroom. I was shocked she didn't put up more of a fight about moving in. She had fought me tooth and nail this whole time about fucking everything. Maybe our talk and getting it all out there worked and she's really gonna try, maybe this is our time. I can only hope we get this shit right. I don't wanna be away from her anymore and I won't be away from my son.

I have another surprise for her and it'll be waiting for us when she's released. The guys assured me that everything would be ready when we get out. They said they'll put all her furniture in the barn at the cabin, and I'm sure they'll get help from Crazy Girl and Ever, because I don't think my brothers know shit about decorating a nursery. I called Crazy Girl to find out where to get some baby clothes. She told me to just go to Walmart because it's right down the road from the hospital, so I left Jacey and Kellen long enough to go shopping to get them the things they need to go home. I always get funny looks from people because of my size and my cut, so you can imagine the looks I got going where all the baby shit is. I found the baby section easy enough, but I needed help because I don't know shit about this stuff. I asked this old lady to help me, she was nice enough. She said I was gonna need an onesie, pants, and a coat because it's cold outside, diapers, a blanket, and a car seat. I get him a tiny fucking clothes set that's dark blue with light blue words that says **"TOUGH GUY"** on the front, and it has a matching hat and little socks. This woman helped me get everything I needed for him, and in the right sizes. While I'm here, I pick up an extra set of clothes for Jacey and me also.

I'm back at the hospital, waiting for the doctor to come in and

release them. When the doctor comes in, she gives us a bright smile.
"Hey Jacey. Are you ready to take your little guy home?"
"Yes, I'm ready to get out of here. Thanks for everything Sierra."
"You're welcome, girl. I'm glad you came to your senses and told him." She looks over to me. The way they're talking, they must know each other.
"Yeah, it took me too long. I should've told him from the beginning, but I was being stubborn."
"I take it you know each other?" I ask, wanting to find out.
Jacey answers, "Yeah, we've known each other for awhile. She was my attending doctor until something happened, and made her switch to being an OB/GYN. She was my doctor throughout the pregnancy and she happens to be Zoey's doctor too."
"Nice to meet you Doctor...?"
I notice something pass through her eyes and face before she responds. "Oh, Dr. Greene. It's nice to finally meet you too, Bear."
"How you know my name?"
"Jacey talked a lot about you during her appointments. Don't hold it against her for not telling you. I don't know her whole story, but I do know she hasn't had it easy."
"We're working on it. Thanks for taking care of them." I'm genuinely happy that she was taking care of my baby, even if she wouldn't tell me.
"No problem. Alright, you guys are free to go. All the paperwork has been signed and the nurse took your IV out. If you need anything, just call me and make sure to setup your pediatric appointment."
Dr. Greene leaves and we get Kellen dressed. I try helping, but Jacey laughs at me because something so little doesn't work when you have huge hands. She just takes over and then gets herself ready. We get him strapped in the car seat just as the nurse walks in with a wheelchair. "The fuck's that for? She can walk fine." Kindly smiling, the nurse says, "It's just protocol. Every patient gets wheeled out, sir." She sits in the wheelchair and I put the car seat in her lap. I go down to bring the surprise to the front exit. I jump out, lighting up a cigarette, and wait for her. When she comes out, her eyes narrow and she's frowning. Fuck, what did I do now?
"Bear, what the fuck is that?" she asks, pointing at the Tahoe I bought her.
"It's a Tahoe, Jacey."
"I can see that, Bear. I mean, what's it doing here, why are we taking it?"

"You needed a different vehicle for the baby."

"Please tell me you did not buy that for me."

"No, I bought it for him," pointing and tilting my chin to Kellen. "Jacey, we needed somethin' to drive him in."

"First of all, my car is fine, Bear. Secondly, I have money. Remember? I can buy my own goddamn car." The longer she talks, the higher her voice rises. She's getting pissed.

"Your car is not fine for him. Where were you gonna put him, in the fuckin' trunk?"

"Not funny asshole. I would have bought something safe for him to ride in."

"We needed it now, Jacey."

"But you get to have your truck and your bike. You expect me to give up my car to drive this?"

"No, Lil Mama. I don't expect you to give up your car. I expect when you're out with our son, you'll drive this."

"Well, what about you, huh? What are you going to do when you have him?" She's clutching the car seat so tight, her knuckles are turning white. By the look on her face, she thinks she's won, but she hasn't though. I one up her.

"I was thinkin' I would drive this too, when I had him. We can share it. Whoever has the baby will drive the Tahoe."

I see her thinking it over, and loosening her grip on the car seat, she gives in. "Okay. That's fair."

"Thank fuck we got that settled. Can we get Kellen home now?"

Smiling, she says, "Yes."

We get him all buckled in and I help her into the back. Jumping in the driver's seat, I head to her apartment. When we get there, I unload Kellen, carrying him up the stairs and into her living room. "Wow, you weren't lying when you said you'd have them clean the place out."

"Nope, not at all. C'mon, let's get the rest of your shit. The guys left some extra boxes." I set Kellen on the floor in her bedroom then grab some boxes, placing them on her bed. She goes to her closet, while I go over to the dresser and start pulling her bras and panties out, and when she comes out, she yells, "Get out of there!" I look over at Kellen' who's fast asleep. Giving her a curious look, I ask, "Why?"

"Just because. I'll do it."

"It doesn't make sense for me not to help, and besides, I already know what type of panties and bras you wear." I say as I reach into the back of the drawer.

"Bear, I swear to God..." She doesn't finish what she's saying, as my hand brushes across something and my eyes go big.

"The fuck is that?" I ask, pulling the object out. It's a green vibrator. I look at her, her cheeks turned bright red. A giant grin forms on my face, and I dangle it in front of her. "Are you embarrassed?"

"Well, yeah kinda."

"Nothin' to be embarrassed about." I walk closer to her. "Look at me. It's a good thing my brothers didn't see this."

"Bear, don't."

"Don't what, Lil Mama? I just wanna know if you think about me when you use it."

"Of course I do," she hesitates, then asks, "Bear, were you with anybody when we were apart?" Hurt crosses her face, tears forming in her eyes.

"You want the truth?"

"Yes," she huffs.

"C'mon," I pull her with me over to the bed. Sitting down, I pull her onto my lap, wrapping my arms around her waist. "At first, I wasn't. I waited for you for a while. Fuck, I thought you had moved on. You wouldn't answer my calls or texts, and I had no fuckin' idea what was goin' on. The night of Ever's graduation party, I couldn't take it anymore. I asked Crazy Girl what was going on with you and she wouldn't tell me, so I went out to the garage to work on my truck and Morgan came out there. She sucked me off, and after that night, I would get head from the whores." She goes to get up but I pull her closer and tighten my hold on her. "Talk to me."

"I don't like the idea of you being with other women."

"Lil Mama, you asked and I won't lie to you. I was angry, please understand where I was comin' from. If it makes you feel better, I jerked off to you for months and when I was with them, I had to think about you."

"No, Bear! That doesn't make me feel better, and actually, that's worse," she says, slapping the shit outta my arms. "Oh, I know where you were coming from alright." The hitting continues.

"You got a dirty fuckin' mind! You know that's not what I was sayin'." I try grabbing her wrists. "Hey, quit hittin' me! It could've all been prevented." She stills, looking into my eyes, while hers fill with tears.

"I'm sorry," she says. "It's all my fault. I shouldn't even be mad."

"It'll be okay, we'll get past it. At least I didn't put my cock in anybody else. They never turned me on, Jacey. I'm not attracted to any of 'em."

She bursts out laughing. "Yeah, well from this point on I better be the only one."

"You got it, and if you're gonna use that again," I point to her green toy I placed on the bed, "you make sure I'm the one usin' it on you. Got me?"

"Yeah, let's get this shit packed."

"Can I ask you somethin'?" I don't know how she'll feel about this question, but I gotta know.

"Yeah," she answers, looking skeptical.

"What was it like, hearin' his heartbeat? Did you know you were gonna have a boy?"

Tears return to her eyes and one rolls down her check as she responds. "His heartbeat was amazing, and I can't believe I let you miss all of that. I'm such a bitch. I didn't find out what he was, but I didn't want to know. I had so many conflicting emotions throughout the whole thing. I was happy about the baby but then again I wasn't, and I think everything would've been different if I would have told you." I give her a nod and stand then, grabbing her up and placing her on her feet. I give her a hard slap on the ass and she fucking moans. Shit, this is gonna be a long six weeks. I just get her back and we gotta wait for her to heal before I can have her again.

After all her clothes, shoes, and shit is packed in boxes and I've put them in the Tahoe, I call Demon, telling him to bring my truck over to get the last of her furniture from her bedroom. I get Kellen loaded up and we head to my place. When she realizes where we are going she asks, "Why are we heading to the pond?"

"Well because the pond is on my property."

"What do you mean?"

"My place, the pond is on my property." I glance over at her.

"I'm so confused."

"My dad bought this place when I was a kid for when we wanted to get away from the city for a while but still be close enough for him to go to work. After he died, when we lost everything, it got sold, and when I got older and had become part of the club, I came out to go see it. There was a family livin' there and I offered them a cash deal to let me buy it. They gave me one look, saw the amount I offered, and they took it, no questions asked. I haven't lived there, but I keep up on the maintenance of it. Even though I had no plans of ever fallin' in love or havin' a family, I had it set aside in case I needed it."

"Bear, I don't know what to say. I was all wrong about you."

"Yeah, but you just thought what everybody else thinks. They don't expect us to have lives outside of the club. They think were just 'bad guys' that live in our own world. Which is true, but if you get to know us, you'd understand there is more to us than just that."

"I'm starting to realize that."

I go past the road to the pond and turn down the next. Going a little way down, surrounded by trees, is the driveway. I turn in and go up until I park in front of the cabin. "Bear, are you fucking serious? This is yours?"

"Yep."

"It's beautiful."

"Yeah, I used to love coming here. Let's get you two inside, show you around." I help her out, then get Kellen and head up to unlock the front door..

"This is seriously amazing Bear. I love it! It has an old, rustic feel, but new at the same time."

"I've done some work on it and put in all new appliances. The fireplace works and I've chopped some wood for it that's stored out back. The living room is over here and the kitchen's that way, with a dining room running directly off it. The bedrooms are this way, there are four total." We start walking toward them, and I continue, "On the left is the master bedroom and bath, which'll be yours. Next to it is another bedroom, which I assume will be Kellen's, and on the right side of the hall are the other two bedrooms, which share a bath." I lead her back to the dining room to show her the backyard, putting Kellen down before we go out. We step through the sliding glass doors onto a giant wooden deck with bench seat railing wrapping around it. Jacey takes time to look at the patio furniture, her eyes lingering at the grill. She looks up after a moment and notices the dock leading into the water.

"You see that clearing over there in the distance?"

She puts her hand over her eyes, shielding the sun. "Yeah. Is that where we always park?"

I nod. "C'mere." I take Jacey's hand and pull her to me, hugging her and rubbing my hand up and down her back. When look down at her, she's looking at me. Tightening my hold on her, I tell her, "I hope you like it out here."

"Bear, it's great. I love it!" I lean down, putting my lips to hers, giving her a slow tender kiss. "Let's go look at Kellen's room." She gives me a smile and nods.

We go back inside, I open the door that I figure would be his, and sure enough, it's the cutest goddamn thing I've ever seen. They used all the furniture Jacey had already bought for him, plus got some new shit to match. "Oh Bear, did you tell them to do this?"

"Shit no, woman, I know fuck all about puttin' a nursery together. It had to have been the girls. Fuck, I had to get help when I went to the store to get him clothes and shit to bring him home." We both laugh. The walls are painted light blue with a banner of wallpaper that has little bears peppered on it. The crib and rocking chair are both made of dark brown wood and a big teddy bear has been propped in the rocker. There's a changing table, same dark wood, that's filled with diapers, wipes, lotions and soaps, plus a whole lot of other shit. I walk over to the closet door and open it. The girls filled it with baby clothes, varying in size.

"Bear, I can't believe they did all this!"

"They're family, this is what family does," I tell her, pride swelling inside me.

"I don't want them to hate me." She lets out a deep breath." I know I apologized, but was that enough? I really am sorry I didn't give you guys a chance."

"I understand why you did some of what you did. The guys are fine, they forgave you, but I think you need to talk to Crazy Girl and Snake."

"Zoey, I can talk to, no problem. My father, however, I think I need some time to wrap my head around that."

"Understandable," I say. "I'm gonna go get your stuff out of the truck. Why don't you get Kellen settled?"

"Okay."

I walk out and start unloading everything. By the time I got everything in the cabin and put away, it's late. "Hey, it's getting late. I think I'm gonna go," I tell her as I put my cut back on.

"Bear? Will you stay with me tonight? Please?"

"Are you sure?" I ask, turning to look at her.

"Yes, I want you to."

"Okay." Taking my cut back off, I walk into the kitchen and look in the fridge. They've stocked it with food so I walk out back and turn on the grill. I pull some steaks out and season them, and when grill is hot, I put them on to cook. Going back inside, I make a salad and boil some corn, still on the cob. I set the table and call Jacey when the food is ready.

"Bear, this is delicious! How did you learn to cook?"

"My mom taught me some. Then I had to start fending for myself, so I learned the rest on my own."

She looks at me with her big, beautiful multicolored eyes and asks,

"So, how is this going to work?"

"What, with you livin' here?"

"Yeah, I mean, you said you won't be. When will you come over?"

"I wanna come over in the mornings before work, and in the evenings, if that's okay. Plus, I'll be here whenever you need me, all you have to do is call."

"You can see him whenever you want, you know."

"I'm not comin' over to just to see him, Lil Mama, I'm comin' for you too. I had one of the hang-arounds that works for a security company put in a top of the line security system. He also installed a monitor system for Kellen, there are cameras everywhere. I'm sure you've seen all the monitors around. You turn those on and you can watch him from any room of the cabin. The code is 2746. Make sure you always have the alarm on, along with Kellen's system, and as long as you do, you two will always be safe." We get done eating and Kellen starts crying, so I feed him and burp him. Jacey changes him and puts him back to sleep. We're both exhausted from the day, so we go into the master bedroom. Jacey puts Kellen in his bassinet, which is on her side right next to the bed. The guys really came through. They thought of everything, I knew they would with the girls help. She changes into her night clothes and I strip down to my boxers, then we get under the covers and I bring her over to me, laying her head on my chest. I give her a kiss on the top of the head, then a thought crosses my mind, and I have to ask her. "You realize this is the first time we'll be going to sleep and waking up together?"

"We've slept together."

"No, I climbed in bed with you after you were already asleep and left before you woke up."

"True. Huh, I guess it is." She lifts her head to look at me. "This is all new for us. Usually we fuck and then I leave. What're we gonna do for the next six week without that?"

"Jacey, I'm gonna make you fall in love with me."

"I already love you."

"There's a difference in loving someone and being in love with them."

"Yeah, I guess."

"You've never experienced it, Lil Mama, but I'm gonna give you the love my parents had, what Crazy Girl and Hanger have. Do you want that?" She says yes. "Then let me love you. Let me show you what it's like to be loved."

"Okay, I'm in this Bear. No more running, remember."

QUIET COUNTRY

"No more runnin'," I echo back. "Goodnight Lil Mama."

"Goodnight Bear." I lean down, giving her a kiss. It doesn't take either of us long to fall asleep.

TWELVE

Jacey

It's been four weeks since I had Kellen, and winter is in full force now. I sit out on the dock, sipping my steaming hot cup of coffee. I love coming out here in the evenings to watch the sun set behind the trees in the distance, it's the most peaceful time of day for me and I can get lost in my thoughts. The cold air hitting your face, breath showing in the air. No more leaves on the trees as the branches are covered in snow just like the ground, the water from the pond is encased in ice. It's beautiful, peaceful, and quiet here in the country. No more sounds of sirens from police cars or ambulances going by. The only time I hear a vehicle is if it's someone coming over to visit.

Since it's too cold to take Kellen anywhere, the guys and girls come over to visit. Bear and I agreed that we don't want Kellen getting sick, so it's best if we keep him at home. We did take him one place, though, before it got too cold, and that was to the diner. Ma and Pop gushed over our baby boy, falling in love with him just like everyone else. It brought tears to my eyes and Ma cried right along with me. She told me she was so happy that everything worked out for us because she was always worried that Bear wouldn't find someone to settle down with. Little does she know that I'm the one holding back, not him.

I've gotten really close with Doc, and he knows more about my past now and understands why I did what I did. The other guys don't question it so I guess my apology was enough for them. Zoey and Ever know I'll tell them in time so they leave it alone too.

I think back to that first night when Bear stayed with me. He said he was going to make me fall in love with him and I didn't understand at the time what he meant, but now I do. Every time I walk in the room and see him with his son, see all the love he has for him, it makes me fall a little bit more. Watching him sleeping with Kellen on his chest or talking to him does something to my heart. Bear comes over every day, but never stays the night, bringing us food and anything else we might need. He's just been really great, taking care of us. For the first time, I think I might actually get the kind of love he was talking about, the kind

Zoey has. I want it, I just don't know if I'm ready quite yet. I'm not running though. I still worry about what he does at the clubhouse, being there with all those whores he was with. I'm scared he's not going to look at me the same, and I'm insecure because my body isn't back to tip top shape. Will he still want me like before? I hear the door slide open. I must've been deep in my thoughts because I didn't even hear him pull up. I turn towards it and there he is, looking as sexy as ever.

"Why are you out here? Where's Kellen?" he asks, as he puts his mouth to mine.

Pulling away from the kiss, I answer, "I was just thinking about things. He's taking a nap."

"C'mon, it's cold out here." He puts his hand out and I take it so he can lead me back inside. He walks me over to the couch. "Sit," he instructs as he points to the cushion. Once I'm down, he sits back away from me, putting my legs in his lap. Taking my shoes and socks off, he starts rubbing my feet.

"That feels like heaven," I sigh, making him chuckle to himself..

"So what were you thinking about?"

"Just some stuff."

"Jacey." He arches an eyebrow and cocks his head slightly.

I don't want him to think I'm keeping shit from him, so I tell him that I was just thinking over the last four weeks and how great it's been.

"Yeah," he agrees, "it has been pretty great, huh?"

"Yeah, I mean, the way you are with Kellen, the way you are with me…I couldn't ask for more."

He gives me that smile that I love so much as he says, "I got somethin' planned for you tonight."

"What? You know we can't go anywhere. It's too cold outside for Kellen."

"I know that, Jacey. We aren't goin' anywhere." I should've known he would plan something for here. He's so protective over his son.

"Okay."

"Stay here, I'll be right back." He gets up and goes outside. When he comes back in, he's carrying bags of stuff and I wonder what he has planned. He goes back out to his truck and comes back a little while later. "C'mon," he says as he takes my hand, leading me to the bathroom. He opens the door and my eyes go wide at what I see. Bear drew me a bubble bath with the jets blasting and rose petals scattered everywhere, plus he placed lit candles all around the room. I turn and look at him, he gives me a smile, and with a shrug of his shoulder he says, "Today's about you, Lil Mama, so just relax and go with it. I have

Kellen, so just stay in here as long as you want."

"Thank you."

"Don't thank me, just enjoy it."

I give him a nod and he turns, walking out and shutting the door behind him. I strip down, then sink into the hot water, leaning back against the tub. I stay in until the water starts to get cold and my fingers and toes look like prunes. Putting on the robe that he left for me, I make my way to the living room. I lean against the wall and watch him sitting on the couch with Kellen on his chest.

One of Bear's big hands covers his little butt, the other supports his head, and he's talking to his son, telling him, *"Do you know how much I love you and your momma? No, you probably don't, but I'll tell you. I love you two more than anything in this world. The love I have for you guys is so deep, I feel it in my bones. I'll always be here to take care of and protect the two of you, no matter what. I just have to make your momma open her heart to me and accept me for who I am. It's my mission to make her smile everyday, make her just as happy as my pop did for my momma. When you get older I'll teach you all the things he taught me, like playing sports and riding a bike. You'll grow up to be a good man, buddy."*

Finishing with a kiss to the top of his head, and there goes my heart again. Clearing my throat, letting him know I came into the room, I go sit down next to him.

"Hey, I'm just gonna put him in his bassinet. I changed and fed him, he just went back to sleep."

I lean over, kissing his little head and give Bear a nod.

Once he has Kellen down, he goes into the kitchen and I follow. He makes us chicken fettuccine with garlic bread and salad. Bear really is an amazing cook. I set the table and light some candles so it can be a romantic dinner., and once we get done eating, I help him clean up the kitchen. After we're done, he tells me to come with him to the bedroom.

"Lay on the bed on your stomach," he instructs, and I'm wondering what the hell's going on, but I do as I'm told anyway. He asks me if I'm still bleeding.

"Um… no, I stopped a week ago."

"Good," he responds, and *Trey Songs' Scratchin' Me Up* starts playing. He comes over, straddling me on the bed as he pulls on the robe, loosening it up. I lift up a little to help him get it from around me, then he grabs the oil sitting on the night table. I close my eyes as drops of oil rain down on my spine. Bear starts to slowly massage it into my skin, using his rough hands to work my muscles over, making sure to reach every part of my backside, not leaving a single inch untouched. I wonder why he's doing all this. Is he trying to make up for something he did with one of those whores?

"Roll over," he commands, standing on the bed. I shake my head no. "I said roll over."

"Bear, I can't."

He sits down on the bed. "Hey," he says as I get the robe back around me and turn over. "Why not?"

"Because."

"Because... why?" He's looking at me, frustration clear in his eyes, waiting for the truth.

"Have you been with any of those whores at the club since I've had Kellen? Or anybody else for that matter?"

"The fuck?" He's looking confused now. "Where the fuck did that come from?"

"I just need to know."

"No, I haven't been with anyone else, Jacey."

"I'm sorry. I guess I'm just a little insecure." Bear asks me why, and I try to explain.

"My body's not the same as it used to be. I just...I don't know if you'll still want me now or look at me the same." The song changes to *Often by The Weeknd*.

"Lay on your back. You're not hiding from me." I slowly lay down.

"Put your arms above your head and don't fuckin' move 'em."

He climbs up the bed, taking his belt off. He puts a belt around my wrists, securing them to the iron bar on the headboard. I couldn't move them even if I wanted to. He then comes back down and undoes my robe, throwing it open, and leans down, kissing my mouth and my neck, making his way further down to my breasts.

Lifting his head to look at me, he says, "You're a goddess, Jacey. You were gorgeous before, but now," he places his hand on my stomach," you've carried my son in here, and there's not even a word to describe how much more beautiful you are to me."

Tears well up in my eyes. "Bear, I have stretch marks."

"No baby, you have warrior marks."

He then kisses each mark on my stomach before sitting up to take off his grey V-neck shirt and his loose fitting jeans, as well as his boxers. When he's completely free of clothing, he comes and lays over me, holding his weight up with his elbows. His hard erection lays perfectly against my clit and he starts rolling his hips against me.

"Bear," I say. "We can't fuck."

"Nobody said nothin' 'bout fuckin' Lil Mama. It's only been four weeks, that doesn't mean we can't do other shit."

He continues moving and grinding against me. He suddenly stops to sit up, grabbing the oil again, holding it over me. Drops land all over my breasts and stomach and he massages every part of my front like he did my back. Bear slides his fingers down between my legs, letting them trace along my lips. I'm so turned on and it's been so long, I feel like I could explode. He lightly runs his fingers over me a few more times until I'm pulling against the restraint of his belt, tipping my head back. His fingers leave the place I want them most as he leans down, kissing and sucking on my neck. His hands are on my breasts, fingers twisting and pulling at my nipples. He knows I like the pain, and I moan loudly, "God, Bear this feels amazing!"

"You haven't felt nothin' yet, Lil Mama." He gets up and goes over, changing the song and putting it on repeat. Earned It by The Weeknd booms through the room as he stands there, gazing at me. He stalks back over to the bed ,leaning down and kissing the top of my feet, moving to my ankles, up my calves. Crawling up the bed, over my body, kissing every part of me and never breaking eye contact.

"Quit looking at me like that."

"Lookin' at you like what?" he asks, grinning.

"Like I'm your prey and you wanna eat me."

The grin forms into a smile as he chuckles. "Oh, Lil Mama, I'm about to do just that. I'm gonna show you how well I eat." He skips over my top half, putting his mouth to mine and kissing me hard, letting our tongues dance. Moving over to my neck, he starts kissing, licking, and biting down. I tilt my head back to give him better access, and his tongue travels slowly down my body until he gets to my nipples, causing a shiver to go through me. He runs his tongue around my nipples, sucking them into his mouth and lightly biting them. My moans grow louder as he continues down over my stomach until he lands on that place I need him most.

"Please, Bear, I need you."

"I got you. I'm gonna give you what you need." He spreads my legs wide open. I'm completely at his mercy, no way to cover myself with my hands still secured by the belt. "You have the sweetest, prettiest cunt I've ever seen. So wet, I'm about to devour you. I've been a starvin' man since the last time I tasted you. On my lips, my tongue, my mouth, I want your taste everywhere. I'm gonna take everything you've got to give." He finally puts his mouth on me, running his tongue front to back. He spreads my lips apart, finding my clit with his tongue. Flicking it over and over until I'm thrashing on the bed, digging my nails into the palms of my hands. Shamelessly and quickly, I'm screaming out his name with the release I needed. He doesn't stop, continuing until I'm squirming away from him. He comes up and lays beside me, watching as I come down from the ecstasy he just gave me. Starting to kiss his way down again,, he goes back to teasing my still sensitive clit.

"Bear, stop. I can't take anymore!"

"Yes you can baby. I'm not done yet. Gotta taste you one more time." He goes back, assaulting my pussy again with his mouth. I feel him place a finger on my asshole, causing me to tense for a second, but then I remember how good it felt the first time, so I relax and let the sensations take over. Pretty soon I'm coming for the second time, screaming out his name once again, and when I open my eyes, he's looking at me while jerking himself off. A few pumps and he shoots his cum all over my stomach and breasts. "Watchin' you cum is the sexiest thing I've ever seen in my life. Swear to fuckin' Christ, Lil Mama."

"Bear, will you untie me?"

"Yeah." He reaches up, finally freeing my hands. I put my hand against his cheek and lean up, kissing him. He goes to the bathroom and comes back with a wet washcloth to clean me up.

"I want to taste you too. Lay down."

"Not tonight, Lil Mama."

"What do you mean not tonight?"

"Tonight was all about you."

"Kellen fucking Rhodes, you better tell me what's going on," I say, glaring at him. "You've been with one of those whores, haven't you? That's why you did all this, trying to make it up to me. You feel guilty, you lying piece of..." He interrupts me with his laughing. I don't know why because this isn't fucking funny.

"Jacey, calm down. I haven't been with anybody. I just did this all for you, but I did wanna ask you somethin'."

I knew there was a hidden agenda, the douchebag. "What?"

"Well, I know it's not in front of everybody, like what Hanger did, but I figure that's not us. I wanna know if you'll be my Ol' Lady?"

"What?" I ask softly.

"Jacey, I don't want anyone else. You're the mother of my child, I love you. Will you be my Ol' Lady?"

"Bear, I can't."

"The fuck? Why not?"

"I'm not ready for that."

"You haven't fuckin' changed at all."

He goes to get up, but I grab his arm stopping him. "Bear, look at me," I say, hoping he'll listen. He turns and I wasn't prepared to see the hurt in his eyes. "Bear, I have changed, and I'm not running. I love you so much, but I just need time to figure shit out, like what I'm going to do instead of being a doctor. We still haven't worked out everything with us."

"What is there to work out? I thought we covered everything."

"I want to know why you aren't still pissed about me keeping the pregnancy a secret."

"Jacey, I am pissed about it, but there's nothin' I can do! I can't go back. He's here now and you're not keepin' him from me. What the fuck do you want from me, you want me to hate you?"

"No, of course I don't want you to hate me."

"We just gotta move on from it. I'm tryin' to get past it and not hold it against you. After I met your mom, I can understand more now of why you did what you did. Anybody raised by that cunt would have done the same thing."

"Yeah, I guess I haven't forgiven myself yet."

"I thought for sure you would say yes. I can't let anything else happen until you decide. I won't keep chasin' you."

"Why do you want me anyway?"

"We're perfect. We're two jagged, broken pieces that fit perfectly together. You just haven't realized it yet."

"You really believe that? I'm scared Bear."

"Hell yes, I believe it or I wouldn't be tryin' so hard to keep you. I would've let you go a long time ago. And Jacey, I know you're scared. I still think it would help if you talked to Snake and find out his side."

"Yeah, maybe. I'm just not ready yet."

"You're never gonna be ready for somethin' like that, you just gotta suck it up and deal. The worst that's gonna happen is your mom told you the truth about everything. If, and I mean if, that happens, I'll be there for you and you don't ever have to see him again. I don't know how it'll turn out, but this is the only time I might have to sit back and watch you get hurt. I don't want that for you, but there's not shit I can do about it, you just gotta get it done."

"Yeah, and you promise you'll be there?"

"I promise, Jacey, but now I gotta go."

"You're not staying?"

"No, you need to get shit figured out and I can't keep hurtin' myself." He gets up, puts his clothes on and leaves. I cry myself to sleep, wondering what the fuck is wrong with me. Why couldn't I just tell him that yes, I wanted to, but I can't yet?

QUIET COUNTRY

It's been a month since that night. Bear has stuck to his word about not letting anything else happen. Not only that, now he barely talks to me. He still comes over to see Kellen and brings us the stuff we need but that's it though, and I fucking miss him so much it hurts. Most nights when I go to bed, I cry myself to sleep. Zoey came over the other day, and when we were talking, I told her I didn't know what was going on between us. I regret not telling him yes when he asked me to be his Ol' Lady. Today is the day. I've called Zoey over to watch Kellen so I can go talk to him at the garage. It's still cold out, but I have to look sexy so I put on a black leather mini skirt and a tank top with the Sinners' logo that I asked Zoey to bring. I have my hair down and curled with my hoop earrings in and my makeup is light, except for some bold eyeliner. Soon enough, I'm ready to go. I've been working hard to get my body back in shape and I'm almost there, so I feel pretty good about myself. I walk out with my hooker heels in hand and Zoey is giving me a curious look.

"What?" I ask her.

"Where are you going dressed like that in the middle of the day?" she asks, smirking. "You're such a bitch, by the way. I'm so jealous, you're looking all good and here I am, fat and frumpy."

Laughing, I tell her, "Thanks. You'll be back to your hot little self too, once you have those babies. And I'm going to go get my man."

I see the smile forming on her face. "Well, it's about fucking time, girl. I'm glad you finally came to your senses about him."

I laugh, grabbing my coat. "I'll be back in a little while. If you need anything, call me."

"We'll be fine. I need all the practice I can get anyway. Take as long as you need. I got Chasyr outside too."

"Thanks Zo."

"No problem, I'm happy for you!"

I grab my keys and head to my car.

I pull up and the second I step out of my car, I hear *Crazy Bitch by Buck Cherry* blasting throughout the garage. Bear's underneath a 1969 black and chrome Camaro that he's been working on. He didn't hear me pull up, so I lean up against the car. He has the hood up and I take a peek underneath. I can tell just by looking at her that she's been completely restored. Trying to be sexy, I cross my arms, pushing up my breasts up, and kick his leg, which makes him slide out from underneath the car. Bear glares at me, and I'm taken back, was hoping for a better reaction, but I suppose I deserve this. "This song remind you of me?" I ask, jokingly. He stands up, pulling out a towel he had sticking out of his back pocket, wiping his hands on it. Even in a dirty white beater and oil covered jeans, he's still sexy as hell.

"What are you doing here?" he demands.

"Well, my car is making a funny noise and I was wondering if you could look at it."

"Where's Kellen?"

"With Zoey. It looks like you need a clean shirt, that one's pretty dirty." I say, taking the few steps to him. I reach out and grab the hem, pulling it up, but he grabs my wrists to stop me.

"I told you, Jacey, that we aren't doin' this anymore. Go pull your car in here and I'll look at it." I go get my car, bring it inside, and take my coat off before getting out. When I step out, he looks pissed.

"What's wrong with you?" I ask him.

"Where are you goin' dressed like that?" he growls out, jerking his chin at me. "Where'd you get the tank? You haven't worn that one before."

"I'm dressed like this to come see you. I got it from Zoey." This is gonna take more work than I thought. He was serious this time, and I have got to fix this shit before I lose him completely.

"I'm not doing this with you." I walk up to him, gripping his beater.

"I want you to ask me again."

"Why, so you can turn me down? I'm not doin' it," he asserts, shaking his head no.

"Kellen fucking Rhodes, you look at me and you fucking ask me again!"

"Fine," he huffs out, looking bored. "Jacey, will you be my Ol' Lady?"

"Bear...umm…" I hesitate, tapping my finger on my lips in an attempt to try to lighten the mood.

"Don't fuck with me."

"Bear, I would love to be your Ol' Lady."

"You're serious?" His eyes grow big, shock written all over his handsome face.

Smiling, I reply. "Yeah, I'm serious. I've regretted telling you no every day. I miss you so much, it hurts, and most nights, I cry myself to sleep. I don't want to be without you anymore." I see a smile taking over his face, and he picks me up in his arms, my legs wrapped around him. He's laughing which makes me laugh too. Then, he gives me the most earth shattering kiss, leaving me breathless.

"I love you, Lil Mama."

"I love you too."

Bear sets me down on my feet, cupping my face in his hands. "Did I make you fall in love with me?"

"You did."

His mouth comes crashing down on mine, our tongues exploring each others' mouths. He breaks from the kiss and walks over to the garage door. "Turn your car on, let me hear it." I do as he says and can hear the clunking noise. I turn it off, get back out, and he closes the door as soon as I'm out of the car.

"I need you to get my baby purring again, Bear."

"Your car's not the only thing I'm gonna have purring." He walks right up to me and bends down to grip my thighs, picking me up and sitting me on the hood of my car.

"You scratch or dent up my baby and I'll have to hurt you."

"Your precious car will be fine. I think you got other shit to worry about right now, like how much my cock has missed his home." He runs his hands up my thighs, pushing my skirt up even higher. Moving one hand in between my legs, I spread open for him to let him feel how wet I already am. "No panties?" he questions, while running his fingers along my slit.

"Didn't want you having too much trouble. Now kiss me." He does just that, making it difficult for my lungs to work once again.

"I missed the fuck outta you, Lil Mama," he says, feather light against my lips.

"God, I missed you too, so fucking much," I whisper back.

"Lay back." Bear drops to his knees, putting his tongue flat against my pussy. He works it up and down, using his fingers to spread me open. Sucking my clit into his mouth, I arch my back, but he places his hand on my stomach to keep me still. When he releases my clit, he starts running his tongue back and forth over me, putting it inside, fucking me with it. When he pulls it out, he flicks my clit which has me bucking my hips against his face. It doesn't take long for me to scream out his name, an explosion letting go within my body. I can hear my screams echoing through the open space of the garage. He quickly pulls me up and has me on the edge of the hood. His jeans are down now, he's lining himself up to my opening and with one hard thrust, he's balls deep inside me. "Shit, you feel fuckin' good, so goddamn tight," he grunts out, pounding my pussy.

"Harder, Bear." He picks up speed as he squeezes me tighter in his embrace.

"It's been so fuckin' long, I'm not gonna last!"

"Me either, you feel so good!" I say, between cries of pleasure. "I'm gonna cum again!"

"I can feel you your squeezing me, so fuckin' good. Let go baby. I'm right there with you." Taking me over the edge, I cry out Bear!, digging my nails into his flesh. He calls out my name in the crook of my neck as he bites down, then when we're done, he lifts his head to look at me "Did you really mean it?"

"Which part?"

"All of it."

"Every word."

"I fuckin' love you. Never thought I'd have an Ol' Lady."

"I fuckin' love you too. Don't back out on me now."

"Not a goddamn chance." We smile at each other. "I gotta get somethin' to clean you up." He pulls out of me and brings back a warm wash cloth, cleaning me up. I realize he didn't use a condom. Smacking his arm I ask, "You trying to get me pregnant again?"

"Maybe." He laughs. "Really, I just got caught up in the moment and forgot."

"Well, it's a good thing I started back on the pills."

"Fuck me. No more condoms? That felt pretty amazing ridin' bareback."

"No more condoms. You going to stay with me tonight?" Bear kisses me again before he walking off. He tells me he will, and I hang around until he gets my car running normal again, then I go back home.

When I get inside, I see Zoey on the couch, bouncing in her seat. "How was Kellen, and what the hell are you doing?" I ask her, laughing..

"Oh, he was so good. I'm waiting for you to tell me what happened."

"Looks like I'm an Ol' Lady now." I smile.

"Ahhhhhh!" she screams out, loud enough that I have to cover my ears.

"Zoey, it's a good thing Kellen's awake or you would've just woken him up."

"I'm just so happy! This is so exciting!" she declares while clapping her hands. "So what happened? I want details."

"I made him ask me again and he didn't want to, but he did. I said yes and then we had amazing sex on the hood of my car. You're not getting any more detail than that."

"Oh my God, that's so hot! I'm gonna have to do that with Hanger. We fucked on his bike and the back of his truck, oh, we need a car!" She zones out, like she's trying to figure out how to make it happen, and I can't help but to laugh. This is why I love her so much.

THIRTEEN

Bear

I went to Hanger not long after Jacey had Kellen. I needed to know if he kept the pregnancy from me, and it turns out, he did know that she was carrying a child, he just didn't know who's. Hanger knew that we had fucked, but thought since she quit coming around, there wasn't anything there. He assured me that if he would've known, he wouldn't have kept something like that from me. Crazy Girl apologized and that's good enough for me. She was in a hard spot, and I can't hold it against her for being true to her friend.

I got my woman, finally after all this time, and I'm not letting go. Chatty used to be the one to do the cuts and patches, but since she's gone, I had to go to Ever. Now, I have Jacey's cut ready to go. It has "Property of Bear" on the back, which is something I never thought I would see, and on the front it reads "Lil Mama". She's the best fucking mother to my child I could ask for. I'll be getting her pregnant again, and when I do, I'll be there every step of the way this time. Jacey's been alone her entire life, so I understand it was natural instinct to hide within herself, but now she has me, Zoey, and my brothers. Hopefully soon, she'll have her father back too. She doesn't know that I called him.

I open the front door, walking in to seeing her feeding Kellen. She bottle feeds, which is fine with me because that allows me to feed him too. I'll never forget the first time she tried to breastfeed him. She put him up to her tit and he latched on just fine, but then she yelled out, "Son of a bitch! It hurts!" From that day forward, it was the bottle for our sweet Kellen. I walk over and lean down to give her a kiss. "I got somethin' for you."

"What is it?" she asks, looking at me. Jacey stands up, putting Kellen in his bouncy seat. I pull the cut from behind my back and show it to her. She goes to grab it, but I pull it back. "Bear, give it to me!"

"Not yet. Before I give it to you, I want you to know that there's no turnin' back once you put it on."

"I know that Bear, shit, there was no turning back when I said yes. I love you. I'm not going anywhere." I give her a smile. Leaning in, kissing her one more time, I hand it over. She puts it on and looks sexy as fuck. "How's it look?"

"Looks fuckin' sexy, Lil Mama. I'd actually like to see you in nothin' but this and some fuck-me-heels." She's got the biggest smile plastered on her pretty face as I grab her, pulling her to me. "Let's do it then."

"We can't, not yet. I have somethin' to tell you and you're not gonna like it."

"What? What did you fucking do?"

"I called Snake and he's comin' over here."

"YOU DID WHAT?" she screams at me.

"I called Snake, he's comin' over." I grab her hands and hold them in mine. "You gotta get it done. You're officially a part of the club now, Jacey. It's time."

She's shaking her head. "I'm not ready! I can't believe you did this!" I see her eyes tearing up.

"You would never have done it. You're strong, you can do this. Get your answers, Lil Mama. I'll be right here with you." I hear a knock at the door. "I'll get it." I walk to the door and open it, stepping outside.

"Snake," I greet him.

"Bear." He nods.

"Remember what I told you. I can't have her hurt any more than she already has been. If you think that's going to happen, I want you to leave now."

"She's my daughter. I've been waitin' for this day for twenty years, man. I'm not gonna hurt her. It's time we had this talk."

"Alright, but if she gets gets too upset, this meeting is over. Got me?"

"I got you. I know you love her and are looking out for her, but this'll be the only time you talk to me like this. You got me?"

"Yeah. Lets go in, and keep in mind, she's really fuckin' nervous." I open the door and we step inside. Entering the living room, I see that she's sitting on the couch, knees bouncing with her hands in her lap, looking nervous as fuck. "Lil Mama," I say, walking up to her. I bend in front of her, getting eye level. "You okay?"

"No I'm not okay, you fucking dick."

I suppress a laugh. "It's gonna be fine. I'll give you some time to talk and if you need me, I'll be..."

She interrupts me. "Kellen fucking Rhodes, you are not going anywhere! You did this, you are staying with me, goddammit." I do laugh then, and she gives me a go-to-hell look.

"C'mon Snake, have a seat." He sits in the chair across from the couch, and I take a seat next to Jacey, holding her hand the whole time. It's quiet for some time, nobody saying anything, and they just stare at each other. I keep looking back and forth between them. "Alright, someone needs to say something, get this shit started." They both look at me, then gazes return to each other again. Jacey speaks first. "I found you awhile back on the internet. I saw pictures of you with other kids, you looked happy."

"My brother's kids. You grew up."

"Well yeah, I haven't seen you in twenty years. Do you have any other kids?"

"No, never wanted anymore."

"Did you even want me?"

"You forgot, didn't you Jacey?"

"Forgot what?"

"What I told you the day your momma took you from me. I told you to never forget that I would always love you and that you were my princess. Of course I wanted you, I always did. You're my little girl."

"So why did you let her take me? Why didn't you ever try to come get me?"

"Your momma threatened to turn the club in to the police if I came after you. I couldn't do that to them, and if I would've come and got you, what kind of life would you have had at the club? I thought you would have a better life with her."

"So you gave me up for the club?"

"No, Jacey. Never. I let you go because I thought you would've had a better life away from the club. I've missed you every day since you were six, when she took you from me."

"Did you really tuck me in at night and tell me stories?" she asks, fidgeting with her hands.

"Every night. Do you remember the story I used to tell you about the king and his princess?"

"Yeah, you would tell me the only boy the princess could marry would be the one able to stand up to the king, so he would know she'd be taken care of and safe." She has tears running down her cheeks and taking her face in my hands, I turn her to look at me. Wiping away the tears I ask if she's okay, and she gives me a nod. "It wasn't all a dream. It was real," Jacey speaks softly, in disbelief.

Snake replies, "Yeah, baby girl. I love you so much, I always have. I thought about you every day that you were gone."

"Mom would never talk to me about you." Hesitating, she asks the question she's been contemplating for a long time. "Will you tell me what happened with you guys?"

"Marie came into the club as a whore. I'd been with her a few times until I met someone else and fell in love, hard and fast. One night, we got into a bad fight. I thought she was done with me, so I got fucked up 'til I didn't know what the fuck I was doin'. Marie came to me and I ended up fuckin' her that night. Well, the woman I loved came back, and we were together for a little while 'til your momma came and told me she was pregnant. I wanted to do the right thing, so I went to my Vixen, told her what happened, and she left me. Later on, I found out Marie messed with the condom so it wouldn't work. She was tryin' to get me to settle down with her."

"Did you do the things she says you did? Did you abuse her and cheat?"

"Yeah, I never claimed to be a nice guy. I did put hands on your momma one time and that's when I found out what she did. I'm not proud of it. I was young, I could of handled it better, but at the time I felt like she had ruined my life. Once you came along, you were my life, other than the club. I took one look at you and fell in love, thought I could be happy for you. Marie made it hard though, always fightin' with me. I cheated because I never loved her. There was only one woman I would've settled for."

Jacey sympathizes. "It doesn't surprise me she did that. She's always looking out for herself, she doesn't care about anybody else."

"What are you talkin' about?" Snake asks angrily. "Did you have a good life?"

I can tell she doesn't wanna tell him the next part, so I squeeze her hand, encouraging her. "She married a man I hate. I never had friends, and my whole life, she's pushed me to become a doctor. She would slap me around and yell all the time, and she made me forget you, told me all these bad things about you. She said you never wanted me."

Anger flashes in his eyes, then his face drops in regret. "Fuck, I'm sorry. If I knew it would've been like that, I would have taken you back. I didn't know where she took you, but I would've found out. Why don't you like the guy she married?"

She looks at me and I give her a nod. "As I got older, he started looking at me differently, not in a way that a father should look at his daughter. When I was sixteen, on the night of my graduation, he tried to rape me, but I fought back and got away. The next day, I came back to Kansas." I look over to Snake. All the color has drained from his face, and his knuckles are white from gripping the chair so tight.

"Get on the phone, Bear. Call Hanger, tell him to get here now and to bring his Ol' Lady." He orders, taking control just like he would at his club. He's not fucking around.

"Zoey's getting close to havin' the baby," I tell him, and with a cold stare, he replies that he doesn't give a fuck, ordering me again to get Hanger on the phone. I do as he asks, and when I hang up, I turn to him, saying, "He said they'll be here in twenty." Snake gives me a nod.

"Can I hold my grandbaby?" he turns to his daughter and asks.

She goes and retrieves Kellen, handing him over to his granddad.

"I guess you're more like me after all, Jacey. You've got a good man there, I approve," he tells her, smiling.

"Yeah, it took us awhile to get here, but we made it."

He takes her hand, pulling her in, hugging her with one arm while holding Kellen in the other. I get my phone out and take a picture. When Hanger and Crazy Girl get here, Snake puts Kellen down and we all go to the dining room, us guys taking seats around the table, while the girls sit on our laps.

Hanger asks, "What the fuck's goin' on? Snake, why're you here?"

Crazy Girl has a confused look on her face, but she keeps quiet, looking around the table. I ask Jacey if she wants to clue them in.

She agrees, "Yeah okay. So, Snake is my father."

"What!?" they both exclaim at the same time, looking at each other, then back to us.

"He's my father. My mom took me away from him when I was six years old. She raised me to believe that bikers were trash, that's why it was so hard for me to give you guys in the club a chance and why I did everything I did to Bear."

Crazy Girl smiles and Hanger says, "That makes sense, sounds like your mom's a cunt. We're good now, all the guys are really. My brother here loves you, so treat him well and we'll treat you the same. You're his Ol' Lady now, which makes you family."

"I never had family before, I was always on my own," she says as she hanging her head.

"Not anymore, you're not. You never really were, since my Ol' Lady thinks of you as family. You always had her back, you were just too lost inside yourself. Hope all that's changed now though."

She looks up at him and I can see the tears trying to break free. "Yeah, it has. Thanks Hanger."

Snakes pipes up. "Alright you girls, go in the other room. We've got business to discuss."

When they get up and go to the living room, Hanger asks about what's going on. Snake fills him in. "So I let her go because I thought

QUIET COUNTRY

her momma would give her a better life, but I guess I was wrong. She tells me that son of a bitch Marie married tried to rape her, so we're goin' to California and gonna handle this fucker."

I respond. "Yeah, I'm good with that, would have already if it wasn't for her tellin' me not to."

"I can't leave Crazy Girl," Hanger interjects.

"You're not gonna leave her because she's comin' to keep Jacey company." Snake informs him.

"Okay, let me go get our shit. What about her mom? What's she gonna think about this?"

"Her momma was a whore for my club. She knows the rules."

"Alright I'll be back." Hanger gets up and heads to the living room. He gets Crazy Girl and says goodbye to Jacey, then they leave. Jacey comes up to me and questions me about what's going on.

"We're goin' to California."

"What? Why?"

"Your dad wants to go handle that fucker."

"Bear, we can't do that!"

"*We* aren't doin' shit. You girls will be at the hotel."

"Bear!"

"Trust me, Lil Mama. Remember, I told you we take care of our own."

"Yeah, okay." I lean down, giving her a kiss. I ditched the cigarettes after we brought Kellen home, but right now, I could really use a smoke.

When everyone's here and ready to go, we hit the road. Hanger and I both have to take cages, but we let Snake lead the way on his bike. Letting Lil Mama control the music, she flips restlessly through the stations, finally stopping on *A Sky Full of Stars by Cold Play*. While we're listening, she decides to start up a conversation.

"So you never did tell me how you learned to dance."

I look over to her then back to the road. "When I was eighteen, I started prospecting for the club. I wanted to get patched in, so when there was an undercover job to do at a male strip club, I took it." She bursts out laughing.

"You had to be a male stripper?"

"Hey now, I like the term 'male entertainer'," I tell her in amusement. "Anyway, I had no idea what I was doin', and the guys that worked there knew I was young and inexperienced, so they taught me everything I needed to know. I guess it just stuck with me."

"What did you go by? Bear the Sexy Grinder?" She busts up laughing again.

"No smartass. If someone said that, you wouldn't think sexy, you'd think of some fat, hairy bastard," I laugh out. "Bear isn't a sexy name, let's face it, so I was known as X. I became the most wanted man there. I had all the fast cash and even faster women."

"X is a pretty hot name. Hmm. So with that, the man-whore was born."

"Yeah, I guess you could say that. I was livin' it up, that's for sure."

"What did you do with all the money?"

"I used a lot of it to buy back the cabin, and some went to my truck. The rest I put up, along with money I make from the club, the garage, and other things."

"So what happened with the strip club?"

"I can't give you all the details, because it's club business and all. What I can tell you is that I ended up getting my patch because of my time there, and I became the Enforcer of the Satan's Sinners. When it was all done, we took down the owners, seeing as how they were tryin' to pull one over on us and the Cobras, and ended up making an ally with their club."

"You've known my dad that long?"

"Yeah, it's been awhile, I guess around twelve years or so. He's always been a good guy, that's why I called him. After meeting your mom, I didn't think she was tellin' you the truth."

"Thank you for that. I was pissed at first, but now I'm so glad you did it."

I kiss her palm. "I know. You get your dad back now."

We stop in Arizona at a hotel to get some rest. The next morning, we're all back up and ready to hit the road. We finally hit California, and when we're in town, we find a nice hotel, and get the girls checked in and settled.

"Jacey, I need the address," I tell her.

"Bear, I don't want to do this." She's back to being nervous, playing with her fingers, can't sit her ass still.

"Lil Mama, you're not doin' anything. You're stayin' here with

Crazy Girl."

"Fine, but I don't want you guys to do this."

"I think it's a little late for that. If it was my daughter, I would do the same. This would have been done already, but I told you I wouldn't do it. Just let your dad handle it, then we'll be on our way back home." She writes down the address, shoving it at me. "Hey, what're you worried about anyway?"

"I just got you and my dad back and Zoey's about to have a baby. I just don't want any of you guys getting in trouble."

Softening my tone, I try to reassure her. "Lil Mama, we've been doin' this for a long time, nothin's gonna happen to us. Got me?"

"I got you. I trust you."

"Good, because I'll always do what it takes to keep you safe."

"I love you Bear."

"I love you too, Lil Mama. I'll be back in a little bit." I pick Kellen up and walk both of them over to Crazy Girl's room. Hanger brought Demon with them so somebody would be there watching over 'em while we're gone.

Snake, Hanger, and myself climb in Hanger's cage and head out. We pull up to a fucking mansion. "Fuck me, it looks like she had a good life," Snake says, staring up at this huge fucking house.

Hanger replies, "It might look like that from the outside Snake, but behind closed doors is a different story most of the time. Don't go second guessing yourself as to why we're here."

I chime in. "She had far from a good life. Let's do this shit."

We all climb out and head up to the door. Snake rings the bell and some rich jackass answers. "You married to Marie?" Snake asks, anger rolling off of him.

"Yes, how can I help you?" We push our way through when we hear a Marie ask who it is.

"Well, if it's not the cunt herself," I say as she comes around the corner.

"Bear, what are you..."She stops herself when she sees Snake, eyes wide, mouth open.

"I told you I'd make you pay one day. Didn't think it'd be twenty years, granted," Snake states.

"What's going on here?" the douchebag asks.

"You two go sit the fuck down."

"If you want money..." he starts to say, fear written all over his face, but we all laugh.

"Money? We have plenty of money. so shut the fuck up and go sit down," Snake orders. They head into the front room and we follow. Once they're sitting, we stand in a line in front of them.

"What's going on Snake, why are you here?" Marie asks. She's trying to look calm, but you can see plenty of fear in her eyes.

"We're here because you took my baby girl away from me. I thought you'd give her a better life, but it turns out I was wrong."

"I did give her a better life, she became a doctor."

"Not by choice," I say.

Snake points to her husband. "Did you know he tried to rape Jacey? I'm here because I'm her fuckin' father and you let someone touch her, you fuckin' whore. You were a shit mother from the start, I shoulda known you wouldn't be good to her. Christ, Marie, you're her goddamn mother, you shoulda fuckin' acted like it!"

"What?" She shakes her head. "No, he wouldn't have done that." She looks over to him. "Richard, tell them you didn't do it. Tell them she's just being the spoiled little bitch she has always been."

He hangs his head in shame. "I'm sorry Marie. I was mad that night, I got drunk and I wasn't thinking clearly. It was a mistake."

I walk up, bending down in front of her, bringing us face to face. "That'll be the last time you disrespect my woman. After this, you don't contact her at all. If I find out you did, I'll be back for you." I stand back up, stepping away from her.

"You can't do that! I'm her mother."

"You!" I point at her. "You should've fuckin' acted like it then, but instead you ruined her goddamn life."

"You know the rules of the club," Snake reminds her and she nods, but has nothing to say. I can smell the fear coming off of 'em.

"Where's the basement?" Snake asks, grabbing Richard up from the couch. "Hanger you stay here and watch her."

She gives us the directions before we walk out of the room, and we haul his ass to the basement, turning the light on before we start our descent. Snake pushes him to go down first, while I follow.

Once Richard touches the bottom step, Snake shoves him down and he tries to scramble away, but he's not going anywhere. I grab him by his shirt, pushing him into the wall, and holding his arms up, I let Snake get a few good hits into his body and face.

Snake tells him, "You tried to rape my daughter, you filthy piece of shit! I should kill you, motherfucker."

Richard coughs from the blows connecting to his body. Still holding him up, I get my hits in, trying really hard to keep control of my anger. I really wanna kill this fucker. There's blood everywhere by the time we get done. We did a number on him: his eyes are swelling shut, lips split, blood covering his face, and he's barely conscious. I get in his face, telling him that neither he nor Marie is to contact my Lil Mama, and if they do, I'll come back and finish what we started down here. Richard nods in agreement. He better hope he does, otherwise there'll be a bigger mess to clean up next time.

We carry him back up the stairs, throwing him down on the couch next to his wife. Marie looks over to him, covering her mouth with her hand, tears forming in her eyes. Do I feel sorry for her? Absolutely not.

"You keep your fuckin' mouths shut, unless you want us to come back. You never saw us, we were never here. And next time, we won't be so nice."

Snake chimes in.

"Wish I could say it was nice seein' you again, but you're just as much of a cunt now as you were back then. Have a fuckin' lovely day. Oh, and where's a bathroom? I gotta get this cocksucker's blood off me."

She gives us directions to a bathroom and we both clean up the best we can before heading back to the hotel.

I go get Lil Mama and my son from Hanger's room, walking them back over to ours. As soon as the door's shut and locked, she turns on me.

"What happened?"

"We beat him pretty good and I told both of them not to contact you again."

"Are you guys gonna get in trouble for this?"

"No, they won't say anythin'. If they did, we'd be back and they definitely don't want that," I tell her.

"Lay down and take a nap, I'm gonna shower, then go over and talk to Hanger."

She gives me a nod as I walk into the bathroom. When I get done, they're both asleep so I give them both a kiss on the head, then shut the door behind me. I walk over to the next room over and knock. Hanger opens up, letting me inside.

"Hey brother, what's going on?" he asks, curious as to why I'm back over here.

"We need to take a different route home. I gotta make a stop."

"Sure thing, we'll just follow you."
The next morning, we all get up and head out.

FOURTEEN

Jacey

On our way back home, I turn up the music, playing *Elle Goulding's Love Me Like You Do*.
"This song reminds me of you." I say, looking over at him.
"Does it?"
Bear's gripping that steering wheel awfully hard. I can see sweat building on his forehead. Is he nervous? What the fuck would he have to be nervous about?
"Bear, what's wrong with you?"
"Nothing, why?"
"You look like you're really nervous, and you're about to detach the steering wheel from the car."
We hit Nevada and soon, we're on the Las Vegas strip. This isn't the way we came.
"Why are we in Vegas? We didn't come this way."
"Jacey, are you all in with me?"
"What do you mean 'all in'?"
"Just what it sounds like. I finally got you, and I'm not letting you go, ever. I've been waitin' my whole life for you. I just never knew it. After my parents, I never wanted love, a relationship, or the responsibility of one, until you. I have everything I could ever want with you, Jacey. Marry me."
"You're fucking crazy."
"Maybe. You love me?"
"Yes, you know I do."
"Then let's do this. What do we need to wait for?" he asks, looking out of the corner of his eye at me.
"You have your best friend and your dad here, and we've got our boy. It's perfect, unless you want a big wedding."
"Okay."
"Okay?"
"Yeah, let's do it. You're right, I have everybody here I would want, so let's do it."

He stops at a jewelry store and when we get out, Zoey has her window down.

"Jacey, what's going on? Why are we here?"

"I'm getting married."

"What? Don't fuck with me! What's really going on?"

I laugh at her.

"I'm serious, we're getting married!"

I see her eyes widen, mouth agape. "Oh my God! We have to get you a dress!"

She's practically jumping in her seat. Hanger smiles and tells her to calm down.

"They're getting married! I'm so excited!" she squeals, clapping her hands. We all laugh.

"Zoey, listen to Hanger. Calm down! You could throw yourself into labor," I tell her, and we definitely don't need that.

"So true," she says, nodding. "Okay, go get the rings then we'll get dresses."

We go into the store and I pick out a white gold band with white and black onyx diamonds for Bear, and he picks out the most beautiful two rings for me. The first would've been my engagement ring if he hadn't decided to do this shit on a whim. It's a square cut onyx diamond with white ones surrounding it and trailing down the sides. He also picked out a wedding band that alternates between onyx and white diamonds, and both are set in white gold bands. Once the argument is over about who will pay, of course he wins, we walk out of the store with our rings. We find a dress shop next, and I pick out a simple white dress, while Zoey searches for one in a maternity size.

"You know you guys are strange, right?" she asks.

"Why do you say that?" I ask, laughing.

"I guess it's your whole relationship. I mean, you guys haven't been together that long."

"Neither have you and Hanger, but you're happy. Technically, it's been about a year of seeing each other, and don't forget that we started fucking around the same time you guys did. If I wouldn't have been so scared and put him through all that bullshit, we could've been together this whole time."

"You're right, it has! You were just so secretive about it. I guess I'm still getting used to you guys actually being a couple. Besides, I'm your best friend and it's my job to make sure you're happy."

"I'm unbelievably happy, Zoey. I never thought I could have this, and now I do and I'm going to hold on to it the best I can."

"You won't have to try hard, that man has been in love with you for a long time."

"I know. I just wish I hadn't wasted so much time. I wish I wouldn't have kept my pregnancy from him either."

"Oh girl, you have all the time in the world now. You just gotta let that go. He understands now why you did it, just let it be. There's no going back, move ahead. He didn't miss Kellen's birth and he's been a great father. You're getting married, leave all the past shit there. Only forward from here girl."

"You're right. How did you get so smart?" Zoey is one of the smartest people I know. She stays quiet and watches people, but when she feels it's the right time, she gives you her opinion, and she always seems wise beyond her years. "It doesn't take smarts, Jacey. You just need somebody on the outside to make you understand."

"Yeah, I guess. Okay, we got our dresses, what's next?"

"Well, are you making him wear a suit?"

"Umm, no." We both laugh, paying for the dresses. When we walk out, the guys are standing against the vehicles. Bear asks what's next and I tell him that he needs to go pick out a suit, keeping a straight face.

"The fuck? I'm not wearing a suit, Jacey," he tells me, so serious. I decide to see how far I can push him. "Yes, Bear, you are."

"Lil Mama." He holds fast.

I throw it back on him, and pointing, I inform him that because this marriage was his idea, he most definitely will be needing a suit to wear down the aisle. I don't know if I can push this any further though, it's hard as hell not to laugh because he looks pissed. "Fine. Let's go." Oh God, I'm about to lose it! I'm already dying laughing on the inside. "Bear?" I coo his name.

"Yeah?" He looks at me.

"I'm fucking with you! You can wear what you have on." Everyone bursts out laughing. He starts to walk toward me and I back up. Every step I take back, he moves one forward until I'm hit the dress shop's brick wall. He pins me against it, looking into my eyes. "That wasn't very nice, Lil Mama."

"Well, you did tell me once that I wasn't that nice." I smile at him and he leans down, smashing his mouth against mine.

"That's enough of that shit! She's still my daughter, Bear," Dad calls out. I can hear Zoey and Hanger laughing, but I could care less right now. He breaks from the kiss, leaving me breathless. I need a second to recover before opening my eyes.

"You're gonna pay for that little joke later," he informs me. I know exactly what kind of paying I'll be doing and it has me aching between the legs.

Once everyone is ready to go, we head to The Luxor to check in. Wouldn't you know, it's Vegas, so there's a little chapel right in the hotel. Zoey and I get ready together while the guys go off to do the same. After my shower, I get my dress on and decide to leave my hair down, but curl it. Zoey puts her black dress on, pulling her hair up in a curly ponytail. We're almost done getting ready, when I get a call on my phone. "Hello?"

"Hi, is this Jacey Thomas?"

"Yes who is this?"

"My name is Daphne Roberts. I've been looking at your building for sale."

"Oh, okay, hi. Would you like to meet up in a couple of days? I'm out of town right now."

"Sounds great, just give me a call when you're ready."

"Who was that?" Zoey asks.

"Someone named Daphne. She wants to meet up and look at the building."

"That's great! It's like everything's falling into place."

"I know! It's kind of scary, like something bad is just waiting to happen." An uneasy feeling takes over. That's the way it's been for the last year though, right when everything's good, something always comes along to knock things down a notch.

"Don't say that, Jacey. Everything will be fine."

We walk down to the lobby of the hotel where the guys are waiting. Bear has Kellen with him and it brings a smile to my face. I swear, I fall in love with him a little bit more every time I see him with our son. Handing Kellen over to my Dad, he walks up to me, taking me into his arms. "You look so fuckin' beautiful. I love you, Lil Mama."

"I love you too. Are you ready to do this?"

"I've never been more ready for somethin' in my entire life."

I place my hand on his cheek, making sure he looks me in the eyes as I tell him, "Me either, Bear. I've never wanted something so much as I want to be your wife." Smiling at each other, I see his eyes glass over, so trying to lighten the mood, he slaps my ass and we head to the chapel. Wouldn't you know, it's Elvis themed. We order the package we want and they take the guys inside, leaving my dad with us girls and Kellen. "Jacey, are you sure you want me walkin' you down the aisle?" I look at my father holding my son. "I wouldn't want it any other way. I love you, I always have. My dreams never let me forget how great a father you were."

"I made a lot of bad choices though."

"You were only doing what you thought was right. I did the same thing. I heard somewhere that you just have to let it be. You can't go back, so move ahead." I give Zoey a smile, our eyes shining with tears. I take her hand. "You've always been the best friend I could ever ask for. I love you."

"I love you too, Jacey. You're more than just a best friend, you're like a sister to me."

I hear the piano playing, and it's time for us to walk out so I take Kellen from my dad. He puts one of his arms through mine and Zoey walks ahead of us, Hanger never taking his eyes off her, and I can see all the love he has for my best friend. I see Bear as I make my way down the aisle, his face mimics Hanger's.

I thought he'd destroy me if I gave myself to him, but I was wrong. I was so utterly wrong. He loves me completely, protects me to the fullest, makes me smile every single day, and he will do whatever he has to do to keep me safe. I realize all of this as I walk toward him. I couldn't ask for a better man for me or for our child.

My mother always thought it was about money, but it's not. Money has nothing to do with someone consuming your every thought or every feeling. Love is what matters, when you would rather sacrifice yourself than to be without that person. When you can't remember what your life was like before that person came into it and you never want them to leave.

"Who gives this woman to this man?" the Elvis impersonator asks.

"I do," my dad replies. He leans in, giving me a kiss on my cheek. "I love you, Princess."

"I love you too, Dad." Before he passes me off to Bear, he tries to stare him down, but Bear doesn't falter.

"You take care of my Princess. If you don't, I will kill you."

He reassures my father that I'll be very well cared for, and I pass Kellen to Dad before he walks away. Bear and I say our I dos, and the guys cheer while Zoey and I cry. Bear turns to Elvis.

We need some time." Elvis nods.

"Take all the time you need. We don't have anybody else coming in for a while." He walks out, leaving us all alone.

"Since we aren't doin' this the traditional way, we don't get a reception, but I wanna play you a song. Dance with me."

He puts on *Canaan Smith's Love You Like That*. Putting his phone back in his pocket, upside down so we can still hear it, he takes my hand in his and spins me around, then pulls me into him.

I can feel his hot breath on my ear as he whispers, "You made me the happiest man alive today, Lil Mama."

I bury my face in the crook of his neck, content.

"I love this song."

"Me too. I think of you every time I hear it." He lifts my head up. "You're mine now, in every way. We've come a long way in the last year."

"Don't forget, you're mine now too. And we have, haven't we?"

"I was always yours, Lil Mama, from the time you stepped outta that hallway and I laid eyes on you for the very first time."

Once we get done dancing, we make our way out of the chapel. Zoey says, "Since it's your wedding night, we're taking Kellen"

"No, you can't do that," I tell her, freaking out because I don't want to be without my baby.

"Yes, I can. He'll be fine. We'll be right next door."

"Are you sure?" Now that I'm thinking about it, it would be nice to have some time with Bear, alone.

"Yes, I'm sure, and you can call or come over anytime you want."

"Hanger, is it okay with you?"

"Yeah, it's fine. Congratulations, by the way," he says as he slaps Bear on the back and gives me a hug.

"Thank you."

We all go out to dinner and head back to our rooms. I get everything ready for Kellen and we take him next door. Once we return, I go into the bathroom to get ready for bed, deciding to give him a little strip show. I step out of the bathroom in a robe with just my panties and bra on underneath. He's sitting on the edge of the bed, elbows on his knees, watching TV.

Once he sees me, he sits straight up, turning it off. I turn the music up, letting *Motivation by Kelly Rowland* play on repeat. Walking over to him, hips swaying side to side, he watches me the whole time. I can see his nostrils flaring, eyes darkening with lust.

Stepping right in front of him, I move my hips with the beat, bringing my hands to his hair, running my fingers through it and pulling it back so his neck is free for me to do as I please. I bend over, running my tongue from his shoulder to his neck, landing at his ear. Giving it a little bite, he lets out a growl. Moving back down to his neck, I suck the skin into my mouth, biting down so his growl comes out louder.

I can feel his hands moving over the backs of my thighs and up over my ass. I stand back up, stepping away from him, and still swaying my hips, I turn away from him. I look over my shoulder toward him and untie the robe, slowly letting it fall to the floor. I undo my bra and it takes its place next to the discarded robe. I cover my bare breasts, and turn to face him.

"Let me see you, Lil Mama."

His voice is an octave lower than normal, eyes so dark they look black. I let my hand fall, showing myself to him.

"Good girl. Panties off now." Moving to the beat, I shimmy out of them, now completely bare, except for my heels.

"Leave the heels on. C'mere." Walking over to him, he grabs me and pulls me down onto his lap.

Kissing me hard, he pushes me into his massive erection. Getting even more turned on, I wiggle around, trying to ease the throbbing between my legs.i get up, dropping to my knees and undoing his jeans. He lifts his hips, helping me to get him free. Once I have his hard cock in my hand, I go to put my mouth on him, but he stops me by pushing on my shoulders. Sitting back on my heels, I ask him what's wrong.

"You don't need to do that."

"Why? I want to."

"I just...I don't want you to feel like you're one of those whores."

I cannot believe he just said that shit. Slapping his arm, I tell him, "Shut the fuck up! Bear, you got shit timing, bringing that up."

Standing up, I start to walk off but he grabs my arm, stopping me.

"I know I just I want you to know your more than that."

"Fuck, I know that. We just got married." I ask, "I did it once before, am I not any good? Is that why you don't want me doing it?"

"Baby, no, you got the best mouth I've ever had. I just wanted you to know you're more than that."

"I know I am, but you please me in all ways, sexually. I want to do the same for my husband. Now lay your ass down and enjoy what I'm about to do. You bring that shit up again, you won't have a cock to be doing anything with anymore. Got me?"

"Yes ma'am, I'll let you control right now, but when you're done, I'm in control of the ride."

He lays back and I straddle his waist, starting at his mouth, kissing and biting his bottom lip. I move my way down, alternating between kisses, bites, and licks until I'm at his belly button. I place my hands at his neck, raking my nails down his chest and stomach, causing his back to arch, and he lets out a low moan. I grip his cock with one hand, licking around the head, working my way down his shaft. Hollowing my cheeks, I suck him into my mouth, going down as far as I can, he lets out, "Fuck."

Working my way back up, I let my saliva gather on him so I can slide easily up and down. Picking up my speed, he places a hand in my hair, tightening his hold and turning me on more. Taking my other hand, I hold his balls and massage them in my hand. I can feel them tightening up, he's growing close. I pull back and wet my finger, then start sucking him in again.

I don't know how he's going to feel about this, but we'll find out. Spreading his legs, I take the finger that I wet and place it at his ass. Slowly working it, in he stills for a second, but let's me continue. I know just where to find his spot. Once I find it, I rub against it, causing him to buck his hips pushing his cock further into my mouth. He tries to pull my head away.

"I'm 'bout to cum." I nod, sucking harder, taking him down to the back of my throat. I move my finger in and out of him faster, massaging his balls, and humming so he can feel the vibrations on his cock.

"Holy shit! Lil Mama!" He growls out loudly as he fills my mouth with his hot semen.

I swallow down as much as I can, but some leaks from the corners of my mouth. Pulling back, I wipe it off using the sheet, and watch his heavy breathing, tattooed arm covering his eyes.

"Fuckin' hell what was that?", he asks, dropping his arm to look at me.

Feeling a little shy, I ask, "Did you not like it?"

"I fuckin' loved it. I've never came so hard, ever."

"Glad I could please you," I tell him, feeling pride that I could make him lose control like that.

"You always please me, Lil Mama," he says as he grabs under my arms, pulling me up. "I love you, wife."

"I love you too, husband." We laugh, then his mouth is on mine, kissing hard.

"Alright, you ready?"

"Ready for what?"

"I got somethin' for you when you were tryin' on dresses."

"What is it?"

Bear gets up off the bed and grabs a bag. He brings it back over, pulling out a blindfold, a whip, a new vibrator, some lubricant, and two sets of handcuffs. I can feel myself grow wetter at just the thought of him using this stuff on me. We've played around with light bondage, him tying me up and the spankings, and he knows how much I love it. We talked about exploring the harder shit, but nothing ever came of it, until now that is. I can't wait to see what he is going to do. "You like?"

"Uh huh."

"I knew you would," he says, giving me that cocky smile. "Stand up." I do as I'm told. He walks me over to the rack where you can hang your clothes. "Arms up." Lifting my arms, he handcuffs them to the rack, my back towards him. "You face the mirror and don't fuckin' look away. You watch what I'm doin' to you." I nod, looking towards the mirror. He walks away to change the song. Bad Girl by Marilyn Manson and Avril Lavigne comes blaring through the iPod. He walks back over to me with the whip in hand. "Spread 'em. If it gets to be too much, you tell me to stop. Got me?"

"I got you."

He runs the whip softly down my spine, over my ass, then lightly over my pussy. I jerk in the restraints, needing more. Pulling it back then bringing it forward, the whip lands on my ass, not hard, but not soft either. I let out a low moan when the second hit comes to the other cheek, just a little harder this time. "You good?"

"Yes."

"You want more?"

"Yes. Please"

He whips my back, this time harder, and I jerk against the cuffs. Three more whips, landing each in a different spot, biting into my skin harder than the last. My moans grow louder with each one. "My dirty girl, how wet are you?"

"So wet. Give me more please."

He stands at my back, placing his mouth on my neck, kissing in the crook. I feel his hand between my legs, causing my head to go back. "I told you not to look away from the mirror." I quickly turn back, watching as he pushes his fingers inside me. "Yes. Oh God please. I need to cum."

"Not yet. You cum when I let you. Got me?"

"Yes." I let out in a growl.

"Since you looked away, you get another hit."

This time it comes with his hand hard on my ass. I jerk and cry out. He spreads my legs further apart, and getting down on his knees, he starts licking me.

"You're so goddamn wet, it's on your thighs, makin' 'em shine for me. Fuck," he says as he continues licking, finding my clit, sucking it into his mouth. I make sure not to break my stare from the mirror. My whole body's shaking, just watching what he's doing to me.

"I'm about to cum!" I scream out, needing this so bad I could die.

"You know what I want to hear."

"Please, Bear, please can I cum?"

"Mmm, such a good girl," he says. "Let go baby, I'm gonna lick you dry."

His dirty words send me over the edge. Finding my release, I come so hard it brings tears to my eyes. Throwing my head back, I scream out his name. Bear stands back up, unlocking the cuffs and carrying me over to the bed. Lying me down, he tells me to lay on my stomach. When I flip over, I feel something cool hit my back and ass. "This is some cooling gel, it'll make the marks not burn." I nod as he rubs it in, instantly cooling my tender skin. When he's done, he feels between my legs noticing I'm still wet as shit. This man makes me soaked just from looking at me. He uses his fingers, pushing them inside. "Up on your hands and knees," he commands. "You've got a sexy ass, but seeing it marked up by me is fuckin' gorgeous." He pushes his fingers back inside, rubbing against my g-spot and bringing me close to another orgasm. "I want to own you in every way."

"You already do."

"No, I mean sexually. I want to claim you in every way possible."

"Yes," I pant out.

He pulls his fingers out, and gripping my hips, he pushes his cock inside. Pumping into me from behind, he goes so deep this way. "Oh god! You feel so good, so big," I moan out. He reaches around, finding my clit and making lazy circles with his finger. My orgasm builds as he thrusts in me. "I'm gonna take your ass now baby."

I nod but ask, "Is it gonna hurt?" I turning my head to look at him.

"Yeah, at first it will, but just relax. I'll make you feel good," he answers as he grabs the lubricant and the vibrator.

Pulling out of me, I watch as he lubricates himself and me, then turns the vibrator on. He places the head of his cock at my asshole. I turn back around, dropping my head as he slowly pushes in. I try to relax, but it hurts. Turning my head, I bite down on his forearm.

"Relax baby, breathe." I do as I'm told.

Bear grabs the vibrator, placing it on my clit as he pushes in a little more. That distracts me from the pain and the stretching he's causing. When he is in completely, he stills, letting me adjust to his size. He pushes the vibrator inside of me, finding my g-spot.

This makes the pain diminish, allowing pleasure to take over. God, I've never felt so full, whimpering as he pulls the vibrator out. Placing it back on my clit and bringing me closer to my orgasm, I start moving back against his cock, biting down on his forearm again, gripping the sheets in my tight fisted hands.

"Fuck, baby. That's it, bring that ass back." His words urge me on as I find my rhythm.

He starts moving with me, matching my speed. It doesn't take long before my head drops down and I cry out his name when the best orgasm of my life hits me. A few more thrusts and he loudly growls my name, then he slowly pulls out. Lying beside me, he asks, "Did I hurt you?"

"No, that was fucking amazing."

He laughs. "It's always amazing with us."

"Yeah it is. You bring something out in me that I never knew was there."

"That goes both ways, Lil Mama," he says as he kisses me, slow and tender. "I love you so fuckin' much, you know that?"

"I do. I love you so fuckin' much too. Oh, and there was a girl that called me today. She wants to look at the building."

"That's good, right?"

"Yeah, I'm going to meet with her when we get back."

"Good. I hope she buys it."

"Me too."

Right before we go to sleep, we call and check on Kellen. Zoey assures me that he's fine, so we fall asleep, holding onto one another.

Hanger or Zoey must've called the guys because as soon as we get back, they throw us a party. Zoey's parents volunteer to take Kellen for us while we celebrate, and everyone is having a great time. Since there are no kids here, the whores and hang-arounds join us. It doesn't bother me having them here it, let those bitches know he's not available anymore. I head to the bar to get another run and Coke when I see Doc just sitting there by himself. I walk up, and patting him on the back, I ask why he's sitting alone. "Hey, Short Shit," he greets me, using the nickname he gave me as we became closer. "I'm just thinkin' 'bout some shit."

"Are you okay, Doc? You know you can talk to me." I worry about him. Most of the time, he has a haunted look in his eyes.

"Yeah, I know. Sometimes, it just takes me back, you know? My brothers finding love, getting married, havin' babies." He takes a pull from his beer and stands. "Coulda been me once. Anyway, you better take care of him, Lil Mama. Hold on to it with dear life and never let go. I'm happy for ya'll, congratulations. Now, go get your husband." He leans over, hugging me, then walks off. I do just that, finding him standing off to the side with Hanger. Before we leave, everyone congratulates us again.

I met up with Daphne a few days after we got back, and sure enough, she bought the building. I feel ecstatic to not have that hanging over my head anymore. She's gonna turn it into a tattoo shop and should have it up and running within a few months. I don't know this girl's story, but she kind of looks lost, and angry, so I hope this helps her.

The following week, Zoey got put on bedrest for the rest of her pregnancy. Bear has moved into the cabin with Kellen and I, and it's been great. I love having him here every night and waking up with him in the mornings before he goes to the garage. We've had one fight since he moved in, and that was when he decided to bring a puppy home. I remember him walking in with her.

"What the hell is that?" I asked, shocked he'd do this without even asking me if I wanted a damn dog.

"A puppy. I brought her home for you."

Glaring at him, I demand, "Kellen fucking Rhodes, why the hell would I want a puppy?"

"Well, when I'm not here, she can protect you. Plus, Kellen can grow up with her."

"So you expect me to take care of a baby and a dog?"

"No, I'll help you."

"You fucking better! She's kind of cute though." The puppy's body is white, and her black markings make it look like she has a black saddle on her back. Her face is half black, half white, and she has an adorable little black nose.

"What do you want to name her?" Bear inquires.

"What kind of dog is she?"

"She's a Staffordshire terrier, better known as a pit bull."

I think for a minute. "Karma."

"Karma… why?"

I just laugh. There's no way I'm telling him, he'll find out soon enough. "I just like the name."

"Okay, I like it."

For awhile, I had to chase her around the house as she tore up anything and every fucking thing in sight. Karma's doing great at the moment though, and she's so good and gentle around Kellen, I kind of love her now.

I go over with Ever to see Zoey while she's on bedrest. That was the first time I had taken Kellen to the club. It's warmed up outside, so we aren't stuck in the cabin all the time. We were talking about Prince Alberts and of course I get curious, especially when Ever tells us that Writer has one. After walking back to the bar, I see that all the guys are there playing with Kellen, so I let them have their fun. I take a seat and hang out for a little bit, watching them in amazement. I still can't get over how great these guys are with him. When it's time to go, Bear walks us to the Tahoe, putting Kellen in his car seat and strapping him in. Before I get in, I ask him if he'll get a Prince Albert for me.

"A Prince Albert?"

Smiling, I say, "You know, a dick piercing."

"I know what the fuck a Prince Albert is. Have you lost your goddamn mind?"

"No. Zoey was telling me about guys in her books that have them."

"Those fuckin' guys aren't real!" he shouts at me,

"Don't you fucking yell at me! Don't you want to give me all the pleasure you can?"

Angrily, he asks, "Are you saying I don't pleasure you?"

"No, I'm saying I want you to get your dick pierced."

"I'm not gettin' my fuckin' shit pierced. End of conversation."

"But Writer has his done." I pout, trying to look cute.

"Stick that fuckin' lip back in your mouth. How the fuck do you know that about Writer?"

"Ever said so."

"I could give two fucks what Writer has! I'm not doin' it! I'm tellin' Hanger Crazy Girl needs to quit tellin' you about that fuckin' book porn she's readin'."

"Fine, I'm going home," I huff.

"I love you." He leans in to give me a kiss, but I turn my head, refusing to kiss him. Bear grabs my face, turning it to him. "You refuse to kiss me again and I'll paddle that ass as soon as I get home." That makes me smile because I know he'll do it.

"Promises, promises. I love you too you, ass," I tell him, standing on my tippy toes while he bends, putting his mouth on mine. When he breaks from the kiss, he turns and walks away, calling over his shoulder, "I'll never break a promise with you, so be ready when I get home!" I watch him walk back inside before I get in and leave. Later that night, he sure in the fuck does keep his promise and I don't think I could sit down right for a couple of days.

Kellen is four months old now and things have been amazing. All the guys have now started calling him Cub, which I think is super cute since he looks just like his daddy. Hell, I've even started calling him that. I think he's going to be big like Bear, all the fat rolls on his chunky little legs. I'm so happy that we could all move forward after what I did. Since I'm married to Bear and his Ol' Lady, the brothers treat me like I'm family, and I've never felt more accepted in my life.

I see my dad a lot. I have yet to go to his clubhouse, but he's over here at the cabin all the time. He absolutely loves Kellen and they're bonding quickly. I've forgiven my dad for everything, knowing that my mother lied, and our relationship keep growing stronger every day.

Karma's doing great too. She's fully trained now, and I even trained her to bite Bear's ass when he pisses me off. She only got him once, leaving teeth marks. I about died laughing, but he got pissed and didn't think it was funny at all, so I had to break her from doing it again.

Zoey had the girls and they're beautiful with heads full of dark hair, but they look just like their momma. Hanger's mom showed up at the hospital. I don't know what's going to happen with that, but I guess we'll find out. Family is so important to Zoey, so if she has any say about it, his mom will be in their life.

With everything that's happened to me, and all the people that I have now, I'm learning to open up and trust more. And tonight, Bear's taking me to my father's club.

FIFTEEN

Bear

I'm taking Jacey to Snake's clubhouse tonight. I used to go watch the fights every week, but since she came along, I've only made it to a few, and I see now how Hanger could give it up. I never really got how he could just change his whole life for some chick, but now I understand completely. Four months old and Kellen already has a nickname: Cub. Everyone love him, and I wish Ripper was here to see him. He and Chatty never had kids, I don't know why, but he would've been a great father and an amazing uncle.

I walk into the house and Karma runs up, wagging her tail so I have to pet her, the cute little shit. The day she bit my fucking ass and left marks because of Lil Mama, I could've killed her. Now I know why she named her Karma. She thought it was so fucking funny, me not so much, and when she saw how pissed I was, she shut that shit down real quick and Karma hasn't done it since.

I go find Jacey in the bathroom, and I lean against the doorframe, watching my Ol' Lady. She's stunning, with her tight shorts and shiny top, her cut worn over it. Her hair's pulled back, and she's looking sexy as hell.

"Are you ready to go?"

She jumps and turns, not hearing me over the music. She's listening to Marilyn Manson's version of *Tainted Love* with Cub in his bouncy seat. "Ahhhh!" she screams and I bust out laughing. "Bear! Fuck! You scared the shit outta me!" she shouts as she reaches over, slapping my arm. I apologize and try to stop laughing, "You look beautiful."

"Thank you."

I walk up to her, putting my face in the crook of her neck, taking in her scent and peppering kisses all along the length. She tilts her head to give me better access. "I'll let you finish getting ready before we end up not going anywhere."

"Wouldn't be so bad to just stay," she says, and gives me a smile.

I smack her perfect little ass. "We gotta go. Bam Bam's fighting tonight and it's his first fight since he was shot."

"I know. I'll be ready in a minute."

I walk over to Cub, picking him up and kissing his forehead. "Hey buddy, you bein' good for Momma?" He gives me his little grin. "Did you miss Daddy today? Daddy missed you and Momma. I love you Cub." I kiss the top of his head again as he starts making those adorable little cooing noises. I carry him out of the bathroom so Lil Mama can finish getting ready.

Once she's done, we take Cub over to Hanger and Crazy Girl. I make Lil Mama stay in the car so she won't open her mouth about where we are going. Hanger doesn't want her knowing anything about the fights, because he knows she'd wanna go. I tell him we'll be back as soon as it's over. They're gonna have their hands full with their two babies.

We get to the Cobras' clubhouse and when she gets out of the car, she immediately starts looking around. "I remember this place. My mother took me from here. This was the last place I saw my father." I take her hand, leading her inside. We meet up with the guys, and they're giving tips to Bam Bam. We don't need to hang around, so I show her around. I see Deuce standing off to the side, so I walk over.

"You taking the bets tonight?

"Yeah. Minimum is a G."

"Put me down a G on Bam Bam." I hand him the money and he looks at Lil Mama. "Why you lookin' at my Ol' Lady?"

"So it is her. Jacey, it's been a long time."

"I'm sorry, but who are you?" she asks, clearly confused.

"I'm Deuce, your pop's..."

She interrupts him. "Vice President, I remember you. I used to play with your son. How is he?"

He chuckles. "Hell of a memory you got. He's good. He's fighting tonight, goes by the name Crawler."

"I hardly remember anything, really, but I think coming here and hearing names brings back a lot of it."

"Well, you guys have a good night. Enjoy the fight."

We walk around some more until she sees Snake. "Hey Dad."

"Hey Princess, you havin' a good time?"

"So far."

"How's my grandbaby?"

"Great, same as he was yesterday when you saw him." Leave it to her to make a smartass comment, making us all laugh.

"Okay, okay," he says, putting his arms up in surrender. "I can't help it if I'm an overprotective son of a bitch." That makes us all laugh again. She really is a lot like him. "You kids have fun and enjoy the fight."

We walk out back where the circle is forming. It's safer for Jacey to be in the front, so I push us through until we're front and center. I stand behind her and wrap my arms around her shoulders, holding her to me, and she lifts her arms to hold onto my forearms. Nobody will fuck with my wife as long as her cut's on, but it doesn't stop me from holding her hand and keeping her at my side the whole fucking time. Bam Bam and Crawler make their way into the middle, then Snake joins them. He states the rules.

"Fight's not over until someone taps or gets knocked the fuck out."

When he's done, he yells Fight! and the show begins. They start circling each other, Bam Bam goes in first, throwing a hook, and Crawler's head flies to the side. Bringing it back up, Bam's ready for him again, giving him an uppercut. Crawler stumbles, then Bam gets him with a leg kick, knocking him to the ground. Bam jumps on top of him and throws punch after punch. Crawler bucks his hips hard, getting Bam off of him.

Shit, I thought that was the end of it! Scrambling up, blood pouring out of Crawler's face, he gets on top of Bam, throwing his own set of punches. He stops, then grabs Bam's arm, sliding his leg over Bam's head and lays to the side, pulling his arm back. Fuck, it looks like it's about to break when Bam finally taps. Well fuck, I lost my money on that one.

"Let's go tell your dad bye and go get Cub."

"Yeah sounds good." We tell Bam Bam he had a good fight, then we find Snake, who's standing with Deuce and Crawler.

"Good fight tonight. Congrats on your win."

"Thanks man," Crawler says, looking at Jacey.

"That's Snake's daughter, Jacey. You remember her, Crawler?" Deuce asks.

"Yeah, I remember her. How you been?" He licks his lips, continuing to stare.

"I've been good. I'm Bear's Ol' Lady now." Good girl.

I gotta bad feeling about this guy. She looks at me and asks if I'm ready to go. I tell her that I am, so she gives Snake a hug and we say our goodbyes.

Once we're in the truck she says, "I don't like that guy. I remember him a little, but he was kind of creeping me out." I place my hand on her leg.

"Yeah, I didn't have a good feeling about him either. When we're there, you stay with me at all times. Got me?"
"Yeah."

Tomorrow is the day I've been waiting for, the day we take down the Italians. We're all gathered in the church room. It's strange not having Hanger here, he's still with Zoey, helping with the babies. Gunner calls the meeting.

"Alright guys, I know it's different without Hanger here, but let's get this shit settled so we can take those fuckers down."

Snake jumps in, saying, "The plan is this: we set up our shooters, surround the building, go in and take all of them out, then get our shit back and call it a fuckin' day."

"Sounds like a plan. Who are the shooters?" Bones asks.

Gunner answers, "We have Ghost and me."

Snake chimes in. "I have Crawler and Diver."

Bones says, "I got Bull and Happy."

Clapper, the Texas President offers, "I'll put one of my guys with each of yours."

Gunner says, "Okay, that should be good." He lays out a print of the warehouse that Pretty Boy made. "Alright, so we can put three guys here and here where the exits are. Put the others on the sides, just in case anybody misses."

"Yeah, sounds good. The rest of us can surround it at the windows and doors. We'll go in and take out anybody that we see. Everyone got it?" Snake asks. The room echo's in yeahs. Church gets called and I head out. Just in case anything was to happen to me, I want my last night to be with my Ol' Lady and my son.

After dinner, we put Kellen to sleep and head to our room, where I draw a bubble bath. When the tub's filled, I turn on the jets and go back into the bedroom, taking Lil Mama's hand and leading her to the bathroom. I strip us both down and help her in. I sink into the hot water behind he, letting it relax me. I pull her against me, rubbing my hands up and down her front, massaging her ample tits. She turns in the water to straddle me. Lining me up to her entrance, she lowers down on my cock. Jacey finds her rhythm, she rides me so fuckin' good, and her nails dig into my skin as she drops her forehead down onto my shoulder. I put one arm behind her back, holding her to me. Kissing and biting at her neck, her cries get louder and louder until she finds her release, calling out my name. I'm not far behind her, and soon I'm growling her name. She lays her head against my chest as I wrap both arms around her. "I'm scared Bear."

"Don't be."

"I don't want anything to happen to you or my dad."

"I know, baby. We're gonna be fine," I tell her. "You know I can't give you all the details, but we have a good plan. Everything will be good."

"You promise?"

"I promise." We get out of the bathtub, dry off, and I carry her to the bed, laying her down. I grab the blindfold from the nightstand and place it over her eyes. Handcuffing her to the bed, I tell her I'll be right back as I walk into the kitchen, grabbing some ice cubes. "You're so fuckin' beautiful, a goddamn goddess." I sit the bowl next to the bed, putting one cube in my mouth. I lean over her ad run the cube over her lips. I move to her neck, letting the water drop down onto her skin, forming goose bumps all over her. I see her mouth drop down, forming in the shape of an o. I work my way down between her full tits until the cube has melted. I grab another and start from there, working my way back up, my tongue catching the running drops of water. "Oh God, Bear," she moans out as she pushes her head back into the pillow.

I get another cube in my mouth and circle her nipples with it, making them rock hard. Moving down to her stomach when that one has melted, I do the same as before, running my tongue back up to catch the water. Jacey arches her back, letting out those soft little sounds that I love. Taking another cube, I place it on her pussy, running it down until I have it at her opening. I let it go with my mouth and take my fingers, pushing it inside of her. Placing my tongue on her clit, I flick and sucking her little nub while pushing the ice cube in and out of her. Her moans grow louder. I work her over harder and faster until I have her screaming out my name, then I go back up her body, freeing her wrists and taking the blindfold off. She has a sated smile across her face, and it's a fuckin' beautiful sight.

"Get your cut on." She stands, walking to the closet, grabbing and putting it on. I lay on the bed to watch every move she makes. When Jacey gets back over to the bed, she straddles me. I rub my tip over her pussy, her head goes back as she lets out a cry of pleasure. I find her opening and push inside of her. She finds a steady rhythm as I watch her gorgeous tits bounce. Reaching up, I take them in my hands, massaging and pulling at her nipples.

"You look so fuckin' sexy ridin' my cock with that cut on."

"You feel so good, Bear." I bring her down onto my chest so I can pound into her tight little cunt. Gripping her ass and throwing my hips up, I slam into her, balls deep. "Fuck, Bear I'm gonna cum!"

"Damn right you are, clutching my cock so hard." Hitting that sweet spot over and over, I throw her over the edge as she cries out my name once again. Picking up my speed, I fuck her harder than I ever have before. "This is mine. You are mine," I grunt out. She moans back, "Yes Bear, god yes!" I feel my balls tighten up and let go, giving her all I have. I can feel her milking my cock as she has another orgasm. When we're done, we stay just like we are, her head on my shoulder as I rub up and down on her back. "I love you Jacey, so much."

"I love you too."

"If something happens to me..."

She interrupts me "You do not do that. You don't talk like that. Youre not leaving us. Got me?"

"Yeah I got you." I tell her. We fall asleep with her on top of me still inside of her.

We're about to have our final church before this goes down. I drop her and Cub off at Hanger and Crazy Girl's, giving them kisses and telling them how much I love them. I always want them to know how much I love them in case one day I don't come back. Since, technically, Hanger's house is on lock down, we have Romeo and Spike on guard. Spike is a prospect for the Cobras, and a damn good one from what I've seen.

We all meet up in the chapel one last time before we head out, going over the plan one more time, making sure everybody understands. When the meeting is over, we all head to our bikes. Some of the guys are taking cages just in case any of us are hurt, and they'll be at the very end of the line.

Gunner, Snake, Bones, and Clapper are all at the front, signaling it's time. Since there are so many of us, we stop about a mile away from the warehouse. We don't want the Italians to know we're coming. Pushing our bikes the rest of the way, we park them on the side of the road before heading toward the woods. We draw our weapons, just in case they have guys set up on guard. We've got to be prepared for anything, keep our heads clear and eyes open.

QUIET COUNTRY

Our shooters get set up as we stay back and wait. I can see they have a couple of men at the front exit, and I'm assuming they would have some at the back as well. That's when I hear the first round of shots being fired, taking out the two guys at the exit. The rest of us run up, getting into position. Snake's at the head of our group as we wait for the door to open, and when it does, Snake doesn't miss a beat as he comes around the door facing the guy, raising his gun and killing him. We wait to see if anyone else is coming, and sure enough, someone is.

"What the fuck is going on?" this guy questions when he sees his guy on the ground.

But that's all he says because then he's shot down too. I hear a few more shots so I know they're coming out the back exit as well. It's our time to go in. Slowly walking, we watch our surroundings with some guys going left and some right. The rest of us go forward. I'm toward the back, and all of a sudden, gunshots blare through the warehouse. Dodger follows me as we duck down, running to take cover, coming to a corner.

I look around it, pointing my pistol. I see one of them, and taking aim, I hit my target right in the side of the neck. Blood squirts out and paints the wall as he goes down. It's not an instant kill shot, so I walk up to him and look him right the eyes.

"This is for my brother Ripper, motherfucker."

His eyes go big but he doesn't try and fight, he just lays there, looking at me. This isn't the time to have a conscience or feel remorse. I make sure to keep eye contact with this piece of shit as I shoot him in his chest, right where his heart would be and two inches lower because that's where they got Ripper.

I take another shot, the last one, putting it in his forehead. As I come out of cover, rounding the corner, I spot another target and pull the trigger, hitting dead center in his chest.

Slowly, we make our way down the hall when I hear a shot behind me. I turn and see Dodger on the ground with a guy standing above him, pointing his gun at me. Fuck, what do I do? Stay calm. Do I have enough time to get the gun outta his hand? No, because if I start walking toward him, he'll shoot. "Drop your gun now!" he commands, so bending at my knees, I lower the gun until it's on the floor. I stand back up, lifting my hands above my head. "Kick it away from you, asshole!" I do, and all I can think about is the fact that I'm gonna die. I'm never gonna see my beautiful wife or my boy again.

He walks up to me and my fighting instincts kick in. As soon as he's close enough, I hit the arm he's using to aim the gun at me.

Catching him off guard, he drops the weapon to the ground. I throw a punch and it makes a solid connection with his face, but that doesn't even phase him. Son of a bitch! He throws his own, hitting me in the stomach, and another landing another on my face and the taste of copper fills my mouth. I rush him, taking him to the ground as we wrestle around, each getting hits on the other. Soon, I'm on top, I have the advantage again. I throw punch after punch until he's unconscious. I feel metal at the back of my neck. Goddammit!

"Get the fuck up," someone orders, grabbing my shirt and pulling me up, pushing me to walk down the hallway further. We pass an open door, but keep walking. He stops me suddenly and I hear, "You get that gun off my brother or you're a dead man." It's Demon. He keeps the gun at my neck, not caring about my brother's threat. How can I play this? Taking my chances, I move to the right, spinning on him. Demon fires his gun as soon as I spin, taking that fucker out. "Thanks brother."

"Glad I was here. Hey, I picked this up for you." He hands me back my gun. Walking together, we check rooms. The ringing of shots starts to die down as we make our way to the back exit and walk out. Looking around, Snake is nowhere to be seen. I have to find him.

"Dodger's down. Where's Snake?" No one answers as I look around. "Where the fuck is Snake?" If something happened to him, it'll kill Jacey. I can't break my promise to her. Bones finally answers, "I don't know, we haven't seen him."

"Did you guys look for him,?" I ask, my voice raised, as I look around at everyone.

Bones answers again. "No, we were waiting for everybody to get out before we started looking."

"I'm gonna go get Snake. Someone needs to go get Dodger." I run back inside, searching everywhere but finding nothing. I can hear footsteps behind me but I don't care enough to see who it is. I have to find Snake. I round the corner, checking those rooms as well. Going down another hallway, coming to the last door, I see him. He's lying there in a puddle of blood. Oh fuck. I drop to my knees, checking for a pulse. It's faint but it's there. Someone drops down next to me, and I look over to see Gunner. "We gotta call an ambulance," I tell him.

"No, you need to get out of here. I'll call, then I'll get out too before they come."

"No, I have to make sure he's okay. Lil Mama will hate me if I don't."

"Bear, listen. When I call the ambulance, the police are gonna come. You have Lil Mama and Cub, and you need to be with them. Let me call, and you can meet them at the hospital."

"Are you sure?"

"Yes. We're wasting time, now go!" I run out, meeting up with all the guys.

"Did you find Snake?" Bones asks.

"Yeah, Gunner's calling an ambulance, so we gotta get outta here." We get on our bikes and head back to the clubhouse. I let Bones know what happened so he can inform everyone else, and I head over to Hanger and Crazy Girl's. I park my bike and the door flies open before I'm even off it yet, so I hurry. Jacey's in my arms, with her legs wrapped around my waist. She peppers kisses all over my face saying, "You're okay, you're here!"

"Yeah, Lil Mama, I'm fine," I confirm as I give her a kiss on the lips. "I have to tell you somethin' though."

"What?"

"Snake was shot. We've gotta get to the hospital."

"What?! Let me go get my stuff." She runs back into the house, and Hanger comes out.

"How'd it go?"

"Snake and Dodger got shot. We gotta get to the hospital. As far as I know, everyone else made it out, and we got all those Italian fucks."

"Alright, we'll keep Cub, just go make sure they're fine."

Jacey comes running back out. I start my bike back up and we head to the hospital. When we get there, she tells them who she is and we're directed to a waiting room. We sit there for about an hour before a doctor comes and tells us that he got the bullet out, that Snake will be fine. We go into his room and she pulls up a chair next to him, taking his hand. "I'm so glad you're going to be fine! You can't leave me, Daddy, I just got you back. Please don't leave me." I see him open his eyes, a single tear rolling down his cheek. He tells her, "I'm not going anywhere, Princess. Didn't they tell you I would be fine? I love you."

"Yeah, they did. Just seeing you lying here... I don't want anybody to take you from me again. I love you Dad, so much." I let them have some time. As I step out into the hallway, I see a cop heading my way. "Would you like to tell me what happened tonight?"

"I don't know what you are talking about."

"Well, you're here seeing someone that was shot, and we have someone sitting in a jail cell, wearing the same type of vest you have on. Also, when we got the call, there were several dead bodies when we showed up at that warehouse."

"Still don't know what you're talking about. Why don't you go harass someone else. I'm just here visiting."

"I'm sure you are." He walks into Snake's room and Jacey comes out.

"I gotta call Hanger. They arrested Gunner." I get on my phone and let Hanger know that Gunner was caught. He says he'll get ahold of our club attorney and instructs us to meet for church. I take Lil Mama back to his place before going to the clubhouse. Hanger starts the meeting like he never took time off. It's good to have our Prez back. While sitting in church, he gets a call from the attorney, and once he hangs up, he runs his hands down his face.

"Alright guys. The attorney has found out that Gunner was pulled over and they found his pistol. That being said, he left before the police and ambulance got there. They have no ties to him being there, so they can't charge him with anything from the warehouse. The attorney advises that it's best if we don't have contact with him while he's locked up. He says it could be bad for the club. We can go through his mom for information on how he's doing and we can give her money for his books." All in agreement, he finishes. *"Snake and Dodger are both gonna make a full recovery. Thank fuck those assholes had shit for aim. I think we've all had a long night, so let's call this meeting and go home. If you have families, make sure you tell them how much you love them. We were lucky not to lose anybody tonight."*

Later that night, as we lay in bed wrapped around each other, I tell Jacey to stop taking her birth control. She pushes up on her elbows to look at me. "What?"

"Get off the birth control. After tonight, I realized life is too short to try and wait. I want you pregnant again, and I want what I missed out on. Stop taking it."

"Bear, I'm not ready for another baby yet."

"You better get ready because it's happenin' soon."

"Bear."

"No, I'll give you some time, but it's happenin'."

Snake and Dodger both made full recoveries and are doing great. Jacey spends a lot of time with her dad, even more than before. I think she feels that she almost lost him again and she doesn't wanna waste anymore time. The Cobras have had some heat from the cops, but the Sinners have stayed out of it. We decided to patch in Demon and Ghost, so we'll be having a patch party for them soon.

Life really is too short to waste. After that night, thinking I was

QUIET COUNTRY

never gonna see them again, I decided I don't wanna wait for shit any longer. I want another baby, I want everything I missed with Cub. Since that night and asking Jacey to stop her birth control, I've asked a few more times. Each time, she shoots down the idea, saying she's still not ready. So for the time being, I'll stop asking, she'll eventually see my reasoning. She's a headstrong woman, so I'm learning. Lil Mama wants to do shit when she's ready, otherwise she fights me tooth and nail, but once I get her in that bedroom, she gives up fast. She may think she controls things and sure, some things she does, but in the bedroom, that's my domain and I'm the one with complete control. That's why I've been fucking her like a madman, any chance I get, I take it. I just hope one of these times the birth control doesn't work and I knock my Ol' Lady up. I kinda like her going against me on some things, though, keeps it interesting. It's never boring with her and that's what makes us so great. She wouldn't be the woman I fell in love with if she always just went with what I say. It makes me fall more in love with her everyday, knowing she's still that same person with the same feisty personality. She doesn't take shit, doesn't let people take advantage of her, and that's one of the reasons why I fell in love with her in the first place. She hasn't changed who she is and I'd never want her too.

It's been a couple of months since everything happened. Gunner got three years in lock up and we miss the fuck outta our VP. We continue going through his momma, making sure he's got enough money for the shit he needs, and she gives us weekly updates on how he's doing. Once he's outta that shithole, he'll be back home where he fucking belongs, with his brothers.

Tonight is the patch party for Demon and Ghost, and since we need a new treasurer, Demon is filling that spot. We have the hang-arounds and the whores here, and so far, it's been a great night. I see some of my brothers over in the dark corners with their pants down and a whore on their knees. Some are on the couches, with one girl riding the fuck out of 'em while they have their face in another's pussy. Some people are playing pool while others are dancing. Jacey's over twirling around with Crazy Girl, so I'm at the bar with Hanger. "Look at 'em, brother."

"Yeah, I see 'em," I respond. "We got lucky, didn't we?"

"We sure in the fuck did. Writer too, you know." He's got that smile on his face that he's had since the day Crazy Girl woke up.

"Yeah. We never see much of him anymore."

"The boy's in love, always with his woman. He's been alone his entire life, not havin' anyone to communicate with."

"He's always had us, though," I tell him, not understanding what he's talking about.

"Yeah, we're his family, but none of us knew how to communicate other than writing it on paper. There's a big difference. Maybe you should think about learnin'," he informs me.

"Yeah, I might have to do that. Crazy Girl changed all our lives, huh?"

"She's somethin' special, for sure. Can't wait to have her officially be mine."

I know he's speaking the truth because that's how I felt about Lil Mama. Laughing, I tell him, "Let's go get our women." We both get up, making our way over to them. I see Hanger grab Zoey, pulling her back to him. I pull Lil Mama to me, dancing behind her to *Runnin' Outta Moonlight by Randy Houser*. We dance to a few more songs then we go sit down.

"I'm gonna call my dad and make sure Cub's okay."

"Alright, sounds good."

She walks out the front door and I turn to the bar. After a few minutes, I feel hands on my back. Fuck me, this isn't gonna be good. I turn, coming face to face with Morgan.

"You need to walk away."

"Ah, but Bear I've missed you. I've been waiting all night for you to be alone."

"Not gonna happen, walk away Morgan."

She leans in closer to my face. "You think I'm scared of your Ol' Lady?"

I see Lil Mama out of the corner of my eye.

"You should be, bitch," Jacey tells her.

It happens too fast, and I definitely didn't see it coming. Lil Mama grabs her by the back of the head, slamming her face into the bar.

"You fucking whores need to learn your place around here. If they tell you to leave them the fuck alone, do it, goddamn it."

She slams Morgan's head into the bar a few more times.

"Lil Mama, let her go," I instruct her.

She lets go and Morgan falls to the floor. Wiping her hands off on a bar towel, my wife says, "Now who's up for one of Crazy Girl's games?"

I can see that she is pissed.

"You guys set it up and we'll be back." I grab her hand, taking her into my room.

"You alright, Lil Mama?"

"Yeah, I'm good."

"You know I wasn't gonna do anything with her, right?"

"Yeah I heard you. It just pisses me off. Why do they have to go after the taken ones?"

"That's what they do, why they're here. They just wanna get fucked by anyone they can," I remind her. "I don't think any of them will be messin' with me anymore."

"They better not," Jacey warns, "or I'll be beating a bitch's ass again."

"I love you, Lil Mama. How's Cub?"

"I love you too. He's good with Dad."

"Good, now let's go get fucked up."

We walk back out and they have the game all ready to go. Of course it's sixes. That's becoming a club favorite. Although I'll never understand why Crazy Girl wants to continue playing, she never wins. By the time it's over, we're all fucked off.

Crazy Girl and Lil Mama have decided to get on top of one of the tables, dancing and belting out the words to *Addicted by Saving Abel*. Hanger walks over to me.

"Should we get 'em down?" He has a smile on his face.

"Nah, let's let 'em have fun," I tell him. I see some of the hang-arounds watching our Ol' Ladies. That doesn't sit well with me.

"You fuckers better turn your heads before we turn 'em for you," I let them know as we walk up to the table, both standing in the same position, arms folded legs and spread, looking up at our Ol' Ladies.

Crazy Girl looks down, smiling. "Well hello boys."

They burst out laughing. Jacey looks down at me.

"Get up here and dance with me."

"Not on your life, Lil Mama."

"But baby." Yeah she's fucked. The song stops.

"C'mon Lil Mama, time to get down."

"Only if you fuck me when we get to the room." The guys start hollerin' and cat callin'.

"You bet your ass I will," I promise, giving her a sexy grin.

"Yes please." Jacey starts giggling.

"You too, Crazy Girl," Hanger tells her.

"You guys always ruin the fun!"

Both of us grab them by the legs, carrying them like cavemen to our rooms.

They yell the whole way, shouting for us to put them down, informing us that we don't know how to have fun. I give Jacey a slap to her ass and chuckle as she moans. I slam my door shut with my foot and lay her on my bed. I walk into the bathroom, and by the time I get back, she's passed out and I can't help but smile. I climb into bed beside her, bringing her over to me and holding her until I fall asleep.

SIXTEEN

Jacey

Today is girls' day with Zoey and Ever, and it's going to be so much fun. I feel like it's been forever since we all got together, and the only one missing is Chatty. I feel like I need this day. I've been a little stressed since the fight Bear took me too. Whenever I'm outside or we go somewhere, I always feel like someone's watching me. I don't want to sound crazy, so I haven't said anything to Bear, and besides, I always have the alarm set and Cub's monitors on, just like he told me to do.

Walking out of the bedroom and into the living room, I see Bear sitting on the couch holding Cub and Karma's laying next to them. He is such a great dad, always talking, singing, or playing with him. Even after all these months, it still takes my breath away watching how he interacts with his son. I guess it's just that when I got pregnant with him, I judged Bear. I didn't think he'd be a good father or be able to take care of us, but boy, was I wrong.

I take a minute to recover as he looks up at me. "Don't forget your cut." That brings me down quick, and glaring at him, I ask, "Are you fucking serious? When do I ever forget my cut, you jackass?" He bursts out laughing. "I swear, sometimes you just like to get me riled up."

"You know I do. I gotta make sure my feisty woman's still in there, wouldn't want you gettin' soft on me."

"That'll never happen and you fucking know it." I tell him. "Dad'll be over in a little bit to take Cub."

"That might be a problem."

"Why?"

"Well since Hanger's mom is back, we were gonna have a playdate with the girls. I guess Hanger's letting her spend time with them, but Hanger still has to be there."

"But Dad'll be over here in just a minute. It's too late to tell him not to come over."

"So will Hanger. It should be fine, maybe he'll just hang here with all of us."

"I guess we should've talked about who was doing what with Cub.

We'll have to work on that. Alright, well let's just see how it goes when everybody's here." I say, just as the doorbell rings. I go answer the door and it's my dad. I let him in and he goes straight for Cub. "Hi to you too, Dad."

"You know I'm here to see that grandbaby of mine, but hi, Princess."

"I know, you're one proud grandpa," I say to him, while laughing, walking into the living room.

"You know it."

The doorbell rings again. I go answer it again, letting Hanger, Zoey, his mom, and the girls all into the house. Once we're all in the living room, Hanger's mom stops dead in her tracks, covering her mouth. "Snake?" she whispers.

"You know my dad?" I ask, confusion taking over. He looks up and when he sees her, he freezes. I look to her and see that her eyes are shining with unshed tears. "Snake?" She questions again, louder this time. "Vixen, is that really you?" he asks, sitting Cub on the ground and coming over to us, grabbing her in for a hug. She holds onto him like her life depends on it. I'm so confused right now, then I remember a previous conversation. "Dad, this is her?"

Hanger asks, "What the fuck is goin' on?" Zoey and Bear look just as confused as him.

"Dad, this is the woman right? The woman you were always in love with?"

"Yeah, Princess, this is her."

Hanger says, "Wait a fuckin' minute. Mom, is Snake the guy you said you loved?"

"Yeah, that's him."

Zoey chimes in. "Well, didn't this get a little more interesting?"

"Sure in the fuck did, Crazy Girl," Bear replies.

Hanger says, "How the fuck is that even possible?"

"Well, I think us girls are going to go. We'll let you guys get this settled," I announce. Zoey's giving me the evil eye because she wants all the juicy gossip, and I walk by her, telling her I'll fill her in later. She smiles and nods. We climb in my Tahoe, and of course they would have Romeo follow us. We go by and pick up Ever, then start the day off by going to lunch. While we're eating, I tell her and Ever the story of my dad and Hanger's mom. Zoey signs to Ever of course, and I never really thought about it before, but I think I should learn ASL.

"Zoey, will you teach me how to sign?"

"*Yeah, sure. Just let me know when you wanna start. So how would you feel if*

Victoria and Snake started a relationship now?"

"What do you mean?"

"I mean with you just getting your Dad back and everything. Are you concerned if they're together, that it'll complicate the relationship you guys are building?"

"I haven't really thought about it, but I want my Dad happy, so I'd be okay with it. She seems really nice, and with you having her grandbabies, I think we'll all be spending a lot of time together."

"Yeah, that's true. So, I have some news." Zoey says, with a huge smile on her face.

"Well, what is it?"

"I'm pregnant."

"That's great Zoey! Congratulations! Bear asked me to go off my birth control and I said no."

"Why would you tell him no?"

"I didn't think I was ready for another baby." Zo listens and nods. "But then, I feel like he deserves the chance to have everything he missed out on with Cub."

"Yeah, I understand. Have you told him you stopped taking it?"

"How did you know I stopped?"

"I know you, Jacey, and I'm guessing you haven't told him."

"No, I haven't. I feel like if I tell him, it'll feel more like a job than in the moment. I don't want the pressure of trying, I want it to just happen."

"That makes sense. It'll happen when the time is right."

"Congratulations, Zoey!" Ever tells her. I'm so glad that Zoey speaks as Ever signs, because I would miss out on a lot.

"Thank you guys. Jacey, I'm sure it'll happen soon. It'll be great too, because this time you'll tell him and he'll be there every step of the way."

Once we're done with lunch, we go get our hair done. Zoey no longer has the pink in her hair and since she is pregnant, she goes for just a trim. Ever and I decide on just trims as well and then we go get our nails done. Ever seems kind of distant today, so I ask Zoey if there's something wrong with her sister.

"I don't know. She seems off, doesn't she?"

"Yeah. Maybe you should ask her."

While getting our pedicures, Zoey turns toward Ever, tapping her on the arm. When Ever looks at her, Zoey asks, "What's wrong with you? Why are you being so distant?"

"I didn't want to say anything yet, but I got a job offer."

"That's great Ever! What's there to think about?"

"It's in New York, Zoey."
"What?"
"It's in New York," Ever repeats.
"Are you really considering taking it?"
"Zoey, it's like a once in a lifetime opportunity."
"What about Writer?"
"If I take it, I want him to come with me."
"He can't just leave the club, you know that right?" Zoey asks.
"I can hope."
"Ever, it's gonna destroy him if you leave."
"I know. I don't want to talk about it anymore."
"Okay."

Zoey, being the person she is, drops the conversation. God, if Ever takes this job, it's going to kill Writer.

Once we're done at the nail salon, Zoey asks, "Now what?"

"I wanna make one more stop."

We pull into the old clinic parking lot, and it's now been turned into a tattoo shop. Looking at the building, they've repainted it, covering it with graffiti style pictures. There's a new sign reading Runaway Tattoos, and I can't help but wonder why she would name it that. I feel kind of anxious going back in, but I really want to see what Daphne did with it.

"What are we doing here?" Zoey asks.

"I'm going to get a tattoo." I tell her. Then ask, "Are you okay with going in?"

"Yeah... I mean it makes me a little nervous, but it'll be fine. I know nobody'll hurt me."

We all walk in and it looks so different. They have the walls painted with different graffiti, much like the outside, and there are framed pictures of tattoos hanging on the walls, and a desk in the front. The girl behind the desk, with wild blue dreads and lots of piercings and tattoos, asks, "Can I help you?"

"Is Daphne here?"

"Yeah, hold on let me get her. Can I tell her who is here?"

"Tell her it's Jacey."

The girl goes into the back and comes back out. "She'll be out in a minute. Would you like anything to drink?"

"No, thank you."

"Alright, well you can have a seat on the couch over there while you wait."

We walk over to the couch and sit, and it doesn't take long for the beautiful tattoo artist to come out. She has blonde and black hair, with a piercing going through her nose. A lot of people can't pull of a piercing like that, but on her, it totally works. She has bright, colorful tattoos running down her arms and across her chest. "Hey Jacey, how can I help you?"

"I love what you've done with the place. How free are you right now?"

"Thanks. Let me check," she walks over to the desk, looking at the planner. "You're in luck. I don't have any appointments until later."

"Great, can you give me a tattoo?"

"Sure, what would you like?" she asks, then looks to the other girl. "Get her the paperwork." I tell her what I want and she tells me to stay here while she draws it up. Daphne comes back about thirty minutes later and shows it to me. "That looks amazing!"

"Alright, come with me." I hand the paperwork back to the girl as we walk back to one of the old exam rooms. Thank God, it's not the one.

"Alright, I want you to lay on your side. Pull your shirt up, and tuck it under your bra." I do as I'm told, waiting for her to get ready. "I'm gonna get the drawing on your skin and you tell me if you like the placement." She hands me a mirror, and I love it. She has kind of curved it on my ribs.

"I love it."

"Okay good. The outline'll be the worst part, so make it through that and you'll be good to go."

"Alright, I'm ready." I hear the sound of the gun buzzing to life. Then it hits my skin. "Oh my God, that hurts like a motherfucker!"

"Yeah, you picked one of the most painful places for your first. Just relax, it'll ease up some." I do as she says, and it's not long before the pain starts to fade, just like she said.

"Can I ask how you came up with the name?"

"Yeah. I was in love once, but he ran away. It reminds me never to let someone in again."

"Shit, I'm sorry."

"It was a long time ago."

I lay there for a few hours. Finally, she says, "It's done. Go look in that mirror and see what you think." I get up and go over to look at my reflection. It's amazing, more than I could've ever imagined. "Daphne, this is amazing! Thank you so much."

"You're welcome, girl. I'm glad you like it. Let me get it taped up."

"Can I show the girls first?"

"Yeah, let me go get them." She walks out and comes back with Zoey and Ever.

"Oh Jacey, that looks great! Bear's gonna love it!"

"Hell, I love it," Ever says.

"Thank you guys." Daphne gets it taped up and I walk to the front and pay.

We head to the clubhouse, dropping Ever off, then we go to the cabin. Once we're back, we walk in and Zoey goes right to Hanger and the girls. I head straight for Bear and Cub. I look to Bear. "Where's Dad?" Hanger and him look at each other and burst out laughing. "What? What's so funny?"

"He's with my mom," Hanger tells me.

"Apparently, they have some catching up to do," Bear says, trying to stop laughing.

"Ew, that's fucking disgusting!" I tell him.

"Not as fuckin' disgusting as catching them kissing in the kitchen." Hanger grimaces.

"Ok, no more. This is so weird," I say

"You got that fuckin' right." Hanger agrees.

"I think it's sweet. They have a second chance at love," Zoey chimes in.

"Always the romantic," I tell her, and we all laugh. "So Hanger, when are you going to take Zoey to watch the fights?"

Glaring at me, he says "I'm not."

"What fights?" Zoey asks, confusion written all over her face.

"One of our guys fight one of the Cobras every weekend," I inform her. Oh no, I thought she would've already known.

She turns to Hanger, throwing her hand on her hip." You've been holding out on me, Hanger?"

"No, babe. Just didn't think you should go."

"You're telling me that my boys have been going and fighting, and you didn't tell me?!"

"Um… yeah." He looks at me, evilly. "Thanks, Jacey."

Trying to hide my smile, I say, "Sorry Hanger. I thought she knew about them."

"Well, I'm going from now on," Zoey informs him.

"No, you're not," challenges Hanger.

"Oh, yes I am."

"We'll talk about this later. I think it's time to get the girls home."

When they leave, Bear asks, "So, what did you do today? Your hair looks real pretty."

"Thanks. We went to lunch, got our hair and nails done…Igotatattooitwasalotoffun." I rush out the last part, not taking a breath.

"Slow down and back up. You got a what?"

"Igotatattoo," I rush it out again.

"I said slow down, Lil Mama." He gets up, coming over to me.

Huffing out a breath and putting my hand on my hip, I repeat, "I got a tattoo."

"You got a tattoo?" he questions, cocking an eyebrow.

"Yes. I went to Daphne's shop and got a tattoo."

"Well, what did you get?"

I slowly lift up my shirt, teasing him. I can tell by the look on his face, he's growing impatient. I get my shirt the rest of the way off and start to pull the bandage, but he grabs my wrist stopping me.

"Let me do it," he says, dropping down to face level with it. When he gets the bandage off, he looks at it, eyes going big, and then he looks up at me with shining eyes.

"Is that a..." I see the happiness and love in his eyes. It's a little overwhelming, so I interrupt him.

"Yeah, I got it for you." I smile and he leans in, kissing all around the tattoo but making sure never to touch it.

"I love it. I can't believe you got a bear claw ripping through your ribs. It even shows a piece of the heart where it ripped through, and you got a smaller one for Cub. She did a fuckin' amazing job."

"You did that though, you know. You ripped your way through to my heart. I love you."

"I love you too, Lil Mama."

"You know, I've been thinking. I love being a mom and I want to do something where I could have Cub with me."

"What would that be?"

"I want to buy a building and turn it into a recording studio. I want to find bands, get them to work with me. I took college courses, so I know how to run all the equipment, and you already know I know how to run a business."

"That's great, Lil Mama. I think you'd be a lot happier. I know how much you love music."

"Yeah, I'm really excited. Will you go with me to find the building?"

"Of course, we'll go next week. You can start calling realtors."

"Sounds good."

We've been looking at buildings all week and I haven't found one that I like yet. They're either too small, not in the right neighborhood, or run down. We pull up to the last one I'm scheduled to look at. The whole outside is brick, connecting with other buildings. There are a couple windows on the outside, but they're tinted so you can't see in. It's in a great part of town, with a lot of shops and restaurants around. The realtor takes us in and the front has a desk and enough room to fit some furniture. The walls are white, which is great, I can do what I want with them. Walking down the hall, there are a couple of offices and a bathroom.

"What's that door for?" I ask, confused because it doesn't look very big and every other building was all on one level.

"This is the reason I chose this building for you. I think you're going to love it," the realtor says. I turn, looking at Bear, and he just gives a shrug of his shoulders. She opens the door and it leads to a set of stairs going down. The whole way, I'm thinking about what he'll I'm getting myself into, until we hit the bottom stair. We walk into the main part of the basement and it's a great size. I would have enough room to fit all the equipment I need, plus furniture, and still have enough room leftover. There's a door which leads to another big room. I could tear down the wall and put glass up, and the bands could practice in here and record. It's great. There's a third room that's a little smaller, but not much, and this would make the perfect playroom for Cub. Smiling at Bear, he gives me a nod. I look at the realtor. "I'll take it."

"Great. I'll get the contracts made up. Do you have your financing ready."

"Oh, I don't need financing. I'll write you a check for the amount." She nods her head, shock pasted on her face. "Have the contracts made up by the end of today. We need to get this going now," I tell her.

"Sure thing, Mrs. Rhodes." Bear smirks at that. "I'll work on it as soon as I get back to the office and give you a call when they are ready to be signed."

"Sounds good. I'll talk to you soon."

We all walk up the stairs and outside.

"Bear, this place is amazing."

"Sure is, Mrs. Rhodes."

"Oh you got jokes, do you?"

"Her face was kinda priceless, when you said no financing."

"It was, wasn't it?" I chuckle as he grabs me around the waist, pulling me to him.

"I really liked hearing the Mrs. Rhodes part though, that's kinda sexy."

"You think so?"

He leans in, catching my neck. "Uh huh." While he sucks in my skin, I tilt my head, giving him better access.

"Well Mr. Rhodes, I think it's time you get me home before we get arrested for indecent exposer." He pulls away laughing. Later that night, after my dad brings Cub back, Bear wants to talk.

"So have you thought more about getting off you birth control?"

Crooking my eyebrow at him, I tell him, "Well, I thought about it, and I stopped taking it ahile ago."

"You did?" A smile forming on his face.

"Well yeah, I mean, at first I didn't think I was ready for another baby, but I am. I want you to be able to experience everything you missed out on with Cub. I didn't tell you because I didn't want it to feel like a job, trying to get pregnant."

"Shit Lil Mama, I love you. So all the fuckin' we do, you could be pregnant now?"

"Well it hasn't happened yet, but yeah, anytime."

Later that night, after Cub's in bed, Bear goes in for round number two. Maybe I should've told him sooner, because round two turned into rounds three and four.

SEVENTEEN

Bear

The weather is turning cold again, and soon I'll be parking my bike because of the snow and ice. As much as I love my truck and the memories of my dad, on my bike, I feel free. Kansas weather is so goddamn unpredictable though, I might get some days where it's warmer so I can still take her for a ride. I wanted to do something special for my Ol' Lady, so I've made some food and brought a blanket out to the dock. Cub's with Snake and Victoria for the day, visiting Ava and Harper. It's not often where it's just the two of us, so I use that time wisely when we get it. "Lil Mama, c'mon!" I yell from the living room. "Just a second!" I wait for her to come out of the bedroom, and when she does, she has her hands behind her back. "What you got?" She gives me that beautiful smile while pulling something from behind her back. "The fuck is that?"

"Bear, it's called a pregnancy test."

"What's it say?" I feel my heart go into my throat.

"It says you're going to be a daddy again."

"Don't fuck with me woman," I tell her, feeling the lump in my throat.

"I'm not. Look, it says pregnant." She holds it out for me to take from her and sure enough, it says pregnant. I grab her, spinning her around in my arms. "Stop Bear! You have to stop or I'm going to puke on you." That stops me and I put her back on her feet. I grab her face with my hands, cupping her cheeks, seeing her eyes match mine with the evidence of unshed tears. "I'm so fuckin' happy! I'm gonna be a daddy again! I love you, so fuckin' much."

"I love you so fucking much too," she says, laughing at me. Moving in, I take her mouth with mine. Opening for me, I slide my tongue along hers, moving my hands down her body. I bend at the knees, gripping her thighs, pulling her up with me. Her legs lock around my waist as I carry her to our bedroom. "I'm assuming it's fine, because we were fuckin' when you were pregnant with Cub."

"Oh yeah, it's totally fine." She smiles against my lips. I slam the bedroom door shut with my foot, and walking over to the dresser, I grab the iPod, turning on Far's cover of *Pony*, making sure to put it on repeat before I walk to the bed, laying her down. I grab her vibrator out of the nightstand. "Clothes off now," I command her. She no longer questions my actions, she just submits and does what I tell her to do, knowing she'll reap the rewards. I remove my clothes as well, and give her the vibrator as I sit on my knees on the edge of the bed. "Turn it on, Lil Mama." She does.

"Now, touch yourself with it." As soon as it touches her clit, her mouth drops open, head going back. "Put it inside you, fuck yourself with it." I grip my cock with my hand, moving up and down matching her rhythm. "Bring it back out and put it on your clit."

"Fuck, Bear." Her words causing me to move my hand faster as I stroke myself. "Look at me. You see what you do to me?"

"God Bear, that's so fucking hot."

"Are you gonna cum for me?"

"Yes."

"Good girl, I need you to cum now. I need inside." She finds the right spot and she shoots off like a fucking rocket. Not giving her time to recover, I crawl up her body, lineup and push inside. "Fuck me, you're so goddamn wet," I say as I pump into her sweet cunt.

"Right there, don't fucking stop! I'm gonna cum again!" Making sure to hit her g-spot with every stroke, she cums quickly, screaming out my name as she rakes her nails down my back. Leaning down, putting my face into the crook of her neck, I roll my hips into her. Pumping harder and faster into her, I growl out her name as I release, sending her into another orgasm. I roll to the side so I don't hurt her, bringing her with me. "The food's probably not any good by now."

"What food?"

"I took some food and a blanket out to the dock."

"Bear," she whispers. "Let's go out there now." Getting up and dressed, she goes into the kitchen and when I get out there, she has made some sandwiches. "We can take these."

"Okay," I chuckle.

We get sat down, looking out at the water, it's so peaceful here. I see headlights out by the other pond, which is weird because you hardly ever see anybody out here. "It's really beautiful," she says.

"Yeah, it is." I put my arm around her as she lays her head on my shoulder.

"You know how I've been learning how to sign? I think you should too, for Writer."

"Yeah, I talked with Hanger a little bit about it. I think the next time you go to see Crazy Girl, I'll go too."

"Okay, I'll let her know." After that, I lay my woman down and show her again how happy I am that she's pregnant.

It's been an up and down year, and today my boy turned one. He's started taking a few steps and he says a few words, Dada being his first, which made my heart swell. We decided to do his birthday at the clubhouse, it's too cold for us to have the kids outside. We made it family friendly so no hang-arounds or whores allowed here today. We grilled out and did the whole cake and presents thing. Kellen got a lot of toy bikes, and his own little cut with Cub stitched in. He also got a lot of clothes, toys, and stuffed bears. The Cobras joined us. You don't see Snake too much without Victoria by his side. I see that fucker Crawler standing in a corner. I still don't like the guy. I grab a beer from the bar and see Writer sitting there. I've been learning to sign so I tap him on the shoulder. He looks up at me and gestures with his hands for the pen and paper, but I shake my head no.

He looks confused until I sign, *What's up brother?*

When the fuck you learn to sign?

Haven't been doing it long, still a little slow.

She's going to leave me and I don't know how to handle it.

Who? He just confused the fuck outta me

Ever. Who else would I be fucking talking about?

I'm not understanding. The fuck you mean, she's leaving you?

She's going to New York. She says she hasn't made up her mind yet, but she has. I know it, I know her.

Why would she leave?

She got a job offer, doesn't want to stick around here. She says it's a once in a lifetime opportunity. She asked me to go.

Shit brother. What did you tell her?

The only thing I could, that I can't go. I can't leave the only family I've ever had. I can't leave the club. What the fuck would I do in New York?

Man I'm sorry I don't know what to say.

There isn't anything to say, she's going to go. She's going to leave me, brother.

I see his eyes glass over as he pushes away from his seat and walks away.

I walk up to Jacey. "Did you know Ever's leaving?" I feel angry for my brother.

"She mentioned she got a job offer. She never said if she was for sure leaving."

"She is. Writer's sure of it," I inform her.

"Oh fuck, how's he dealing with it?" she asks, and I can tell she's feeling the same as I do about it right now.

"Not good. It's gonna kill him when she's gone."

"I know. We just have to be there for him."

Responding, I tell her, "Yeah well, us learnin' to sign is good. It's two more people he's got. He's gonna need all of us to get through this shit."

"Yeah," she replies. This is gonna hurt all of us. Writer's a good dude and a great brother. I wrap my arms around Jacey, giving her a kiss on the top of her head.

Two week later, Ever's officially gone. He was right, he knew his woman. Writer's a fucking mess, and I think the good part of him left with her. He's hurting bad, he doesn't give a shit about anything anymore. He's drinking all the time and doing any drug he can get his hands on. He stays in his room most of the time, but I don't think it'll be long before the anger sets in. When it does, we all need to be prepared for the shit show of a disaster that'll be. Christ, I don't know why she'd leave him like that, they were so fucking happy.

Writer wanted to get into the next fight and I think it might do him some good to get the aggression out. Hanger's been helping him get ready, so tonight's the night Crazy Girl's parents are watching all the kids. That's right, she talked Hanger into letting her go, but I think it's more about Writer than anything else. Crazy Girl and Writer have some kinda special bond after she taught him how to sign. She's been torn up seeing him like he's been, and now he's gonna go in there and fight.

I walk into the cabin to pick Lil Mama up and sitting on my goddamn counter is a dozen red roses. The fuck?

"Lil Mama?" I say, as I walk into the bathroom to see what the fuck she's doing. I'm fucking paranoid now.

Why the fuck would she be getting some flowers?

I see her, and she's looking sexy as fuck. She's not showing that much yet, but I can't wait to really see our baby growing inside of her. She's went up a couple of sizes in her jeans, but she still wears the same tops she always has. Tonight, she has on a Sinner's tank with her cut and a pair of tight fitting blue jeans, paired with black boots. Jacey comes up, wrapping her arms around me.

"Thank you so much for the flowers, they're beautiful!" I grip her wrists, pulling away from her. I can see the hurt in her eyes, especially when I tell her that they weren't from me.

"What do you mean you didn't get them?"

"Just what I said. I didn't fuckin' get 'em."

"Well where did they come from then?"

"You tell me."

"I don't know! The card says *I love you, from Bear.*"

"Where's it at?"

"Right here," she says as she goes and gets it.

I look at it and it, and sure as shit, it says they're from me, but I didn't write that or get the flowers.

"That's not my writing."

"I just thought you had somebody at the flower shop write it for you."

"Have you gotten anything else?"

"Yeah, I got this box of chocolates and a bear."

"I'm throwin' it all in the trash. I'll let the guys know, and figure out who sent it. Did you eat any?"

"I haven't opened it," she says, while handing over the other shit.

"Yeah, that's fucking scary. Is it time to go?"

"Yeah."

I walk out, throw the shit in the trash, then we load Cub up in the car and drop him off at Sophia and Grant's. When we get to the Cobras clubhouse, I keep Lil Mama with me at all times. I find Hanger, letting him know we need to have a church meeting tomorrow.

Next, I find Snake and tell him to be at our clubhouse for church. I can tell Jacey's scared, she's looking over her shoulder constantly. I place my bet with Deuce and hope I win this one, my money's on Writer. There's a lot of hang-arounds tonight, so the bet was higher. Three Gs higher. We meet back up with Hanger and Crazy Girl in the front of the circle.

Once again, I stand behind Lil Mama and wrap her up in my arms. Hanger has Crazy Girl the same way, but she can't seem to stand still.

QUIET COUNTRY

Our brother is going against Crawler, and the Cobras wanna win this fight. When they're both in the circle, it gets worse with Crazy Girl.

You can hear her screaming, "Get him, Writer! Knock him out! You better get his fucking ass, Writer!" while throwing her arms around like she's punching. I look to Hanger and he's just shaking his head, then the three of us bust out laughing at her.

Lil Mama asks, "Why you screaming?"

"It's just so exciting! I can't believe he didn't let me know about this!" she answers as she points her thumb over her shoulder to Hanger. That makes everybody laugh again.

Snake gives the rules, steps back and the fight is on. Writer watches Crawler, taking his time. He steps in and throws a jab. Crawler drops his hands just a little, but Writer sees it, throwing a leg kick to the head. Oh fuck, he knocked Crawler out. He jumps on him, throwing two more punches to the head before they pull him off. Goddamn, that was a fast fight. I guess he wasn't fucking around and needed to get some aggression out. I collect my money from Deuce, ready to get the fuck outta here.

"Do you wanna go home or hang for a bit?" I ask, hoping she'll wanna leave.

"After what happened earlier, I want to go home." I give her a nod and we head back, picking up Cub on the way.

Lying in bed she asks, "How does somebody know where we live?"

"I don't know baby, but I'm gonna find out. I won't let anything happen to either of you, I promise."

"I know you won't. I just don't feel safe being here by myself."

"You won't be. You come with me to the club tomorrow and then you'll have a prospect with you at all times."

"Okay." I run my fingers through her hair, hoping she'll be able to sleep.

The next day, we're in church, with Snake here, and Hanger calls the meeting. *"Alright Bear, what's going on?"*

"Somebody's fuckin' with Lil Mama and we gotta find out who."

"The fuck you mean?" Snake asks angrily.

"Somebody is stalking her. They know where we live. They sent her flowers, candy, and a stuffed animal for Christ's sake," I tell them.

"When I come here, I'm bringin' her with me and if I can't be with her, I want a prospect with her."

"*You got it. Hunter, you start trying to find out who's doing it. Pretty Boy, I want you with her if Bear's not.*"

"No problem. I'll keep her safe," he tells me.

"I know you will."

"I'll come over more often too, and I'll put one of my guys on her as well," Snake adds.

"Yeah, sounds good. She's pretty freaked right now."

The meeting is called and I head back out to the bar. "Is everything okay?" she asks.

"Yeah, it's settled. You'll be safe." She nods, grabbing for me. I wrap her into my arms, kissing the top of her forehead. I hope to hell I can keep my promise.

Over the last month, it's been busy, between always making sure Lil Mama's safe and all of the Sinners working on remodeling her building. Hanger has called church, so we're all gathered, waiting for the meeting to be called.

"*Brothers, it's been a month since the stalking issues with Lil Mama. What new information do we have?*"

"It's still happening. She receives cards, letters, anything really that can be sent through the mail," I tell inform them.

"The person is smart. Nothing's hand delivered anymore, and she's scared all the time. She doesn't feel safe at home anymore, even with the prospects on her. I was thinking she should come stay here with Cub."

"*Yeah that might be best until we know something.*"

"The mail never has return addresses, and everything's typed. There's no way to check the handwriting," Hacker adds. "I haven't seen anybody watchin' her, no cages drive by the house, and no one follows when she goes anywhere."

"*Okay, have them come here to stay, see if it continues. If not, see what happens when she goes back home.*"

"Sounds good. I'll get 'em packed up," I tell him.

"*How's the remodeling on the building coming?*"

"It's good, we're just waiting for some shipments, then it'll be ready," Bam Bam answers.

"*Good. Okay, so if nothing else, meeting's over. Let's get the fuck outta here.*"

QUIET COUNTRY

We've been staying at the club for a month and the day they came here, everything stopped, no more mail. There's no cards, letters, nothing. This shows me that someone was watching her, even if Pretty Boy couldn't see anybody, they were there. They knew I was moving her to the club. If my brothers hadn't seen the shit being sent, they'd probably think I had lost my fucking mind.

It's time for us to go back home. I love the club and my brothers, but it's not a place for babies to live. She's getting bigger every day, looking sexier with her growing belly. I try doing shit for her, like rubbing her feet or massaging her back. When she gets cravings in the middle of the night, I make a trip to the store, getting her what she wants. Thank fuck the pucking stopped, it was pretty fucking disgusting, having to hold her hair and rub her back while her head was in the toilet.

She's tired all the time, but I think that has something to do with the parties. When they're in full swing, Lil Mama has to stay in the bedroom with Cub, and it's loud so he doesn't get a lot of sleep. She's angry all the time, tired and sleepy. It's taking a toll on us and she misses being at our home. Karma stays in the bedroom and she's starting to feel cooped up too, unless she goes outside. That's when she can run free.

As soon as we walk into the cabin, returning home, the smile returns. "I'm sorry for the way I've been lately." I walk up, putting my arms around her.

"I understand, baby. You're home now. Things will go back to normal. Everything stopped, so let's continue to hope that nothing else'll happen."

"Yeah, but if anything else does happen, I'm going to Hanger and Zoey's. I love the guys, but they drove me crazy."

"Sounds good," I say, laughing. "They aren't used to babies bein' around."

"I know, that's why I can't hold it against them," she tells me, smiling. "I'm pregnant, so don't hold it against me for the way I acted either."

"I won't, don't worry about it."

Just a few days after Jacey got home, everything started back up. She started receiving the letters and cards again, and a week later, she received some panties with a letter saying they would like to see her in them. I'm getting real tired of the shit, I'm about to lose it. This person has to fuck up soon so we can get something on time.

Her four month check up went great, and she's seeing Dr. Greene again, as is Zoey. I can't describe the feeling I get when I hear my baby's heartbeat inside of the woman I adore, but any resentment I had left from missing out on Cub is gone now. I swear, hearing the heartbeat and the first cry is the best goddamn feeling in this entire fucking world. Dr. Greene says next month will be the visit when we find out what we're having. Lil Mama keeps asking what I want, but it doesn't matter to me, as long as the baby is healthy. Secretly though, I'll be nervous as fuck if it's a girl.

The building finally got done and it's fucking amazing. We haven't let Jacey see it yet. She told us what her vision was for it and it's to the fucking T of what she wanted. It's perfect. We worked hard to get everything right and I can't wait for her to see it.

EIGHTEEN

Jacey

I've been home for a couple weeks and the shit started right back up. The cards and letters in the mail came back within a few days. It's escalated to lingerie and boxes of stuff being delivered. Pretty Boy's always here, but my dad sends different guys. They have made sure that they receive the mail, then show it to Bear. He shows me what comes, but doesn't talk much about what's happening. I'm trying not to let it bother me. I've realized I can't put my life on hold because of this. Bear doesn't let me do anything alone so now, even if I go out onto the deck, I have someone with me.

Today, Bear's taking me to see the building. This'll be the first time I've seen it since I bought it and the guys started remodeling. We pull up and everything looks the same, except for the window decal saying J.R. Recordings. Walking in the front door, all the walls are painted in a deep red, the trim black. There are black leather couches and chairs with glass tables. The old brown desk has been replaced with a new black shiny one, a computer sitting on top of it. This is amazing! There's one thing I didn't ask for, and I love it.

"Bear, who did those framed drawings?"

"Writer." I look at him with a mixture of confusion and pride. Writer has changed so much, and not for the better. Just like we all thought, it killed him when Ever left, and he's been in a downward spiral since. He doesn't give a shit about himself. I don't know if we'll ever get the old Writer back, although we all hope we will. For him to be a part of something and it be for me is awesome, the drawings are amazing. I didn't even know he had talent like that. They take up most of the wall behind the couch. Writer has made one that says family, that's placed in the middle, and surrounding it are portraits of all of us: Cub, Ava and Harper, Zoey, Ever, all the guys, and me. They're truly incredible and I've never seen anything like it. On the wall behind the desk he has made a big drawing the reads J.R. Recordings done beautifully in black, red, and white.

We walk into the offices, which are decorated like the front lobby.

Opening the door for downstairs, we walk down the steps. I cover my mouth, tears forming in my eyes as I look around. "Oh Bear!"

"C'mere, Lil Mama," he instructs as he pulls me to him, circling me in with one arm, holding Cub in the other.

"This is amazing!"

"I want you to have all your dreams come true," he tells me, kissing the top of my head. "This is a good start."

"My dreams started coming true when I got you and Cub." I look up at him and he smiles down at me.

The walls are done in a light grey color, sticking with the black trim and black furniture, and they have the table set up with all the recording equipment. The walls have been tore down, replaced with half walls. The second room's set up with all the guitars, mics, drums sets, and everything else the bands will need. Glass separates that room from the rest, and the third room also has the wall tore down. They have a half wall put up with half a door, so I can see Cub when he's playing, and they've filled the room with toys for him.

"We made sure to sound proof the room the band'll be in so it won't be loud out here," he tells me.

"God, Bear, this is more than I could've imagined. You guys did an amazing job."

"Thanks, Lil Mama. I'm glad you like it."

"Like it? I fucking love it."

"Now you just gotta find your first band."

"Yeah speaking of, we need to go to Insanity this Friday night."

"Why?"

"They have an open mic night and there's this band playing. I checked them out on the computer and they'e amazing. I want them."

"Okay, sounds good."

Friday night, we walk into Insanity, it's calmed down a lot since the first and only night we came here. Everyone is sitting at tables, listening to the band performing on stage. We take our seats in the middle of the room. The band is good, but not who I'm here to see. They finish up their set and walk off the stage as some other guy walks up.

"Are you guys ready for The Betrayed?" Everyone claps around us.

"That's not good enough! I said are you ready for The Betrayed?" That gets the audience hyped up as they clap louder, shouting and screaming out.

"That's more like it! Welcome The Betrayed!" He walks off the stage as the band comes on.

The first song of the set has a haunting beat, and when the lead singer comes in, I'm amazed. This band plays rock music, but the singer has such a soulful voice, blending perfectly with the guitars.

"Is this the band?" Bear asks.

"Yeah." I respond, not taking my eyes off the stage.

"They're fuckin' amazing!"

"I know." Once the set is almost over, I look to Bear. "You stay here. I'm going up there."

"You stay where I can see you."

"I will." I walk up to the stage right as the song ends. The lead singer looks down at me, giving me a cocky smile. He walks away from the mic, bending down in front of me. He's a good looking guy, just like the rest of the band. The lead singer has long brown hair with facial hair to match, and muscled arms with tattoos going from his wrist up to his elbow on his left arm. He looks to be about my age, maybe a few years younger. "What can I do for you, beautiful?"

Chuckling, I say, "I love your band."

"Oh yeah? You wanna come in the back? I can show you something else you would love." He's got a cocky ass attitude to match the smile.

"I'm a married woman."

"That's fine, I'll show you what your husband is lacking."

"Oh honey, you see that guy over there?" pointing over to Bear, standing with his arms crossed. "That would be my husband and I don't think he's lacking in anything." Smiling, I turn back to the lead singer. I see him swallow hard, the smile's left his face.

"I'm sorry, most women come up here looking for something else."

"Yeah, well I'm not most women."

"What did you come up here for then?"

Handing him my card, I answer, "If you're interested, come see me at the table. I'll be here for a little while longer." He takes the card from my hand and I turn, walking away. I get back and sit down.

"What'd he say?"

"Well, he's a big flirt, but I gave him the card, so now we wait."

Twenty minutes later, the four guys come over. "Why don't you guys have a seat?"

"How about we stand and you tell us what's going on?"

"I believe my Ol' Lady said sit. You flirt with her again, I'll make it to where you won't have a voice to use anymore. Got me?" Bear chimes in. They all grab chairs.

"Sorry about him. That's my husband, Bear. He's a little over protective, if you can't tell. I came here because I love your band and I want to sign you."

"The card says J.R. Who's that?"

"That's me, Jacey Rhodes," I tell them, sticking out my hand. "Nice to meet you guys."

"I'm Dawson, the lead singer. This is Elijah, he's on guitar. Rico, he's bass, and Colton on drums." Dawson says, each one shaking my hand.

"Why should we sign with you? How many bands do you have?"

"Well, I have a passion for music, and you'll actually be my first band. I believe in you guys, love your sound. Within a year, we could have your album done and a tour set up, and you'll get a nice bonus for signing on. I have degrees in business and music. I used to be a doctor and ran my own clinic, so I know what the fuck I'm doing. If you sign with me, I promise you won't regret it, but if you don't, I can guaren-fuckin-tee you won't find anyone as good as me."

"How much?" Dawson asks.

"Why don't you guys think about it? Give me a call and we can discuss numbers."

"Alright, we'll talk about it."

That following Monday, I got the call I had been waiting for and met with The Betrayed. We decided on a number, and everything is set, ready to go. The only thing they have to do is get a manager.

Today I have Pretty Boy and for some reason, my dad sent Crawler, which I'm not too happy about. There's a knock at the door, and putting Cub down, I run to answer it, not even thinking about checking the peephole. I turn the alarm off and throw the door open. I'm greeted by Crawler, holding a gun to my face.

"What are you doing?" I ask, trying to keep the calm in my voice.

"It's time for you to come with me."

"Where's Pretty Boy?"

"Oh he's out there, knocked out, I asked him nicely to take a break, but he refused. How else was I gonna get to you?" I make a run for it, going back into the living room, grabbing Cub. Before I can get to my room, he's there, grabbing the back of my hair and pulling me down.

Karma is growling, but hasn't done anything until I say the magic word, attack. I land on my back with Cub still in my arms, he's screaming now. Karma latches onto Crawler's leg, shaking it like it's one of her toys. He screams out from the pain. I cover Cub's ears as he lifts his gun, firing it. I scream and sit up, wrapping Cub tighter into my arms, trying to comfort him and trying to get up off the floor. Karma yelps out as the bullet hits her and she falls over.

"Jacey, I don't want to hurt you. You need to come willingly so I don't have to."

"Please Crawler, just leave us alone."

"I can't do that. It's time to go now." He pulls me up by my shirt, walking me to the door with the gun at the back of my head. Once we're outside, I can see Pretty Boy laying there at the bottom of the steps, bleeding. I've got to step over him on the way to the car. When he shuts us in the backseat, and before he gets in front, I try the handle, but he has the goddamn child safety locks on. Then we're driving away.

He drives about fifteen minutes and pulls into a rundown house. It makes me sick to know I'm this close to home, and so was he this whole time. The house is small with dirty white paint that's peeling off. Crawler gets me out of the car and I'm still clutching Cub to my chest, who's calmed down some since the ride. He takes us into the house, with old creaking floors and cobwebs covering the walls. The wallpaper's peeling off just like the paint was, and it's bare, no furniture or anything, so I know he doesn't live here. He opens the first door on the left. It's a bedroom, empty except for a ratty mattress on the floor. He takes me over, sitting me down on it.

"What do you need for him?"

"Why are you doing this?"

"I'll explain everything later. What do you need for him?"

"Diapers, milk, wipes, clothes, and a sippy cup."

He pulls out his phone, calling someone and telling them to bring him a list of things.

"When they get here, if you make a noise or try to run, I'll kill you both," he says as he shuts the door. I think I hear a lock click behind him, but I'm not sure so I get up and turn the knob.

Of course, it's locked. I look around the room, trying to see if there's anything I can use to get us out of here. The windows are boarded up. I see another door so I go over and open it. It's a closet and it's completely empty. I go sit back down and feel something in my pocket. I forgot I have my phone, pulling it out to check for service. Nothing, no service at all. Throwing it down, I sit holding my son, trying to come up with a plan to get us out of here alive.

I've tried not looking at my phone to save on the battery. I don't know how long we've been kept in here, I'm guessing at least a couple of hours. Hearing the door start to open, I scurry to get my phone under my ass. I make it just as the door fully opens, and Crawler comes in, shutting it behind him. He has food for me and all the things I needed for Cub.

"Here. Eat. I got one of these things for him," he says as he tilts his chin towards Cub, sippy cup in hand.

"You're the one that sent me all that stuff?"

"Well yeah. Didn't you like it?"

"No. How did you find out where I lived?"

"I followed you the night of the fight. Of course, I stayed back far enough so Bear wouldn't notice, but I had to make sure you got home safely."

"Are you crazy?"

"No. He doesn't really love you not like me. He won't come for you he'll just move on forget all about you."

"Why are you doing this?"

"Because Jacey, you were always mine."

"What the hell are you talking about?"

"Do you remember we used to play together?"

"A little bit, not much." God, that was so long ago.

"Yeah, you were young, six when your momma took you away. I was older than you."

"You know Bear is going to find me and kill you," I tell him.

"I don't think so." Pacing the floor, he continues. "This was always the way it was supposed to be. You were the princess and I was the VP's son. We were destined to be together."

"You're fucking crazy!" I hear the familiar sound of Bear's motorcycle go by. It brings tears to my eyes, knowing he has no idea he just rode by us. "Can you leave me alone so I can eat and take care of my son?"

"Yeah, but just remember what I told you. I'll kill both of you if you try to leave."

"I know. I just want to be left alone."

When I hear the lock click on the door, I get an idea. I take the phone over to the window, lifting it up. I have one bar. Maybe I can send a text.

> **Jacey: Bear help 15 mins from home take the road u just went by house will b on left side old dirty white.**

I hit send and wait. Finally, right before my phone dies, it says the text was sent.

NINETEEN

Bear

When I left the house this morning, I had a bad feeling. I should've stayed my ass at home, but I didn't listen to it, deciding to go ahead and go to the garage to get some work done, just like I do everyday. I couldn't take it anymore, the feeling got worse and I had to leave early. I don't know what it is, just a feeling like something bad is going to happen, something's not right. I get to the clubhouse and everyone is there except Pretty Boy because he's with Jacey. Walking in, I see Hanger sitting at the bar. Pulling up a seat next to him I ask, "Hanger, can you call church?"

He looks over to me. "Why?"

"Something's not right, brother. I can feel it."

"With what?"

"I don't know man. I think with all this shit with Lil Mama."

He shouts over the music, "Guys, church now!"

Everyone walks down the hall to the chapel. Taking our seats, he calls the meeting. "Bear, what's going on?"

"I don't know. Do you guys have anything? Anything at all? I feel something's about to happen."

"Whoever it is knows what the fuck they're doing, Bear. We've done everything we can. I can't find shit all on this person," Hacker says.

"The fuck is going on?" I ask. "Do we have any ideas on who it could be?"

"None, that's the fucked part of it all."

"Could it be the stepdad?" Hanger asks.

"Not unless he has people watching her. I thought we handled that though." I get a call from Pretty Boy, and I know something's wrong now. "Yeah?" I talk into the phone.

"Brother, we got a problem."

"What?"

"It's Crawler. Snake sent him today. I didn't even see it coming when he knocked me out and took 'em."

"The fuck? You tellin' me he has my Ol' Lady and my boy?"

"Yeah man, I'm sorry."

I hang up the phone, looking at Hanger. "It's Crawler. He took her and Cub. I'm callin' Snake."

"Fuck. What reason would he have to do this?"

"I don't know, but come to think of it, he gave me a weird feeling when he first saw Jacey. She felt the same way." I dial Snake's number and his phone rings twice, then he answers. Before he can say anything, I tell him, "Crawler kidnapped Jacey and Cub."

"WHAT?" he yells into the phone. "No fuckin' way."

"I just got word that it's Crawler. Why did you send him and not a goddamn prospect?"

"I didn't send him. I sent Spike. I haven't seen him all day, so I assumed he was there."

"Pretty Boy said Crawler was sent by you. He knocked him out. He didn't even see it coming."

"You have any idea where they are?" he asks, his breathing deepening with his growing anger.

"Not yet, but when I find them, he's a dead man. Got me?"

"I'm on my way." He hangs up.

"I'm riding to the cabin to check things out. I'll keep you updated."

"I'll come with you," Doc says. We leave the clubhouse and ride to the cabin where I find Pretty Boy on the front porch. He's got a gash on his head, dried blood smeared everywhere.

"You might wanna have Doc look at that," I tell him as I go into the house. They are hot on my trail, and with the bond that Jacey and Doc have formed, I knew he wouldn't be sitting this one out.

"I'm sorry, Bear. He told me Snake sent him so I thought it was okay. He asked me to take a break, but I refused," Pretty Boy says. "He pulled his pistol and hit me, that's all I remember."

"Not your fault for gettin' knocked out." I turn my cold stare on him, telling him, "What is your fault, however, was not gettin' me on the phone when he pulled up. If anything happens to either of them, brother or not, I will kill you."

"I know. I wouldn't expect anything less." He drops his head. I know he feels guilty, but I'm too fucking pissed and worried to give two fucks about him right now.

I get to the hallway and laying there is Karma, bleeding. I get down, making sure she's still alive. She's hanging in there, but if I don't hurry, she'll be dead.

"Get a vet now!" I yell, not caring who does it.

I check the whole house, and nothing's missing or out of place.

There are drops of blood going from the hallway, out the door, and down the steps. I'm hoping it's his blood, that Karma got him before he shot her. Other than that, it just looks like she left without taking anything. The alarm didn't notify me, so she had to have opened the door. My phone beeps with a new text, and pulling it out, I see it's from Lil Mama. Thank fuck! She tells me where she's being kept at, and it's not far from here. She heard my bike go by. That son of a bitch didn't think this through very well.

Pulling my phone out again, I call Snake. "I'm almost there."

"I got a text from her. I know where she's at, meet me at that dirty old house that you pass on the way here."

"You got it." I hang up and text her back, letting her know I'm on my way. Getting the keys to my truck, I drive a little ways away from the house. The guys park their bikes behind my truck. We pull our guns just in case they're not alone. I don't want to give him reason to do anything to them, so we walk the rest of the way. I try to see in the windows on the porch, but they're all boarded up. Doc and Pretty Boy go around the house as I very softly step up onto the porch and knock on the front door. Sure enough, Crawler opens up. I push on the door, knocking him down with it.

"Where are they, you motherfucker?"

"Bear, what a surprise. I have no idea what you are talking about." He goes to get up, but I knock him back on his ass with my foot.

"Tell me where they are and I might consider letting you live." I hear Lil Mama scream from a door on the left.

"Are they in there?" I ask, pointing to the door.

"I don't know what you're talking about."

I throw a punch to his face. He spits blood and a tooth out onto the floor. Crawler looks up at me, smiling. I walk toward the door, turning the knob only to find it locked. I'm about to kick the door when I feel him at my back. He pulls at me then kicks his leg, sidesviping mine and making me fall to the ground. He throws a couple of his own punches, busting my lip. Doc and Pretty Boy come running into the house, getting him off of me.

I stand back up. "Let him go." They do as they're told. I take the steps to him, throwing another punch, making him stumble. I walk up and give him a couple more hits until he's back on the floor. I straddle his waist, putting all my strength in the hits. I hear someone tell me to stop, but I can't make out who it is.

Blood flies everywhere as another hit lands on his face. At one point he passed out, but I can't stop. I just keep hitting him over and over as I think about him trying to take my family from me. I won't let anyone take my family from me again. It's deathly quiet in here until my fist connects again, and I hear the cracking of the bones breaking in his face. Blood's everywhere and soon it feels like I'm hitting mush. Someone tries to get me off of him.

"Bear, he's dead. You killed him. That's enough." That's still not enough to get me off this scumbag.

"Bear, where are they? Where is my princess and Cub?"

Coming back to reality, I realize it's Snake. I gotta get them. I stand up, seeing the mess I created, and walk over to the door. "Lil Mama, get as far away from the door as you can!"

"Okay, I'm away from it!" she yells back, and as soon as I hear those words, I kick it open. Standing in a corner, back facing the door, is my Ol' Lady.

"Lil Mama," I say, so she knows that it's okay to turn around. When she does, she has Cub clutched to her chest.

"Bear?" she questions

"C'mere, Lil Mama." She runs over to me, putting Cub in one arm and throwing her free arm around me. I wrap them both up in my embrace, peppering kisses all over their faces. "Bear, are you okay?"

"I'm fine, it's not my blood," I reassure her. "Are you guys okay?"

"Yeah, he didn't hurt us. I'm so happy you found us! I love you. Is Karma okay?"

"I don't know, one of the guys has a vet comin' to get her. I got your text. I love you too. And I still think you need to have Dr. Greene check you out."

"Okay." She looks over my shoulder. "Dad, why did you send him?"

"I didn't, Princess, and now I have a missin' prospect. Do you know why he took you?"

"Yeah, but I'd really like to get out of here before I start talking about it."

"Let's go back to the clubhouse. We can talk about it and get the doctor to see you."

She then sees Doc and Pretty Boy, her eyes shine with unshed tears. "Pretty Boy, I'm so glad you're okay!"

"I'm so sorry, Lil Mama," he tells her.

"Hey, come here. It wasn't your fault." He walks over to her and she gives him a one arm hug. He's lucky he gets out of this one. I take Cub out of her arms.

"Doc, are you okay?" He runs up to her, grabbing her up in a tight hug.

"I'm so fuckin' glad you guys are okay!"

"Me too, Doc."

Cub is looking at me as he puts his hand on my face, saying Dada. My vision goes blurry as my eyes fill up with my own set of tears. If I would've lost them, I would've died myself.

"Yeah buddy, it's Dada," I tell him, seeing the smile form on his face.

Snake had a full gas can in the bed of his truck, so Pretty Boy dowsed the inside, along with Crawler's body and the front porch. I pulled out the lighter I still carry, and once ever one's outside, I light that bitch on fire and we stand there watching it burn.

We make it back to the clubhouse and she gives the doctor a call while I take a quick shower, getting all the blood off of me. I walk her down to the chapel where Snake and Hanger are waiting for us. I left Cub with Crazy Girl and the girls. We take seats at the table.

Snake starts, asking, "Why did he take you?"

"He was fucking crazy."

"Jacey, come on."

"What, Dad? He was." She cocks her eyebrow at him.

"He took me because he said it was where I belonged. I was the princess of your club and he was the VP's son. We were destined to be together. So, like I said, he was fucking crazy."

"Before you left, it was talked about, but not a minute afterward. I had no idea that he'd hold onto that, and I can't say what this is gonna do between the clubs."

"What do you mean? He kidnapped them, Snake!" Hanger chimes in.

"I know that, and I'm with you guys, but Bear killed my VP's son. He's not gonna take that lightly."

"I don't give two fucks! His son took my Ol' Lady and my boy! He fuckin' deserved to die," I tell him, my anger bubbling to the surface.

"I agree. I'll see what I can do, but I gotta go find my missin' prospect." He stands, walking over to Lil Mama, kissing the top of her head.

"I'd have killed him myself if he would of hurt either of you. I love you."

"I love you too, dad." We walk out, going to my room so she can lay down with Cub. I walk to the bar, waiting for the doctor when Romeo calls me from the gate to tell me that she's here. A few minutes later, she comes in with a machine, looking around the club, taking everything in. Her eyes stop on Hacker, all the color draining from her face. It's like she's seen a ghost. I look to Hacker and his eyes are huge, face red with anger.

"Dr. Greene?" I question, walking up to her. She jumps, completely off in her head.

"What?" She turns to me. "Oh right, Bear. Where's Jacey?" she asks.

"She's this way." I start leading her to the room. "Are you okay?"

"Yeah, I'm fine just a little jumpy, is all," she responds.

I hear Hacker shout, "WHAT THE FUCK IS SHE DOING HERE?" I look over and see that Dr. Greene has stopped, her eyes closed, breathing heavy.

"Hey, is there somethin' I should know about?" I ask her.

"No, it's fine," she answers, recovering. "I'm just not his favorite person."

We get to the room pushing the door open. "Lil Mama?"

"Hmm?"

"Dr. Greene's here."

She rolls to the side. "Hey Sierra. How are you?"

"I'm good, worried about you though. What's going on?"

"I had an accident, and Bear just wants to make sure that everything's good with the baby."

"Okay, let's find out. I brought a sonogram machine with me so you can see the baby. I believe you're close enough to find out what you are having, too."

As she sets up the machine, I grab Cub, putting him in the play pen we have setup. I go sit on the edge of the bed, taking Lil Mama's hand. The machine is ready to go, and her shirt's pulled up, pants pulled down a little bit. Dr. Greene puts the gel on her stomach and places the wand on the gel, moving it around. "Bear, can you go turn the light off?"

"Yeah." I turn the light off, and look at the screen, seeing our baby.

"The heartbeat looks great, everything looks normal. Here's the head, legs, and arms," she says as she points to each of them.

"Do you want to find out the sex?" I look over and Lil Mama's looking at me. We nod at the same time, smiling and looking back at the doctor. "Okay, it looks like she's being cooperative. Congratulations!"

"It's a girl? We're having a fuckin' girl?" I ask. I start sweating, nerves kicking in.

"Yep, you sure are."

"Lil Mama, we're having a fuckin' girl!"

Laughing, she says, "Yeah Bear, I know, I heard her."

"So everything is good with her and the baby?"

Dr. Greene confirms, "Yes everything's great."

"Thank you so much, Doctor."

"Bear, please call me Sierra."

Smiling, I say, "Okay, Sierra."

Turning to Lil Mama, "I'm gonna walk her out, I'll be right back." She nods and I give her a kiss before walking out. We leave the room, heading back into the bar. Hacker's gone so she gets to leave with no problems. I go back to the room, asking if Jacey if she's ready to go home.

Later that night after Cub is in bed, I lay down next to her. "Bear, did you call the vet? How's Karma doing?"

"She's fine, baby. Don't work about her, she's a tough little shit. So were you, babe. I was so fuckin' scared today. I've only ever been scared one time, until the moment I thought I'd never see the two of you again," I tell her.

"I know. I was scared too. He said he wouldn't hurt me unless I tried to run, but I didn't trust that," she says.

"Yeah. You don't know how fuckin' happy I was to get your text."

"I didn't even know for sure if you got it. It said sent, but then my phone died."

"Enough about all of that bad shit. So, we're having a girl. How do you feel about it?" I ask.

"I'm so happy! I promise I won't fuck her or Cub up like my mom did me."

"Baby, I know you won't. You're an amazing mom, definitely not like your cunt of a mother. You love Cub so much and you will our daughter too."

"I love you too, you know?" she says, smiling,

"Oh, I know, and I'm about to show you just how much I love you."

"Oh really?" she questions as she tilts her neck so I can nuzzle in it.

Uh huh is the last thing I said until I pushed inside of her bringing myself home. I made love to her for the first time, slowly, passionately, never rushing or picking up speed, telling each other how much we loved one another until we came together, calling out each other's names. Every single time is incredible and amazing with my Ol' Lady, but tonight, what we shared between the two of us is something I never thought I would get to experience. I started my life in the Sinners hating life, love, just about everything, but in the end, I have what my parents always had, a love I'll never find twice. I have a life full of love with my club family and this woman. I have just about everything I could ever want or need, and it'll be complete when my little girl gets here. I fought hard to get what I wanted and this moment right here made every single second of it worth fighting for.

EPILOGUE

Jacey

6 months later

I went back to work in the studio a couple of weeks after the kidnapping. The Betrayed got their manager, which Dawson doesn't look happy about. He's dealing with it though and they're amazing, just like I knew they would be, and soon the world will know it. I had to take some time off when I had Kelcey. Bear kept an eye on the studio for me, making sure everyone was working. I had to show him how to work the equipment and the guys knew a little as well, so that helped.

When Bear held our beautiful daughter in his arms for the first time, he had the same look when we had Cub, face full of wonder and pride, but this time he let the tears fall. The only other time I've ever seen tears from him was when Ripper died.

Bear had a surprise for me, too, and let me tell you, I have the absolute best husband ever. Do you remember that argument we had about the Prince Albert? Well, he went way beyond that! Since I couldn't have sex for six weeks, he went and got the Jacob's Ladder piercing. As soon as my six weeks were up, I was on him, finding out what all the fuss is about. Holy shit, I thought his cock felt good inside me before, but feeling those piercings going in and out of me at the same time as his massive cock took me to a whole new level of ecstasy.

I think over the last two years about how far we've come. In our family, that's including the guys at the club, we've lost some and gained some. There have been weddings and babies, deaths and funerals. People finding love and losing it, some getting a second chance with their first.

Speaking of which, my dad and Victoria got married after the first day of seeing each other. They were inseparable, so it's not really a surprise. They loved each other all that time and because of a misunderstanding, plus my bitch of a mother, they couldn't be together. It was a beautiful ceremony in the back of the Cobras' clubhouse, and both clubs got along great. Crazy Girl and I helped decorate everything, and of course, we were the bridesmaids.

Ava and Harper were the flower girls and Cub was the ring bearer. Hanger walked her down the aisle, giving her away to my dad. It was perfect, really, and now they're both so happy. I love her and she's great with the kids. I think Hanger has gotten over all of his issues with her, thanks to Zoey. She was elated when they got married because it meant Hanger and I are step brother and sister, making her my sister in law, which didn't feel new. She was really like a sister to me anyway, and this just made it official.

Not too long after the wedding, my father was shot again. It was worse this time, he lost so much blood and ended up needing a transfusion, so everyone got their blood checked and one of us was a match. I've asked what happened, but all I ever hear is that it's club business.

Hanger and Zoey had a little boy named Damien, and soon they'll be getting married. I think she keeps holding off, hoping Chatty and Ever will come back. Ever is really busy in New York, so who knows? I haven't talked to Chatty, but from what Zoey says, she has no plans of coming back. All of us miss both of them, and Gunner too.

Bear and I have had a lot of ups and down in our journey, but we made it. We fought, we loved, and we won in the end. Through it all, I found out I never really wanted to be a doctor. My whole plan went to shit, but I found a new one, a better one, One where I decide what happens in my life and one that has made me happier than I ever thought possible.

I hope you all loved our story and if you want more, Night Sky will be next. It's coming soon and it's the story of Ever and Writer.

THE END

ACKNOWLEDGEMENTS

First and foremost I gotta give a shout out to Jana Whaley. You have been there from the beginning with me on this crazy ride. I'm looking forward to many more with you. You are my insight and half my brain when it is needed.

Michelle Slagan thank you for taking me on as my PA. You have helped me so much in this book world.

My betas you ladies are amazing and thank you for taking the time to read my books. You have become more than just my betas you have become my friends and that I cherish. You are always there for me giving me input and your opinions when I need it.

To everyone else that has helped me and been a part to make Jacey and Bear's book the amazing story it is I want to say thank you.

ABOUT THE AUTHOR

When I am not working or taking care of my kids I spend my free time writing. I love to travel, but I haven't been able to do much of it lately so hopefully next year I will get to meet some of you at a signing. I'm so excited for 2016 because you will be seeing more than just MC from me and great things are to come. I love to talk to my readers so feel friend to find me on Facebook.

Until the next time
Love, Colbie Kay

Here are some places you can follow me and keep up with my Sinners.

<u>Colbie Kay on Facebook</u>
<u>Colbie Kay on Twitter</u>
<u>Colbie Kay on Goodreads</u>